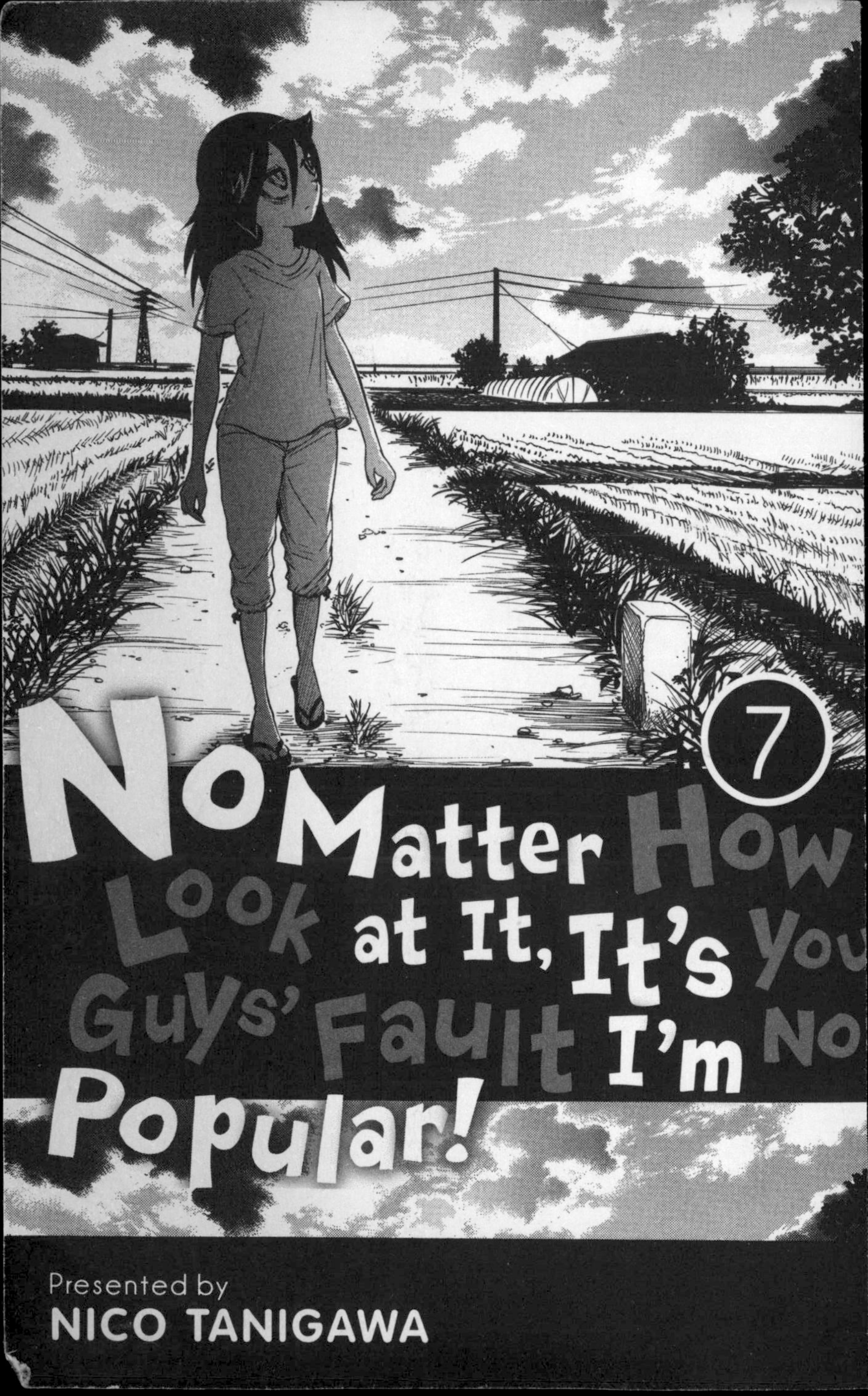

7

No Matter How Look at It, It's You Guys' Fault I'm No Popular!

Presented by

NICO TANIGAWA

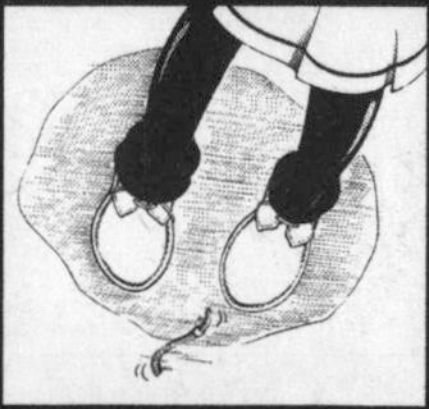

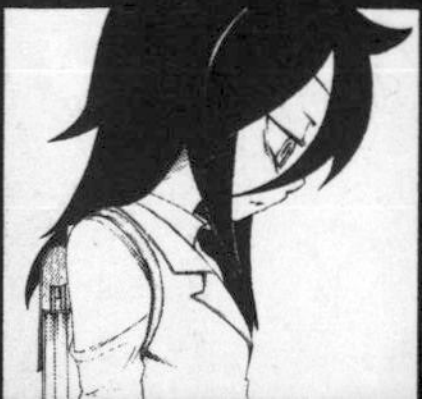

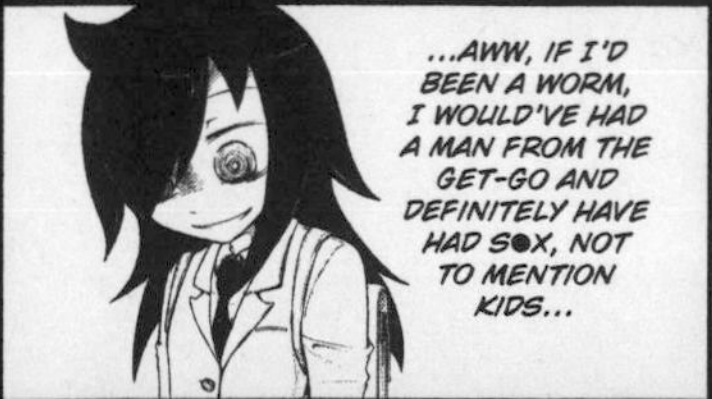
...AWW, IF I'D BEEN A WORM, I WOULD'VE HAD A MAN FROM THE GET-GO AND DEFINITELY HAVE HAD S●X, NOT TO MENTION KIDS...

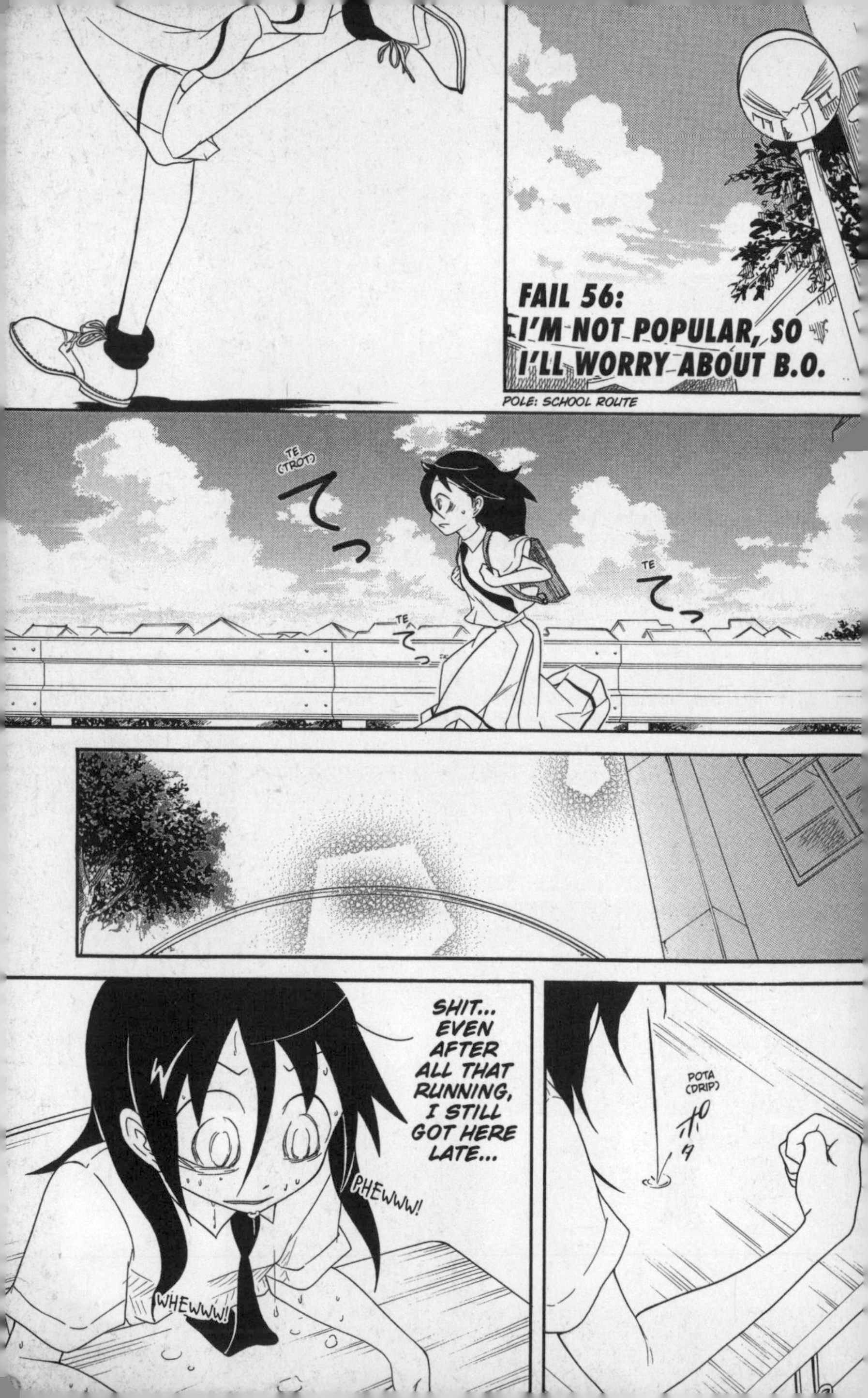
FAIL 56:
I'M NOT POPULAR, SO I'LL WORRY ABOUT B.O.
POLE: SCHOOL ROUTE
TE (TROT)
TE
TE
POTA (DRIP)
SHIT... EVEN AFTER ALL THAT RUNNING, I STILL GOT HERE LATE...
PHEWWW!
WHEWWW!

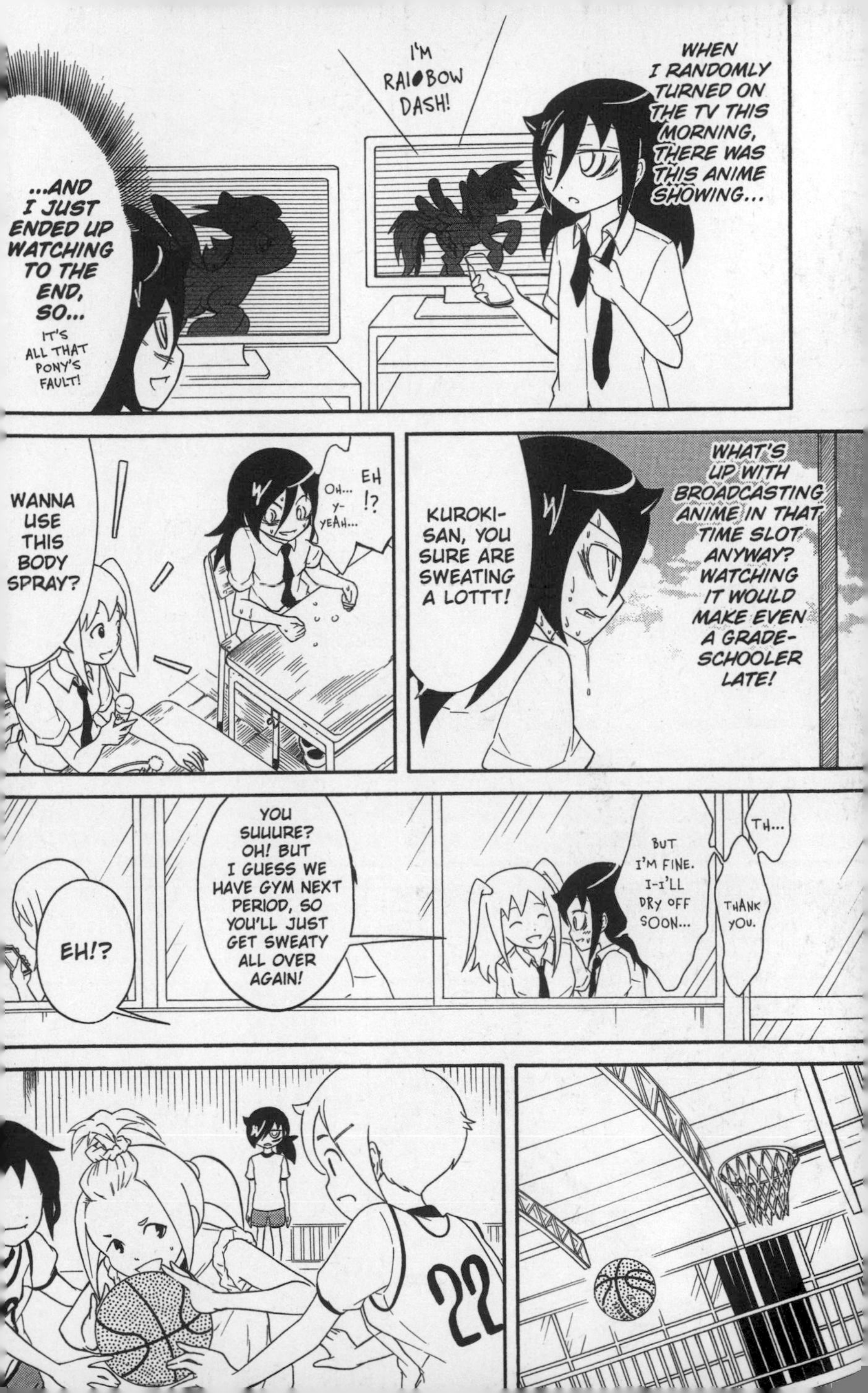
WHEN I RANDOMLY TURNED ON THE TV THIS MORNING, THERE WAS THIS ANIME SHOWING...
I'M RAI●BOW DASH!
...AND I JUST ENDED UP WATCHING TO THE END, SO...
IT'S ALL THAT PONY'S FAULT!
WHAT'S UP WITH BROADCASTING ANIME IN THAT TIME SLOT ANYWAY? WATCHING IT WOULD MAKE EVEN A GRADE-SCHOOLER LATE!
KUROKI-SAN, YOU SURE ARE SWEATING A LOTTT!
EH !?
OH... Y-YEAH...
WANNA USE THIS BODY SPRAY?
TH...
THANK YOU.
BUT I'M FINE. I-I'LL DRY OFF SOON...
YOU SUUURE? OH! BUT I GUESS WE HAVE GYM NEXT PERIOD, SO YOU'LL JUST GET SWEATY ALL OVER AGAIN!
EH!?
22

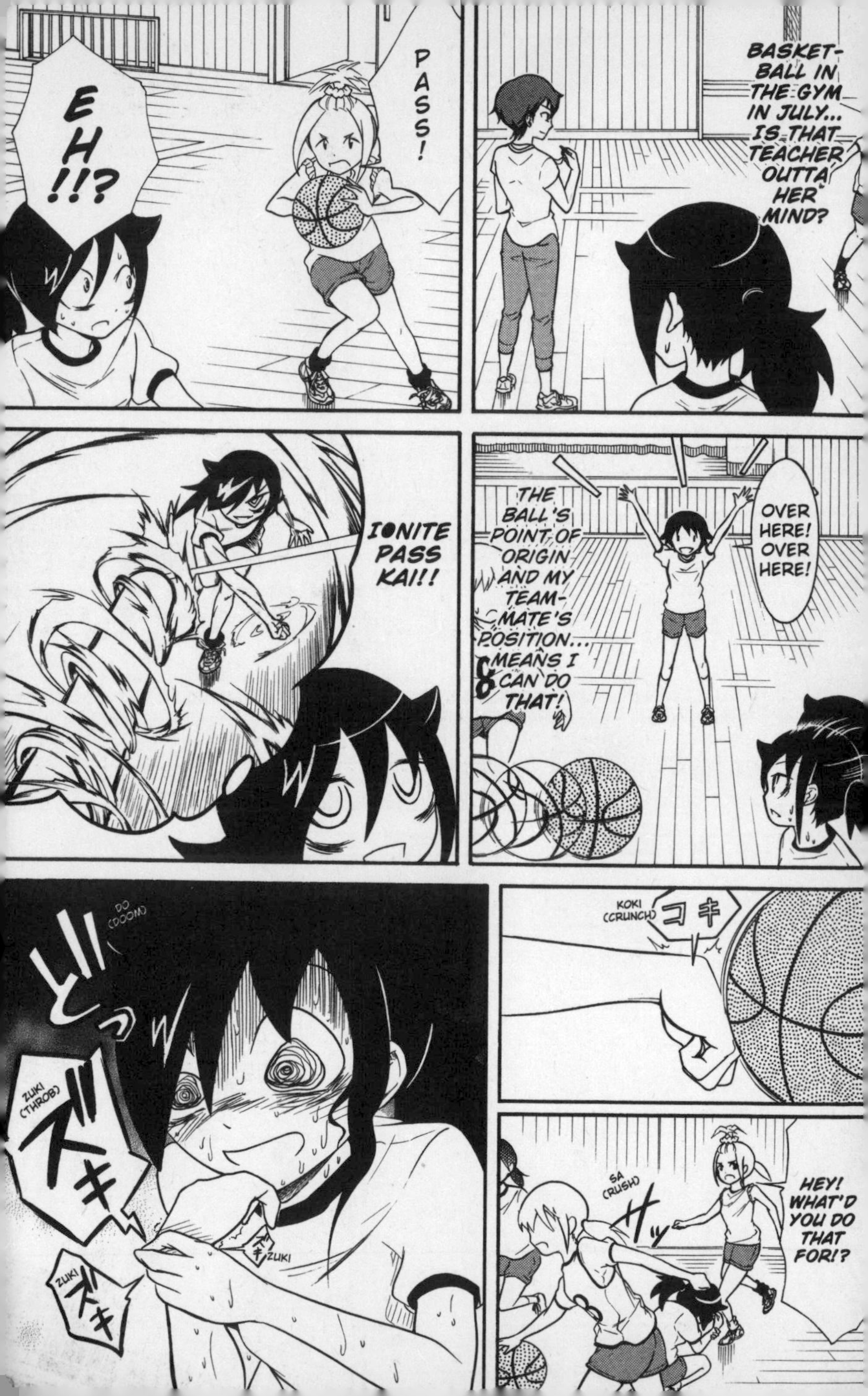
BASKET-BALL IN THE GYM IN JULY... IS THAT TEACHER OUTTA HER MIND?
PASS!
EH!!?
OVER HERE! OVER HERE!
THE BALL'S POINT OF ORIGIN AND MY TEAM-MATE'S POSITION... MEANS I CAN DO THAT!
IGNITE PASS KAI!!
KOKI (CRUNCH)
コキ
HEY! WHAT'D YOU DO THAT FOR!?
SA (RUSH)
サッ
DO (DOOM)
どっ
ZUKI (THROB)
ズキ
ZUKI
ズキ
ZUKI
ズキ

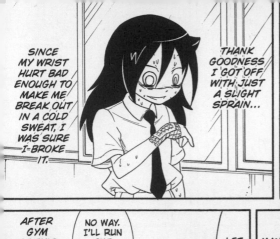

THANK GOODNESS I GOT OFF WITH JUST A SLIGHT SPRAIN...
SINCE MY WRIST HURT BAD ENOUGH TO MAKE ME BREAK OUT IN A COLD SWEAT, I WAS SURE I BROKE IT.
LOOKS LIKE I CAN EVEN HOLD A PEN OKAY.
SHUUU (SPRAY)
シュ
MAN, IT'S HOT!
LET ME USE THAT TOO.
NO WAY. I'LL RUN OUT DOUBLE-QUICK IF I LEND IT AROUND.
SHUUU
シュー
AFTER GYM AT THIS TIME OF YEAR, THE STENCH OF BODY SPRAY IS UNAVOIDABLE...
GIRLS ARE ONE THING, BUT BOYS SHOULDN'T FUSS SO MUCH ABOUT EVERY LITTLE BODILY ODOR!
......
GATA (CLATTER)
ガタ

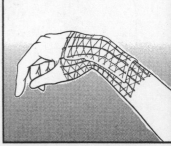

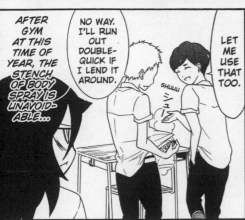

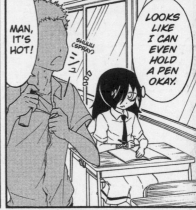

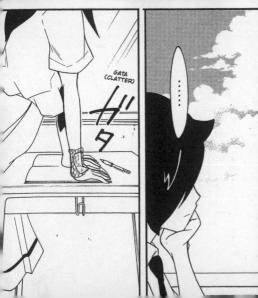

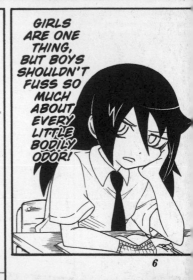

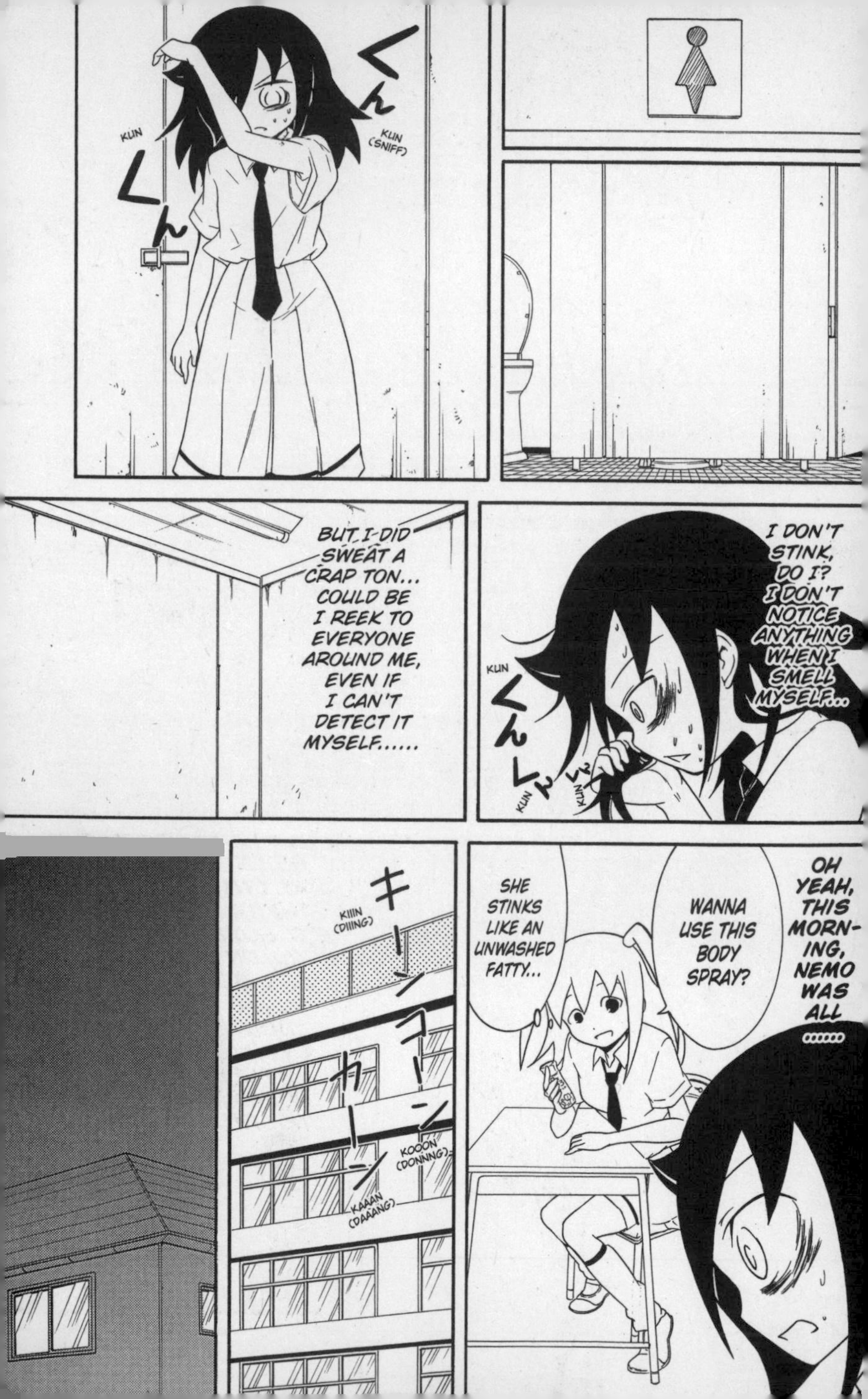
くん
KUN (SNIFF)
KUN
くん
I DON'T STINK, DO I? I DON'T NOTICE ANYTHING WHEN I SMELL MYSELF...
KUN
くん
KUN
KUN
BUT I DID SWEAT A CRAP TON... COULD BE I REEK TO EVERYONE AROUND ME, EVEN IF I CAN'T DETECT IT MYSELF......
OH YEAH, THIS MORNING, NEMO WAS ALL ......
WANNA USE THIS BODY SPRAY?
SHE STINKS LIKE AN UNWASHED FATTY...
キーンコーンカーン
KIIIN (DIIING)
KOOON (DONNNG)
KAAAN (DAAANG)

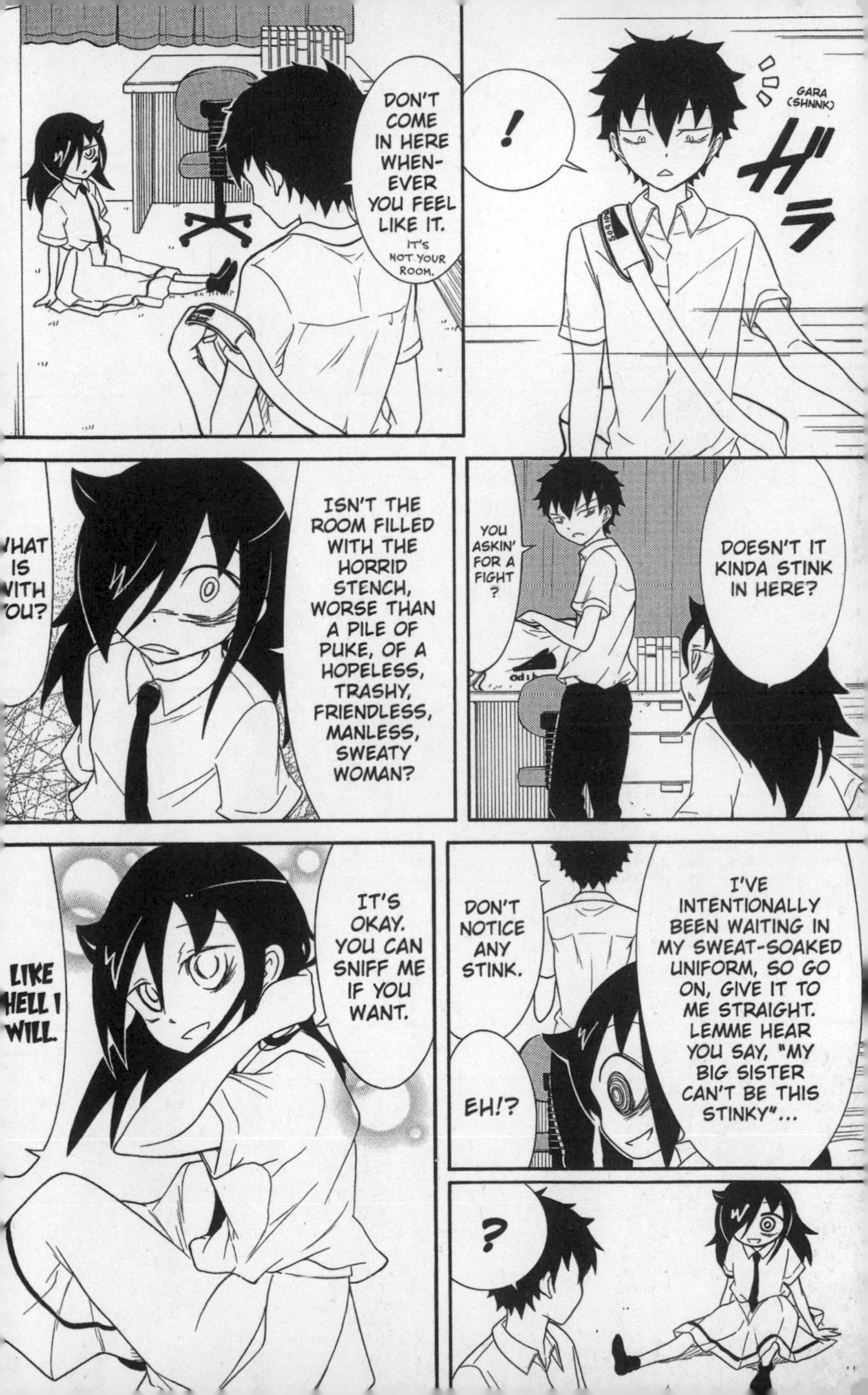
ガラ
GARA (SHNNK)
!
DON'T COME IN HERE WHENEVER YOU FEEL LIKE IT.
IT'S NOT YOUR ROOM.
DOESN'T IT KINDA STINK IN HERE?
YOU ASKIN' FOR A FIGHT?
ISN'T THE ROOM FILLED WITH THE HORRID STENCH, WORSE THAN A PILE OF PUKE, OF A HOPELESS, TRASHY, FRIENDLESS, MANLESS, SWEATY WOMAN?
WHAT IS WITH YOU?
I'VE INTENTIONALLY BEEN WAITING IN MY SWEAT-SOAKED UNIFORM, SO GO ON, GIVE IT TO ME STRAIGHT. LEMME HEAR YOU SAY, "MY BIG SISTER CAN'T BE THIS STINKY"...
DON'T NOTICE ANY STINK.
EH!?
?
IT'S OKAY. YOU CAN SNIFF ME IF YOU WANT.
LIKE HELL I WILL.

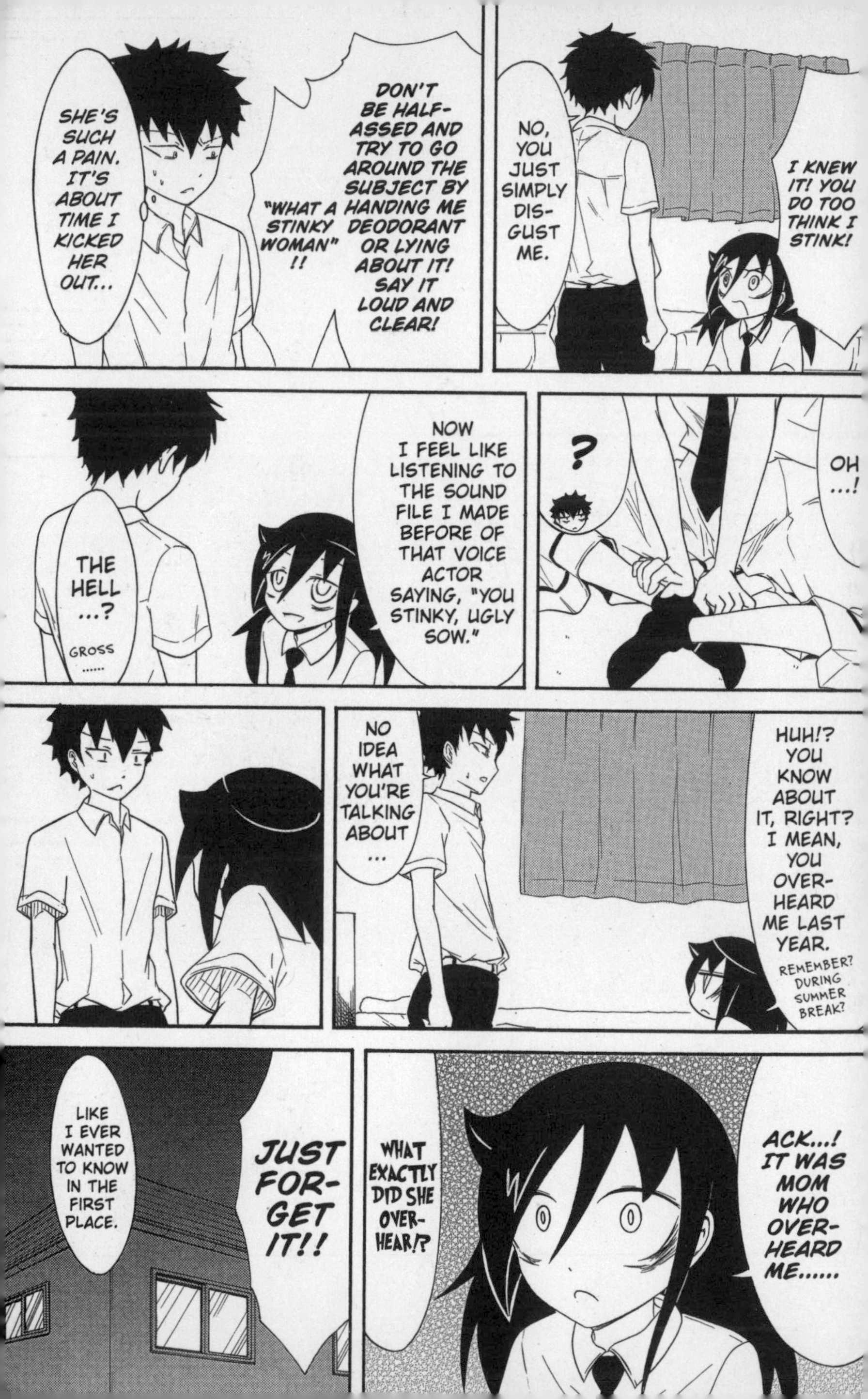
I KNEW IT! YOU DO TOO THINK I STINK!
NO, YOU JUST SIMPLY DISGUST ME.
DON'T BE HALF-ASSED AND TRY TO GO AROUND THE SUBJECT BY HANDING ME DEODORANT OR LYING ABOUT IT! SAY IT LOUD AND CLEAR!
"WHAT A STINKY WOMAN"!!
SHE'S SUCH A PAIN. IT'S ABOUT TIME I KICKED HER OUT...
OH...!
?
NOW I FEEL LIKE LISTENING TO THE SOUND FILE I MADE BEFORE OF THAT VOICE ACTOR SAYING, "YOU STINKY, UGLY SOW."
THE HELL...?
GROSS......
HUH!? YOU KNOW ABOUT IT, RIGHT? I MEAN, YOU OVERHEARD ME LAST YEAR.
REMEMBER? DURING SUMMER BREAK?
NO IDEA WHAT YOU'RE TALKING ABOUT...
ACK...! IT WAS MOM WHO OVERHEARD ME......
WHAT EXACTLY DID SHE OVERHEAR!?
JUST FORGET IT!!
LIKE I EVER WANTED TO KNOW IN THE FIRST PLACE.

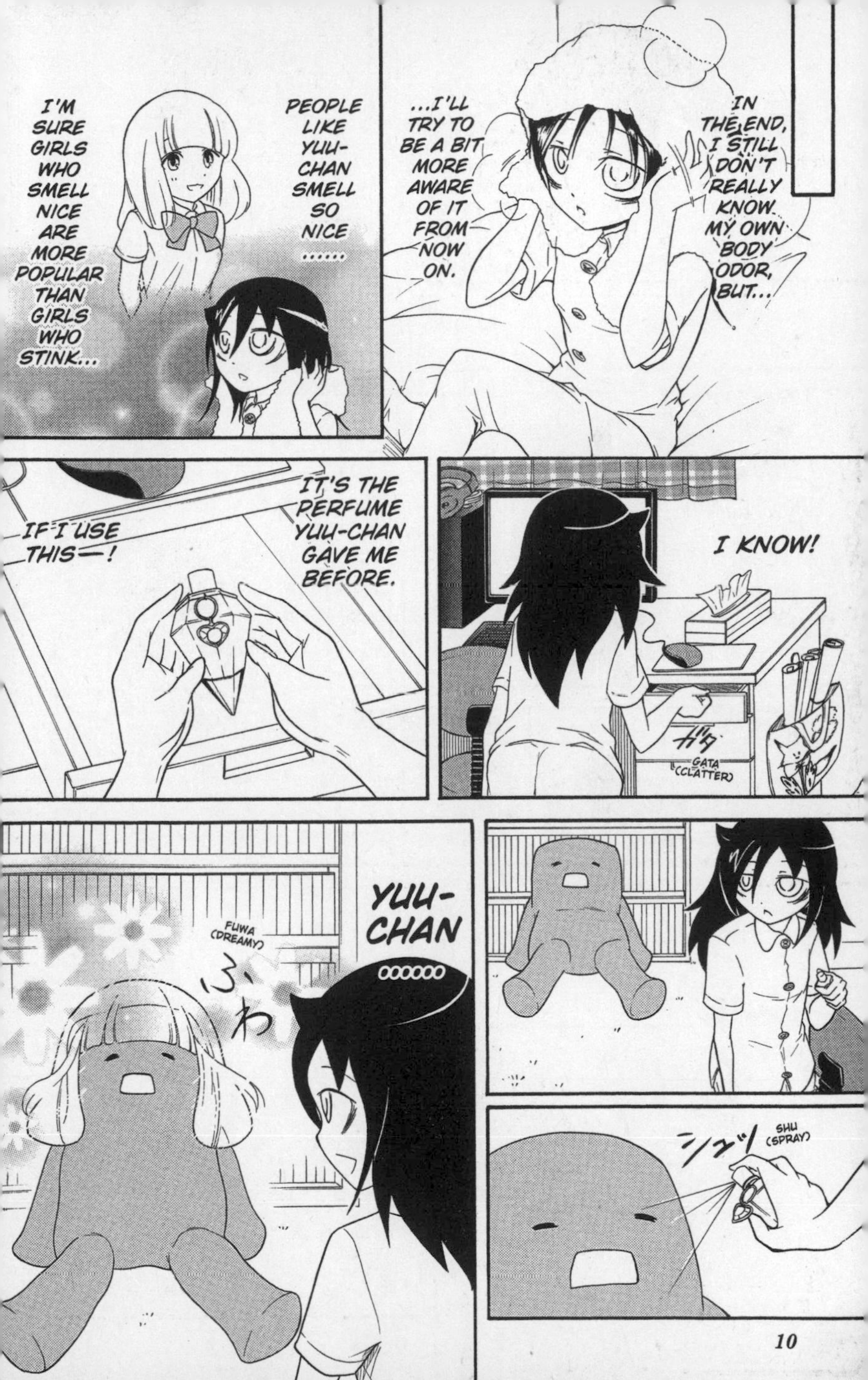
IN THE END, I STILL DON'T REALLY KNOW MY OWN BODY ODOR, BUT...
...I'LL TRY TO BE A BIT MORE AWARE OF IT FROM NOW ON.
PEOPLE LIKE YUU-CHAN SMELL SO NICE ......
I'M SURE GIRLS WHO SMELL NICE ARE MORE POPULAR THAN GIRLS WHO STINK...
I KNOW!
GATA (CLATTER)
IT'S THE PERFUME YUU-CHAN GAVE ME BEFORE.
IF I USE THIS—!
SHU (SPRAY)
YUU-CHAN oooooo
FUWA (DREAMY)
ふわ

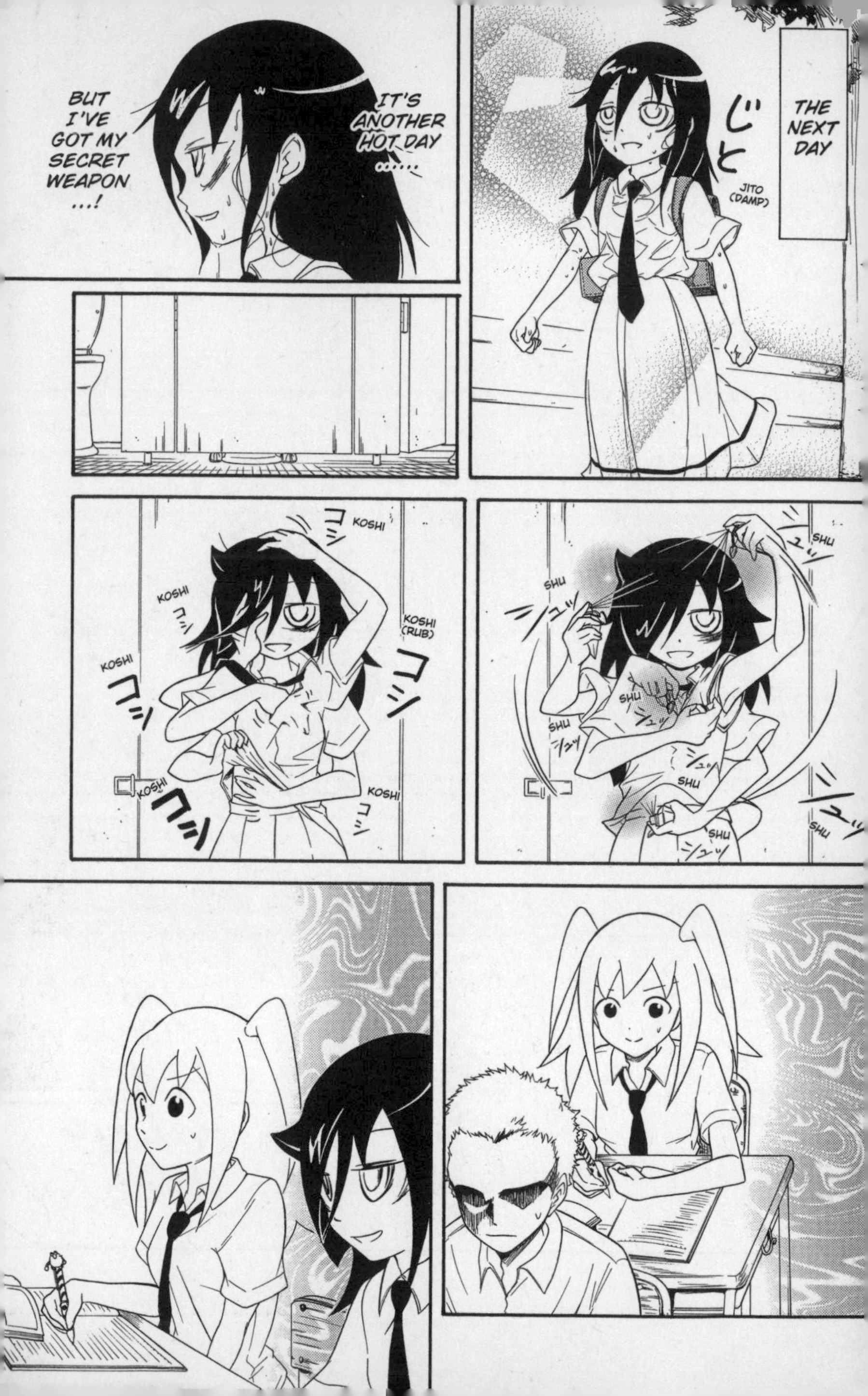

THE NEXT DAY
じと
JITO (DAMP)
IT'S ANOTHER HOT DAY......
BUT I'VE GOT MY SECRET WEAPON ...!
SHU
シュッ
SHU
シュッ
SHU
SHU
シュッ
SHU
SHU
シュッ
SHU
シュッ
KOSHI
コシ
KOSHI
コシ
KOSHI (RUB)
コシ
KOSHI
コシ
KOSHI
コシ
KOSHI
コシ

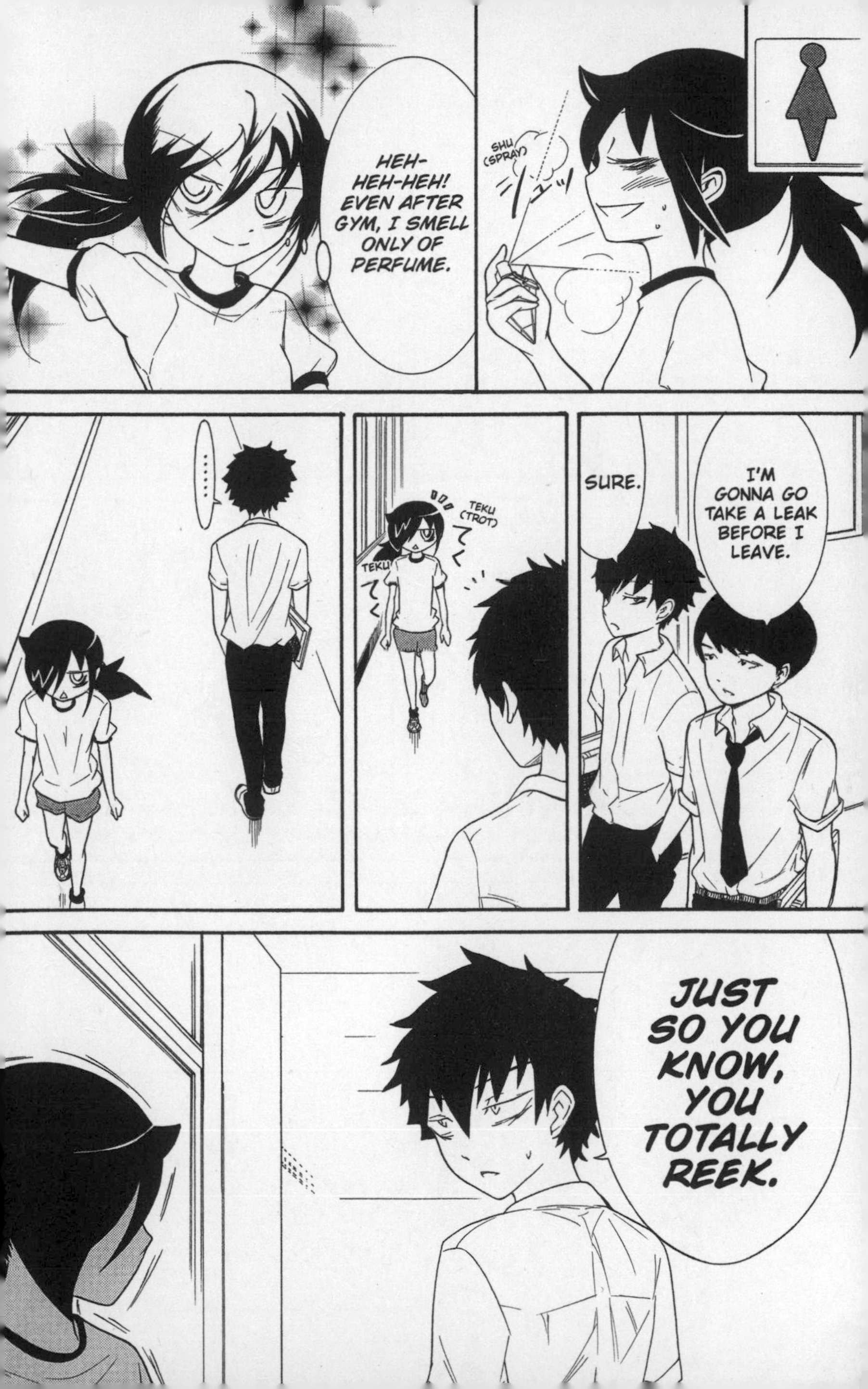
SHU (SPRAY)
HEH-HEH-HEH! EVEN AFTER GYM, I SMELL ONLY OF PERFUME.
I'M GONNA GO TAKE A LEAK BEFORE I LEAVE.
SURE.
TEKU (TROT)
TEKU
......
JUST SO YOU KNOW, YOU TOTALLY REEK.

No Matter How I Look at It, It's You Guys' Fault I'm Not Popular!

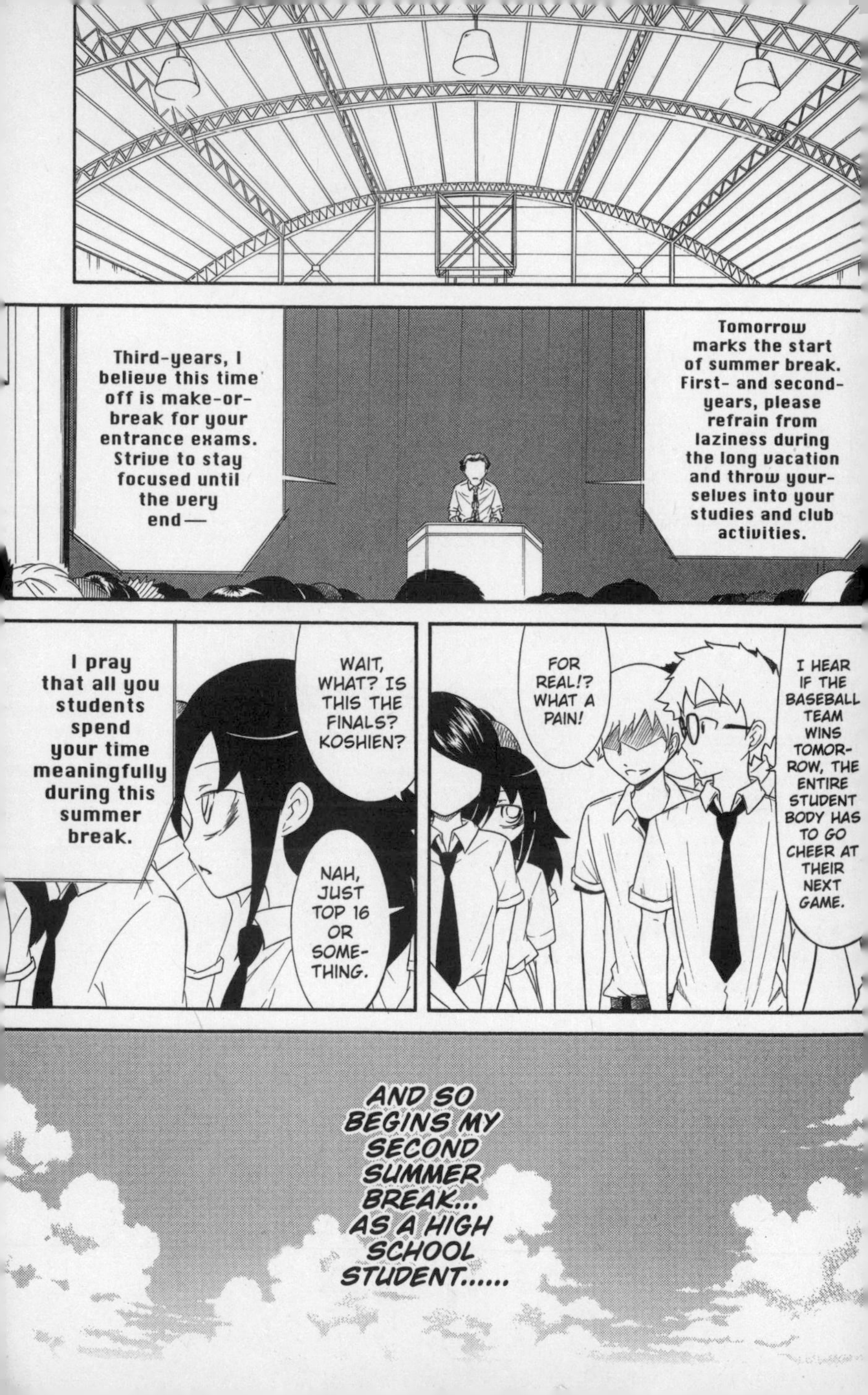

Tomorrow marks the start of summer break. First- and second-years, please refrain from laziness during the long vacation and throw yourselves into your studies and club activities.
Third-years, I believe this time off is make-or-break for your entrance exams. Strive to stay focused until the very end—
I HEAR IF THE BASEBALL TEAM WINS TOMORROW, THE ENTIRE STUDENT BODY HAS TO GO CHEER AT THEIR NEXT GAME.
FOR REAL!? WHAT A PAIN!
WAIT, WHAT? IS THIS THE FINALS? KOSHIEN?
NAH, JUST TOP 16 OR SOMETHING.
I pray that all you students spend your time meaningfully during this summer break.
AND SO BEGINS MY SECOND SUMMER BREAK... AS A HIGH SCHOOL STUDENT......

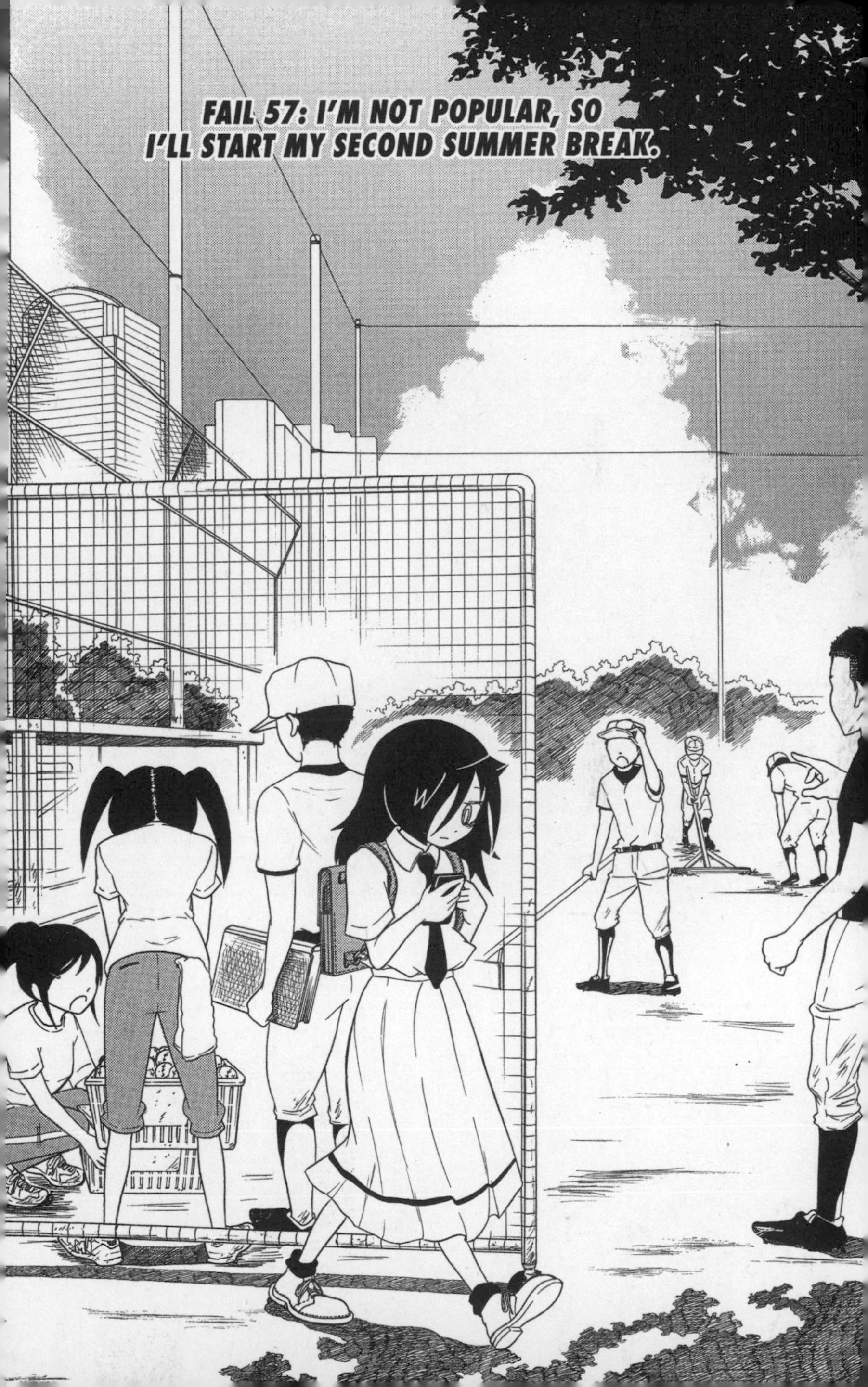
FAIL 57: I'M NOT POPULAR, SO I'LL START MY SECOND SUMMER BREAK.

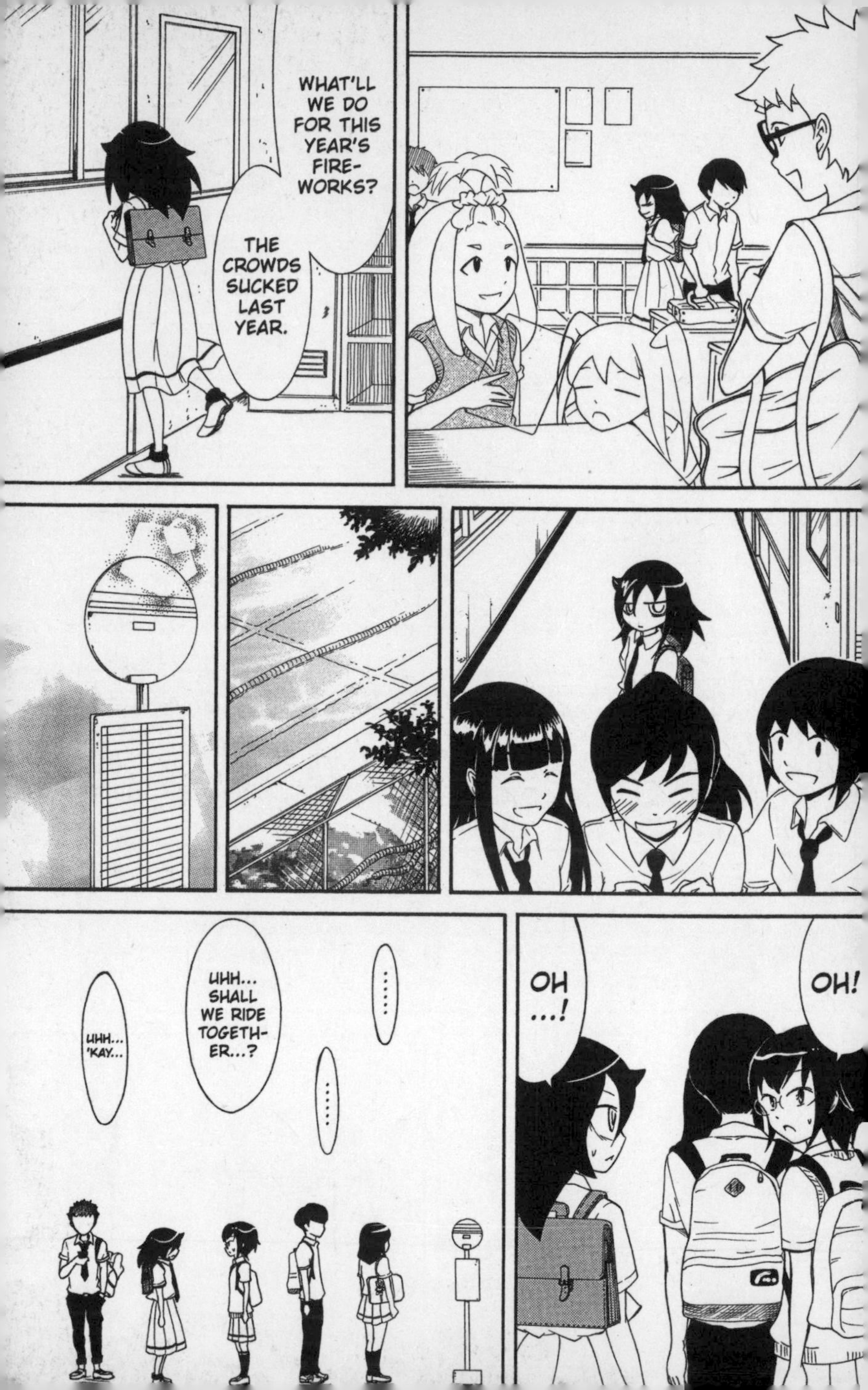
WHAT'LL WE DO FOR THIS YEAR'S FIRE-WORKS?
THE CROWDS SUCKED LAST YEAR.
OH!
OH ...!
......
UHH... SHALL WE RIDE TOGETH-ER...?
......
UHH... 'KAY...

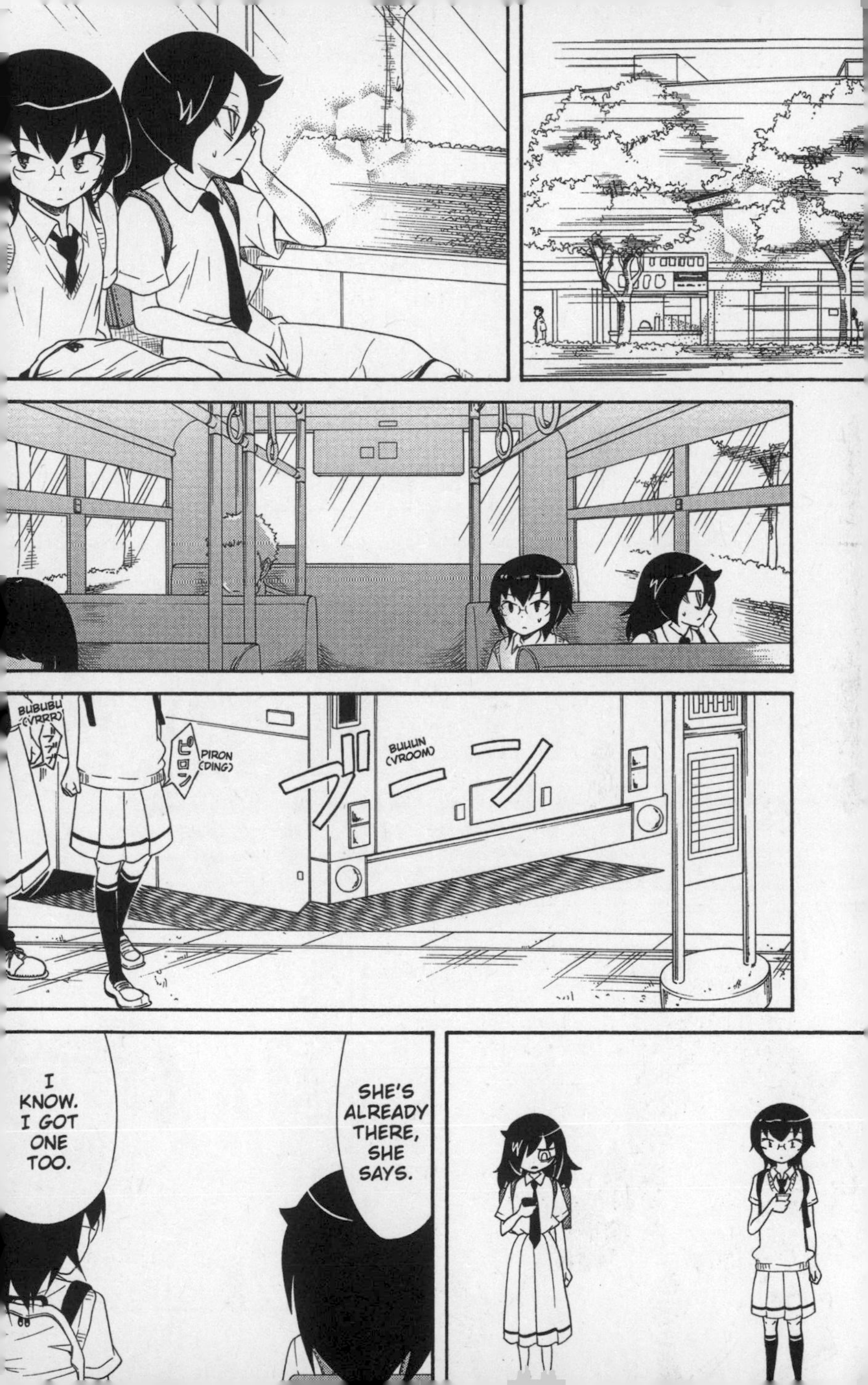
ブーン
BUUUN (VROOM)
ピロン
PIRON (DING)
ブブブ
BUBUBU (VRRR)
SHE'S ALREADY THERE, SHE SAYS.
I KNOW. I GOT ONE TOO.

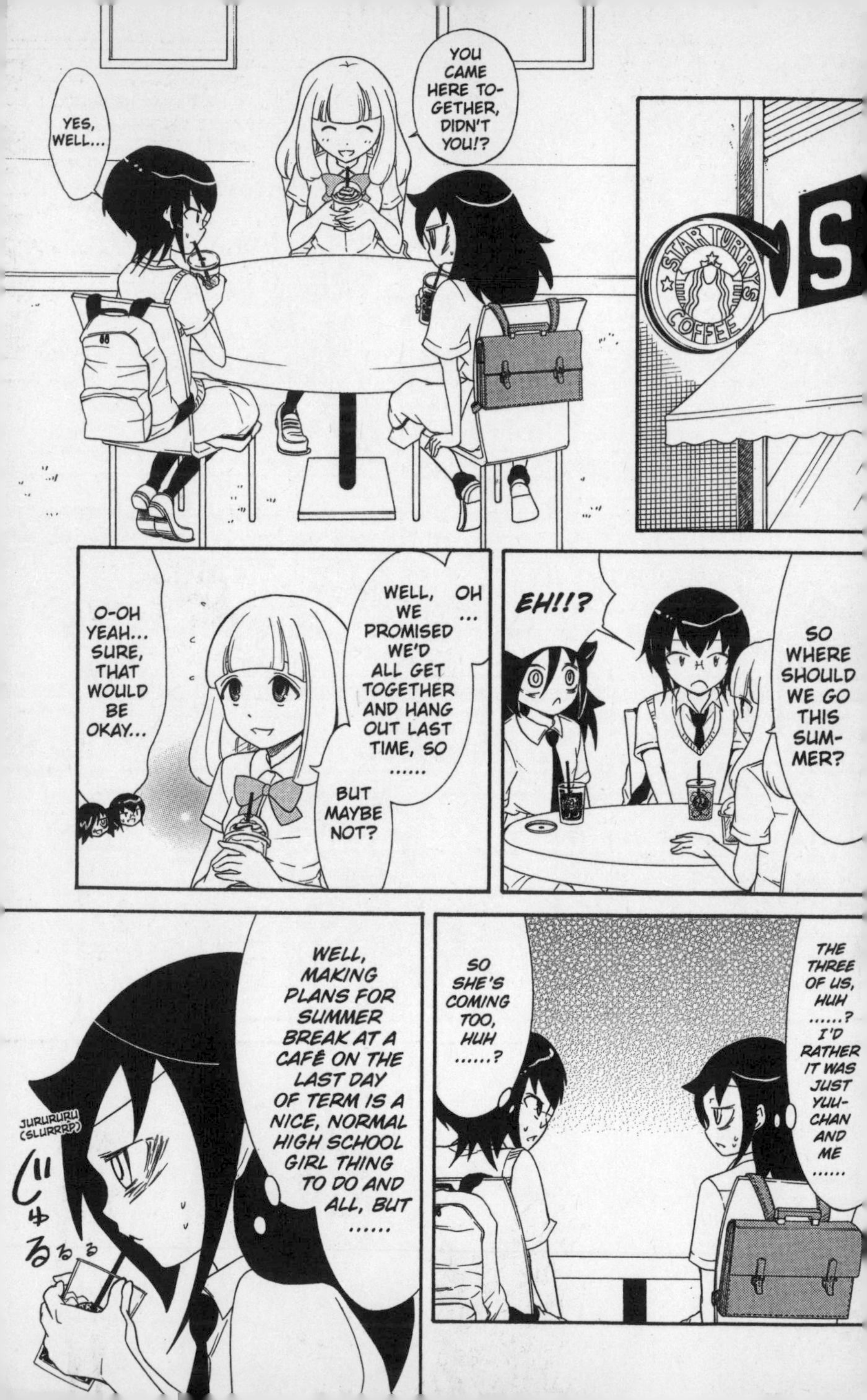
STAR TURRYS COFFEE
S
YOU CAME HERE TO-GETHER, DIDN'T YOU!?
YES, WELL...
SO WHERE SHOULD WE GO THIS SUM-MER?
EH!!?
OH ...
WELL, WE PROMISED WE'D ALL GET TOGETHER AND HANG OUT LAST TIME, SO ......
BUT MAYBE NOT?
O-OH YEAH... SURE, THAT WOULD BE OKAY...
THE THREE OF US, HUH ......? I'D RATHER IT WAS JUST YUU-CHAN AND ME ......
SO SHE'S COMING TOO, HUH ......?
WELL, MAKING PLANS FOR SUMMER BREAK AT A CAFÉ ON THE LAST DAY OF TERM IS A NICE, NORMAL HIGH SCHOOL GIRL THING TO DO AND ALL, BUT ......
JURURURU (SLURRRP)
じゅるるる

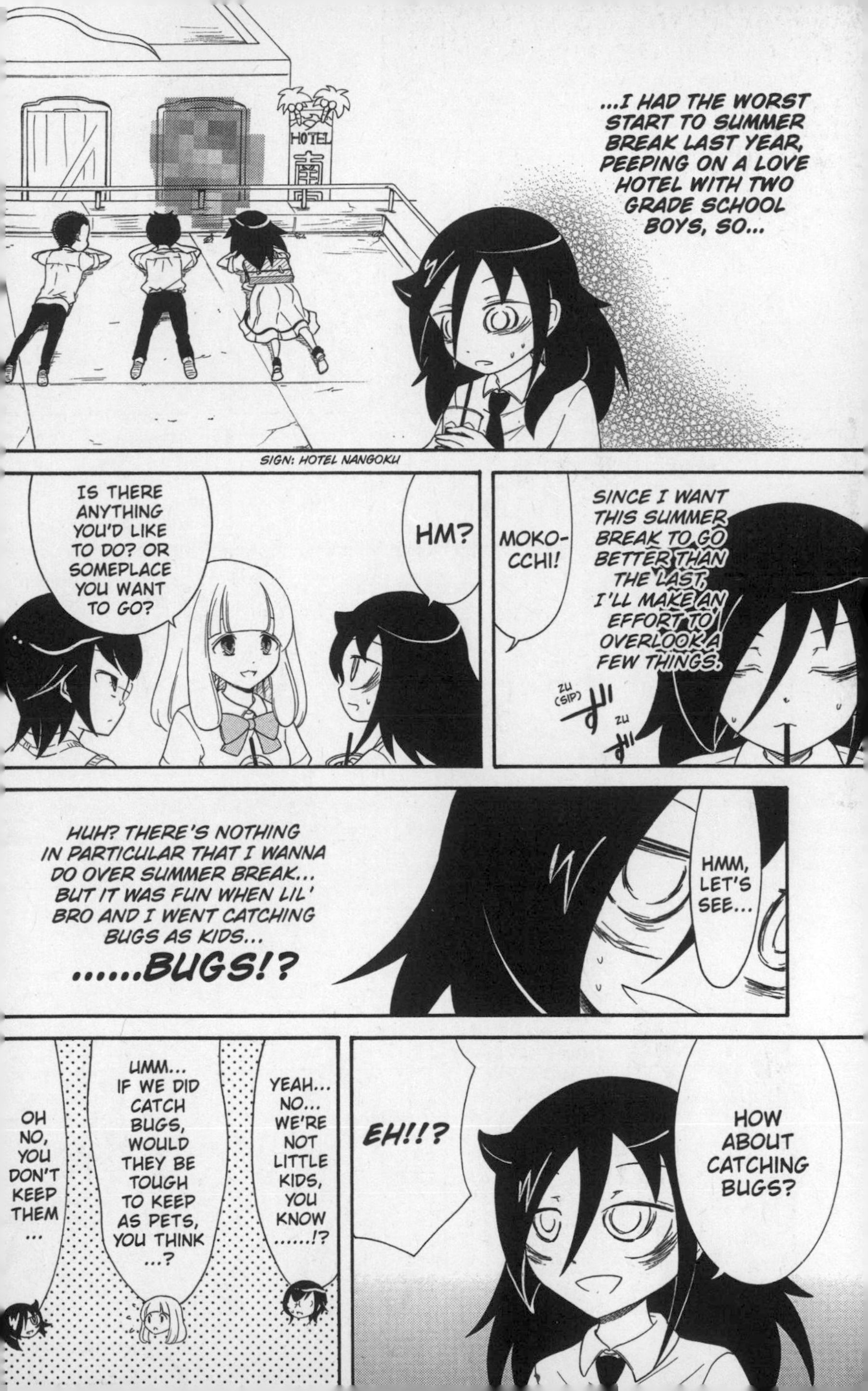
HOTEL
...I HAD THE WORST START TO SUMMER BREAK LAST YEAR, PEEPING ON A LOVE HOTEL WITH TWO GRADE SCHOOL BOYS, SO...
SIGN: HOTEL NANGOKU
SINCE I WANT THIS SUMMER BREAK TO GO BETTER THAN THE LAST, I'LL MAKE AN EFFORT TO OVERLOOK A FEW THINGS.
ZU (SIP)
ZU
MOKO-CCHI!
HM?
IS THERE ANYTHING YOU'D LIKE TO DO? OR SOMEPLACE YOU WANT TO GO?
HMM, LET'S SEE...
HUH? THERE'S NOTHING IN PARTICULAR THAT I WANNA DO OVER SUMMER BREAK... BUT IT WAS FUN WHEN LIL' BRO AND I WENT CATCHING BUGS AS KIDS...
......BUGS!?
HOW ABOUT CATCHING BUGS?
EH!!?
YEAH... NO... WE'RE NOT LITTLE KIDS, YOU KNOW ......!?
UMM... IF WE DID CATCH BUGS, WOULD THEY BE TOUGH TO KEEP AS PETS, YOU THINK ...?
OH NO, YOU DON'T KEEP THEM ...

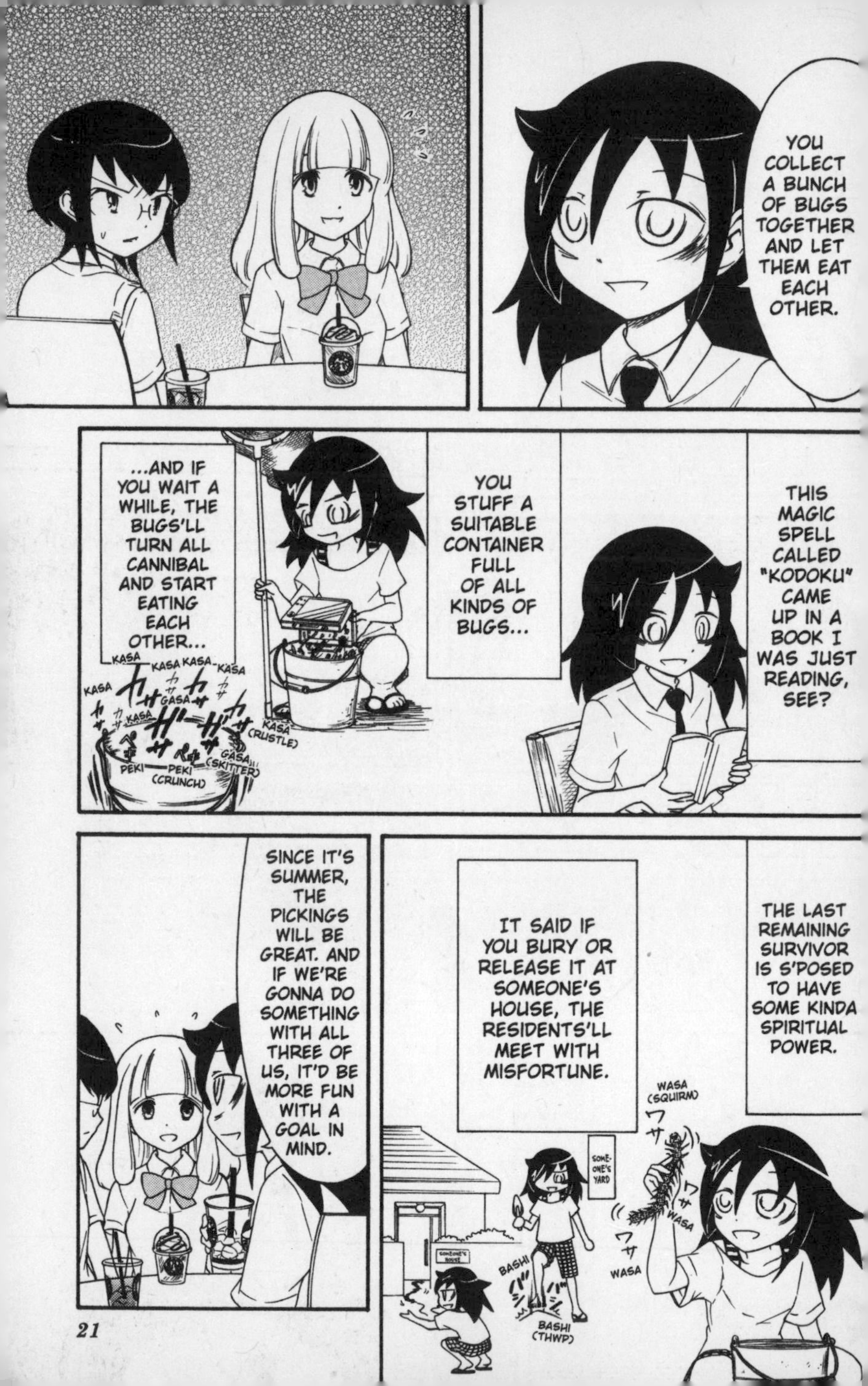
YOU COLLECT A BUNCH OF BUGS TOGETHER AND LET THEM EAT EACH OTHER.
THIS MAGIC SPELL CALLED "KODOKU" CAME UP IN A BOOK I WAS JUST READING, SEE?
YOU STUFF A SUITABLE CONTAINER FULL OF ALL KINDS OF BUGS...
...AND IF YOU WAIT A WHILE, THE BUGS'LL TURN ALL CANNIBAL AND START EATING EACH OTHER...
KASA (RUSTLE)
KASA KASA KASA KASA KASA
GASA GASA (SKITTER)
PEKI PEKI (CRUNCH)
THE LAST REMAINING SURVIVOR IS S'POSED TO HAVE SOME KINDA SPIRITUAL POWER.
IT SAID IF YOU BURY OR RELEASE IT AT SOMEONE'S HOUSE, THE RESIDENTS'LL MEET WITH MISFORTUNE.
WASA (SQUIRM)
WASA
WASA
SOME-ONE'S YARD
BASHI
BASHI (THWP)
SINCE IT'S SUMMER, THE PICKINGS WILL BE GREAT. AND IF WE'RE GONNA DO SOMETHING WITH ALL THREE OF US, IT'D BE MORE FUN WITH A GOAL IN MIND.

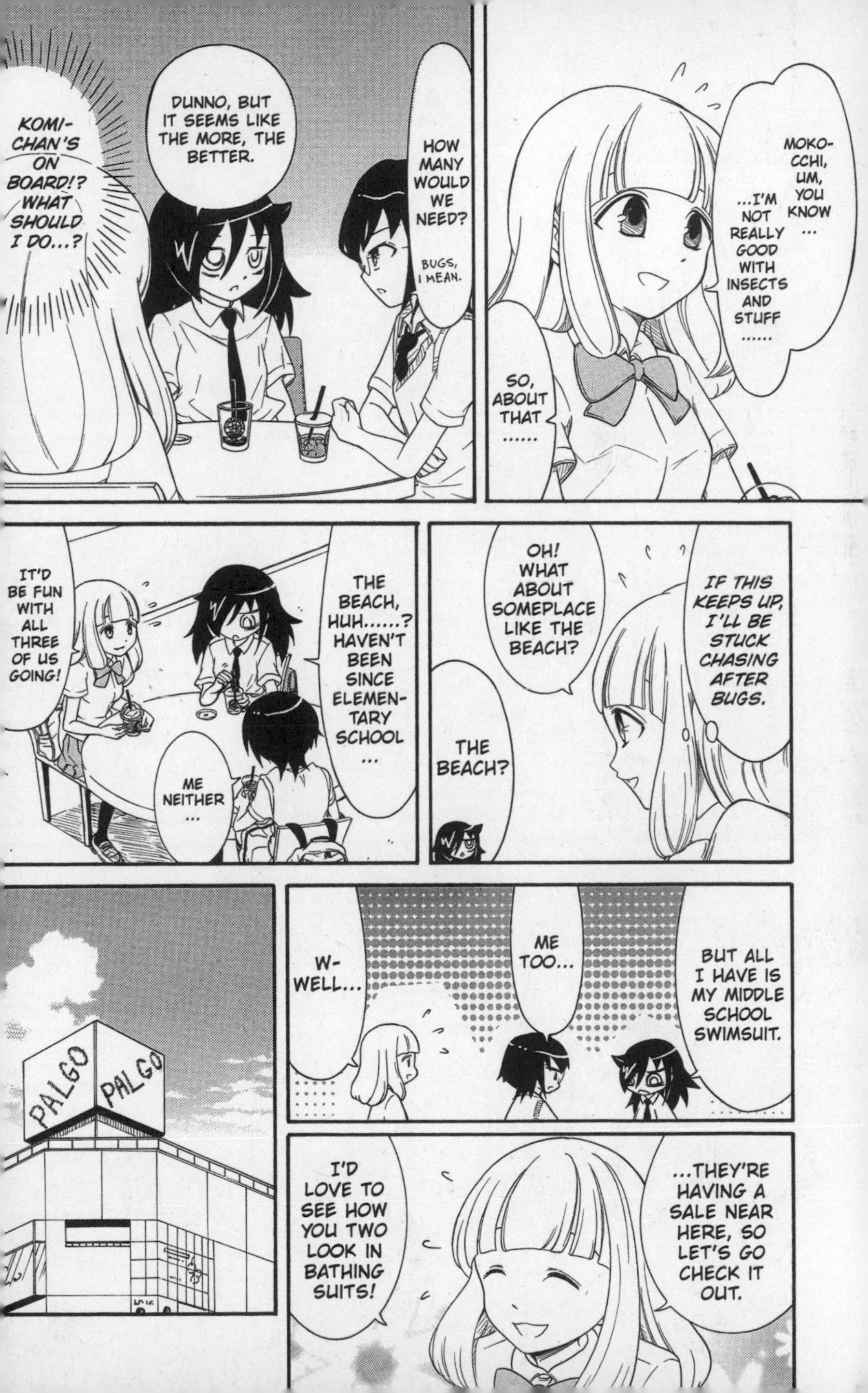
MOKO-CCHI, UM, YOU KNOW ...
...I'M NOT REALLY GOOD WITH INSECTS AND STUFF ......
SO, ABOUT THAT ......
HOW MANY WOULD WE NEED?
BUGS, I MEAN.
DUNNO, BUT IT SEEMS LIKE THE MORE, THE BETTER.
KOMI-CHAN'S ON BOARD!? WHAT SHOULD I DO...?
IF THIS KEEPS UP, I'LL BE STUCK CHASING AFTER BUGS.
OH! WHAT ABOUT SOMEPLACE LIKE THE BEACH?
THE BEACH?
THE BEACH, HUH......? HAVEN'T BEEN SINCE ELEMENTARY SCHOOL ...
ME NEITHER ...
IT'D BE FUN WITH ALL THREE OF US GOING!
BUT ALL I HAVE IS MY MIDDLE SCHOOL SWIMSUIT.
ME TOO...
W-WELL...
...THEY'RE HAVING A SALE NEAR HERE, SO LET'S GO CHECK IT OUT.
I'D LOVE TO SEE HOW YOU TWO LOOK IN BATHING SUITS!
PALGO
PALGO

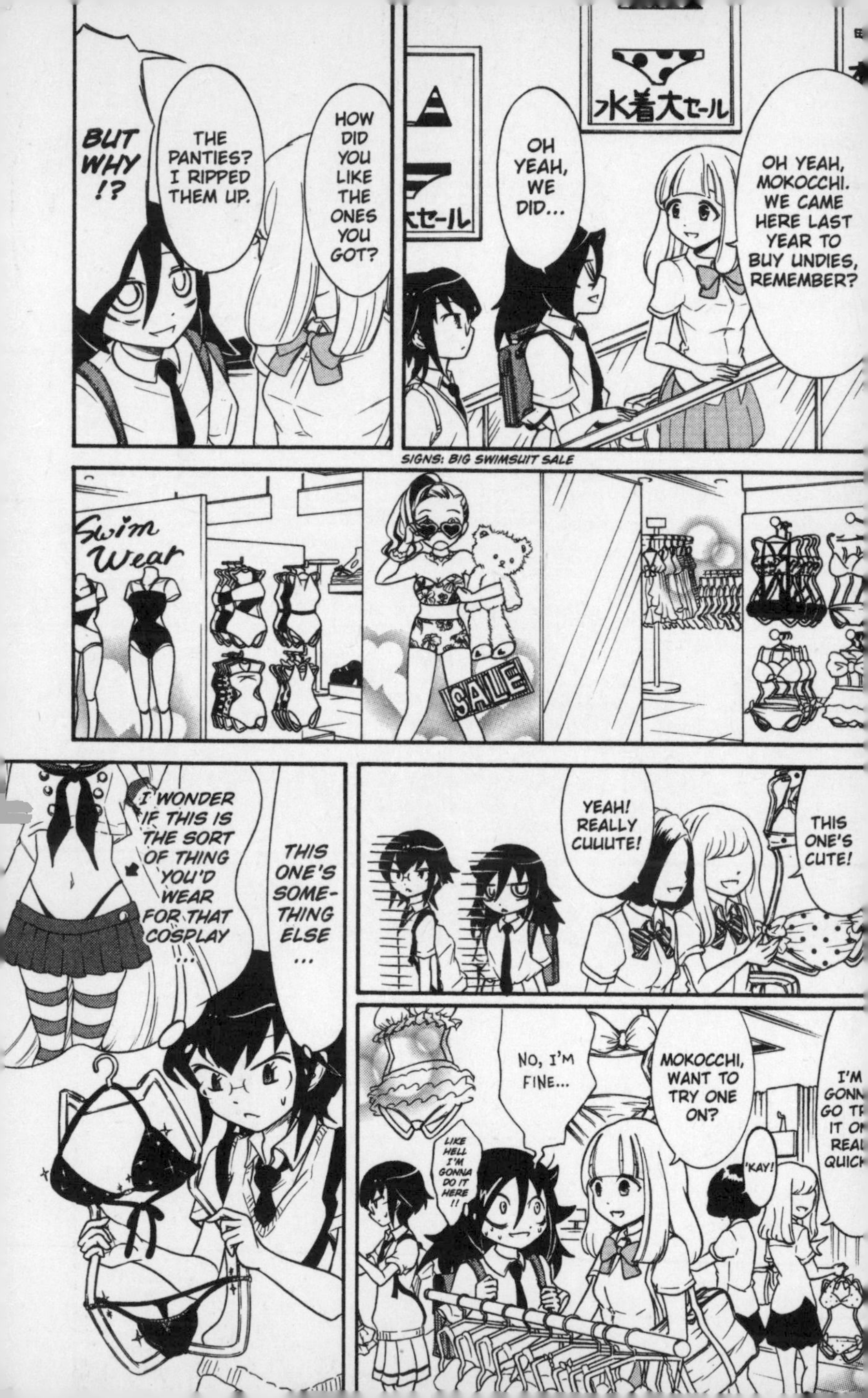
水着大セール
OH YEAH, MOKOCCHI. WE CAME HERE LAST YEAR TO BUY UNDIES, REMEMBER?
OH YEAH, WE DID...
大セール
HOW DID YOU LIKE THE ONES YOU GOT?
THE PANTIES? I RIPPED THEM UP.
BUT WHY!?
SIGNS: BIG SWIMSUIT SALE
SALE
Swim Wear
THIS ONE'S CUTE!
YEAH! REALLY CUUUTE!
I'M GONN GO TR IT O REAL QUIC
'KAY!
MOKOCCHI, WANT TO TRY ONE ON?
NO, I'M FINE...
LIKE HELL I'M GONNA DO IT HERE!!
THIS ONE'S SOME-THING ELSE...
I WONDER IF THIS IS THE SORT OF THING YOU'D WEAR FOR THAT COSPLAY...

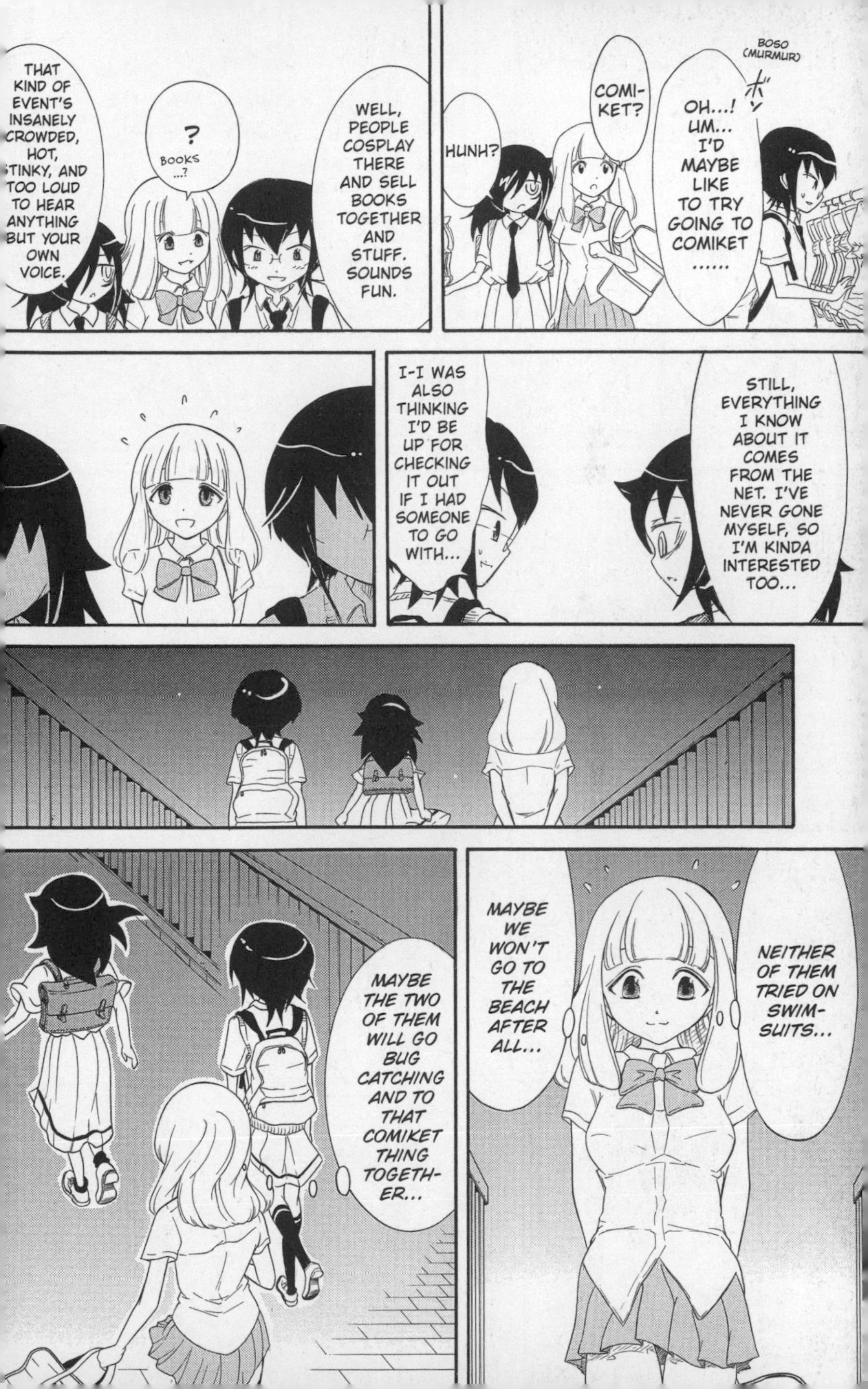
BOSO (MURMUR)
ボソ
OH...! UM... I'D MAYBE LIKE TO TRY GOING TO COMIKET ......
COMI-KET?
HUNH?
WELL, PEOPLE COSPLAY THERE AND SELL BOOKS TOGETHER AND STUFF. SOUNDS FUN.
? BOOKS ...?
THAT KIND OF EVENT'S INSANELY CROWDED, HOT, STINKY, AND TOO LOUD TO HEAR ANYTHING BUT YOUR OWN VOICE.
STILL, EVERYTHING I KNOW ABOUT IT COMES FROM THE NET. I'VE NEVER GONE MYSELF, SO I'M KINDA INTERESTED TOO...
I-I WAS ALSO THINKING I'D BE UP FOR CHECKING IT OUT IF I HAD SOMEONE TO GO WITH...
NEITHER OF THEM TRIED ON SWIM-SUITS...
MAYBE WE WON'T GO TO THE BEACH AFTER ALL...
MAYBE THE TWO OF THEM WILL GO BUG CATCHING AND TO THAT COMIKET THING TOGETH-ER...

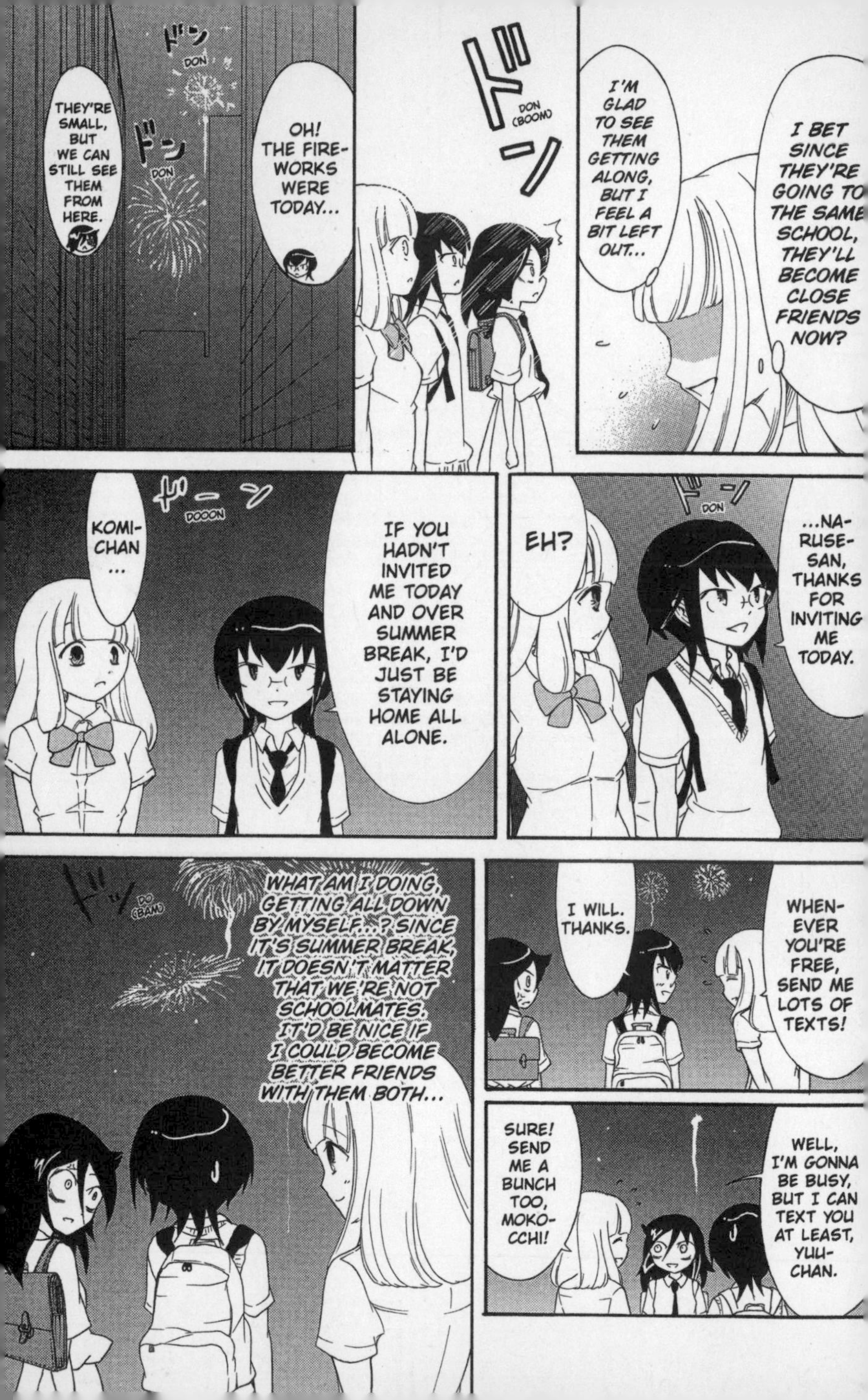
I BET SINCE THEY'RE GOING TO THE SAME SCHOOL, THEY'LL BECOME CLOSE FRIENDS NOW?
I'M GLAD TO SEE THEM GETTING ALONG, BUT I FEEL A BIT LEFT OUT...
ドーン
DON (BOOM)
ドン
DON
OH! THE FIREWORKS WERE TODAY...
ドン
DON
THEY'RE SMALL, BUT WE CAN STILL SEE THEM FROM HERE.
ドン
DON
...NARUSE-SAN, THANKS FOR INVITING ME TODAY.
EH?
ドーン
DOOON
IF YOU HADN'T INVITED ME TODAY AND OVER SUMMER BREAK, I'D JUST BE STAYING HOME ALL ALONE.
KOMI-CHAN...
WHENEVER YOU'RE FREE, SEND ME LOTS OF TEXTS!
I WILL. THANKS.
WELL, I'M GONNA BE BUSY, BUT I CAN TEXT YOU AT LEAST, YUU-CHAN.
SURE! SEND ME A BUNCH TOO, MOKOCCHI!
ドン
DO (BAM)
WHAT AM I DOING, GETTING ALL DOWN BY MYSELF...? SINCE IT'S SUMMER BREAK, IT DOESN'T MATTER THAT WE'RE NOT SCHOOLMATES. IT'D BE NICE IF I COULD BECOME BETTER FRIENDS WITH THEM BOTH...

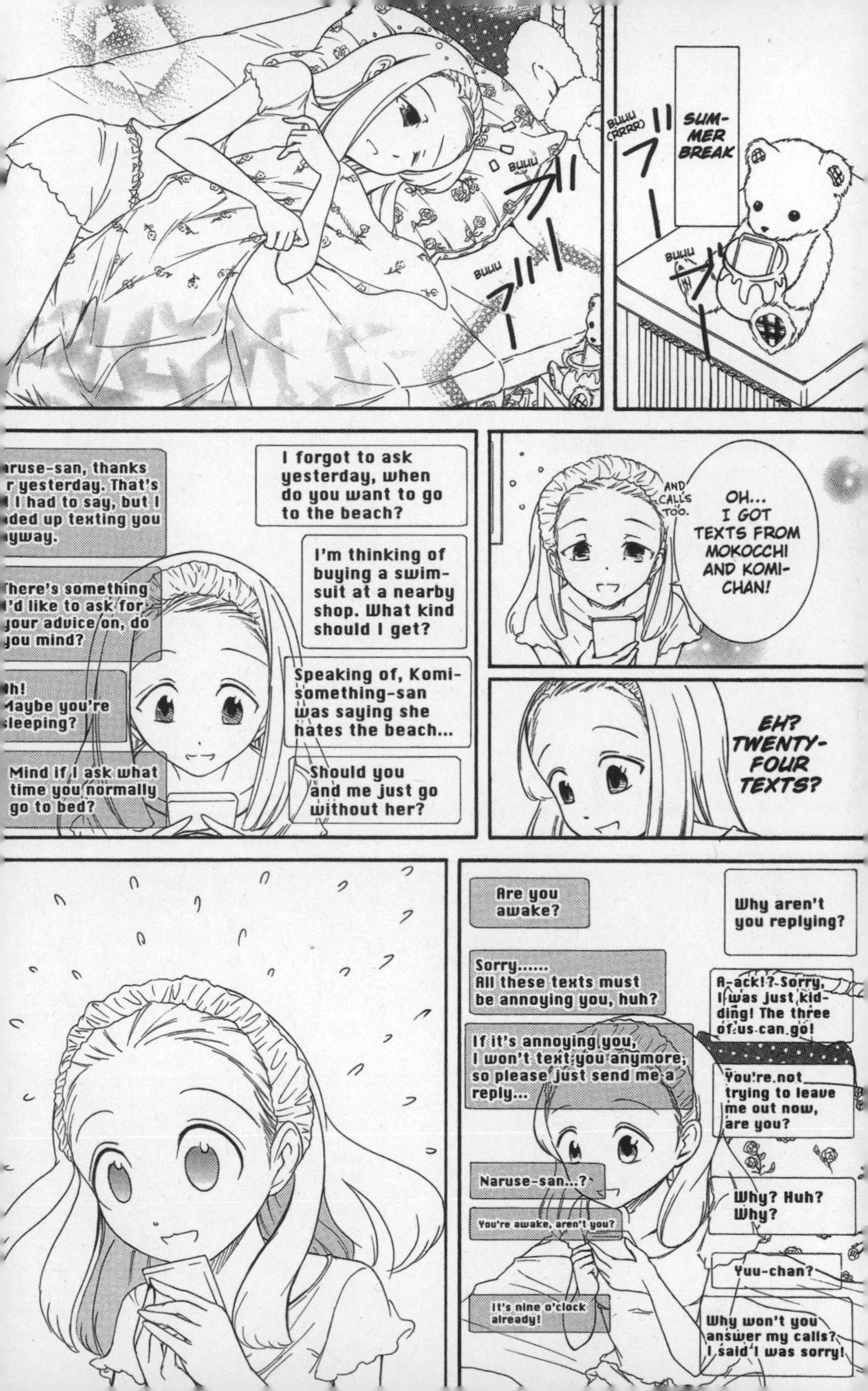

SUM-
MER
BREAK
BUUU (RRRR)
BUUU
BUUU
BUUU
OH... I GOT TEXTS FROM MOKOCCHI AND KOMI-CHAN!
AND CALLS TOO.
EH? TWENTY-FOUR TEXTS?
I forgot to ask yesterday, when do you want to go to the beach?
I'm thinking of buying a swim-suit at a nearby shop. What kind should I get?
Speaking of, Komi-something-san was saying she hates the beach...
Should you and me just go without her?
aruse-san, thanks r yesterday. That's I had to say, but I ded up texting you yway.
There's something I'd like to ask for your advice on, do you mind?
h! Maybe you're leeping?
Mind if I ask what time you normally go to bed?
Why aren't you replying?
A-ack!? Sorry, I was just kid-ding! The three of us can go!
You're not trying to leave me out now, are you?
Why? Huh? Why?
Yuu-chan?
Why won't you answer my calls? I said I was sorry!
Are you awake?
Sorry...... All these texts must be annoying you, huh?
If it's annoying you, I won't text you anymore, so please just send me a reply...
Naruse-san...?
You're awake, aren't you?
It's nine o'clock already!

No Matter How I Look at It, It's You Guys' Fault I'm Not Popular!

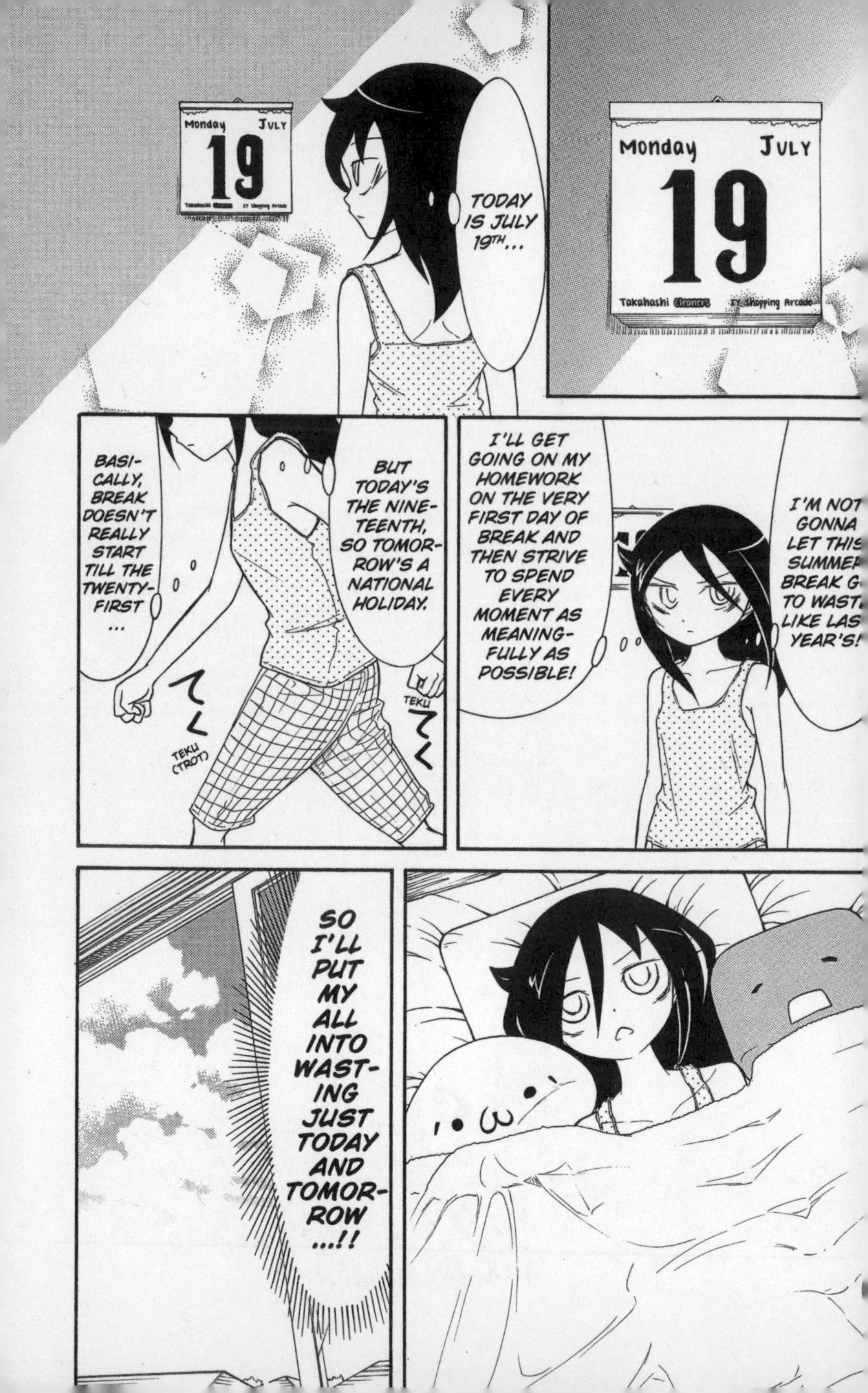
Monday JULY 19
Takahashi Cleaners
Monday JULY 19
TODAY IS JULY 19TH...
I'M NOT GONNA LET THIS SUMME BREAK G TO WAST LIKE LAS YEAR'S!
I'LL GET GOING ON MY HOMEWORK ON THE VERY FIRST DAY OF BREAK AND THEN STRIVE TO SPEND EVERY MOMENT AS MEANINGFULLY AS POSSIBLE!
BUT TODAY'S THE NINETEENTH, SO TOMORROW'S A NATIONAL HOLIDAY.
TEKU
BASICALLY, BREAK DOESN'T REALLY START TILL THE TWENTY-FIRST...
TEKU (TROT)
SO I'LL PUT MY ALL INTO WASTING JUST TODAY AND TOMORROW...!!

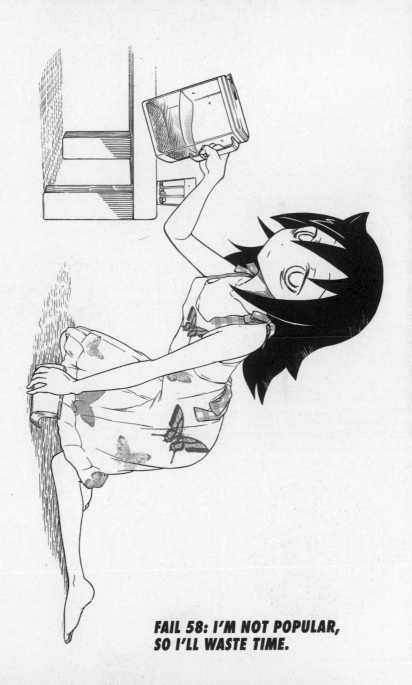

FAIL 58: I'M NOT POPULAR, SO I'LL WASTE TIME.

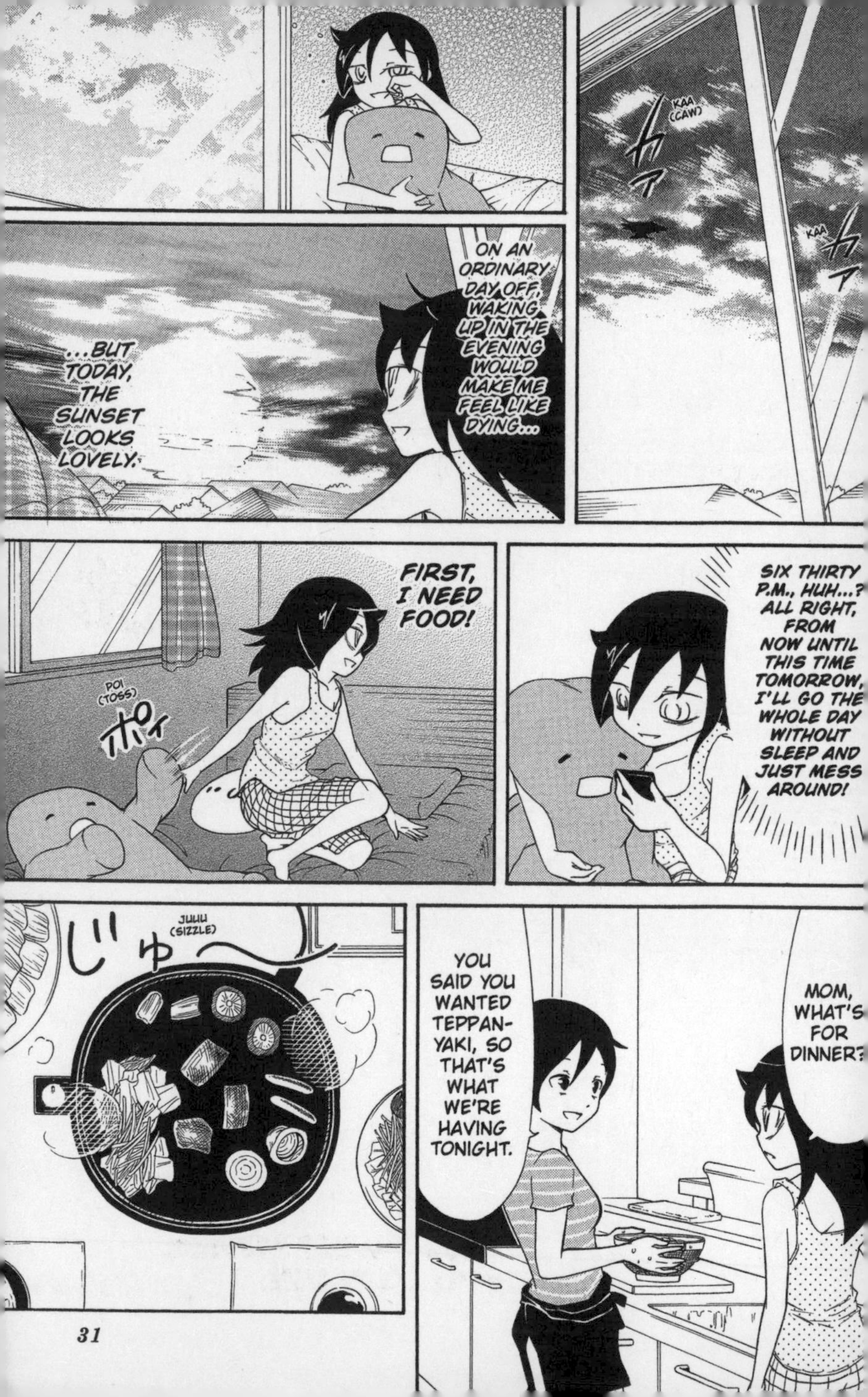
KAA (CAW)
KAA
ON AN ORDINARY DAY OFF, WAKING UP IN THE EVENING WOULD MAKE ME FEEL LIKE DYING...
...BUT TODAY, THE SUNSET LOOKS LOVELY.
SIX THIRTY P.M., HUH...? ALL RIGHT, FROM NOW UNTIL THIS TIME TOMORROW, I'LL GO THE WHOLE DAY WITHOUT SLEEP AND JUST MESS AROUND!
FIRST, I NEED FOOD!
POI (TOSS)
MOM, WHAT'S FOR DINNER?
YOU SAID YOU WANTED TEPPAN-YAKI, SO THAT'S WHAT WE'RE HAVING TONIGHT.
JUUU (SIZZLE)

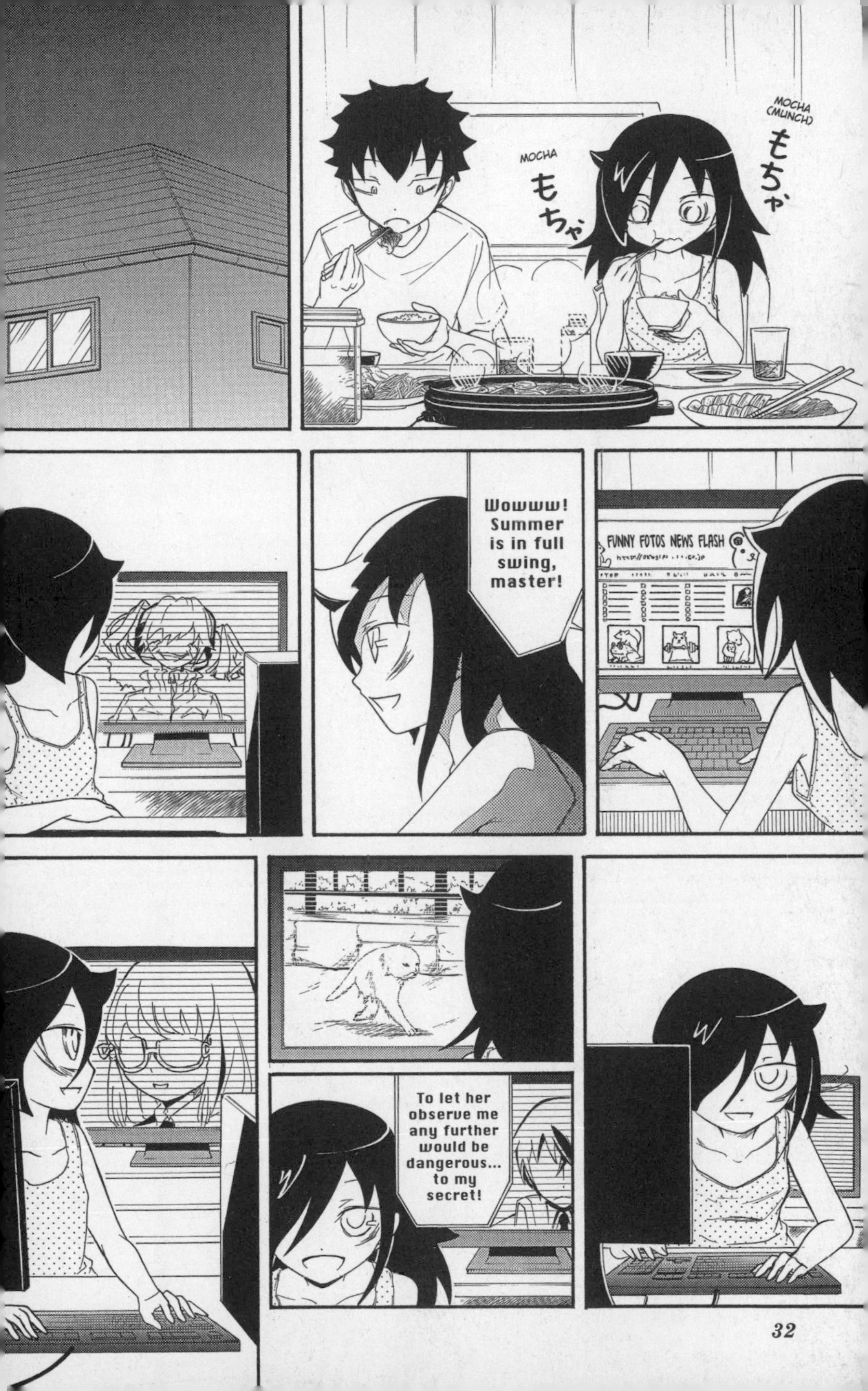
MOCHA (MUNCH)
もちゃ
MOCHA
もちゃ
FUNNY FOTOS NEWS FLASH
Wowww! Summer is in full swing, master!
To let her observe me any further would be dangerous... to my secret!

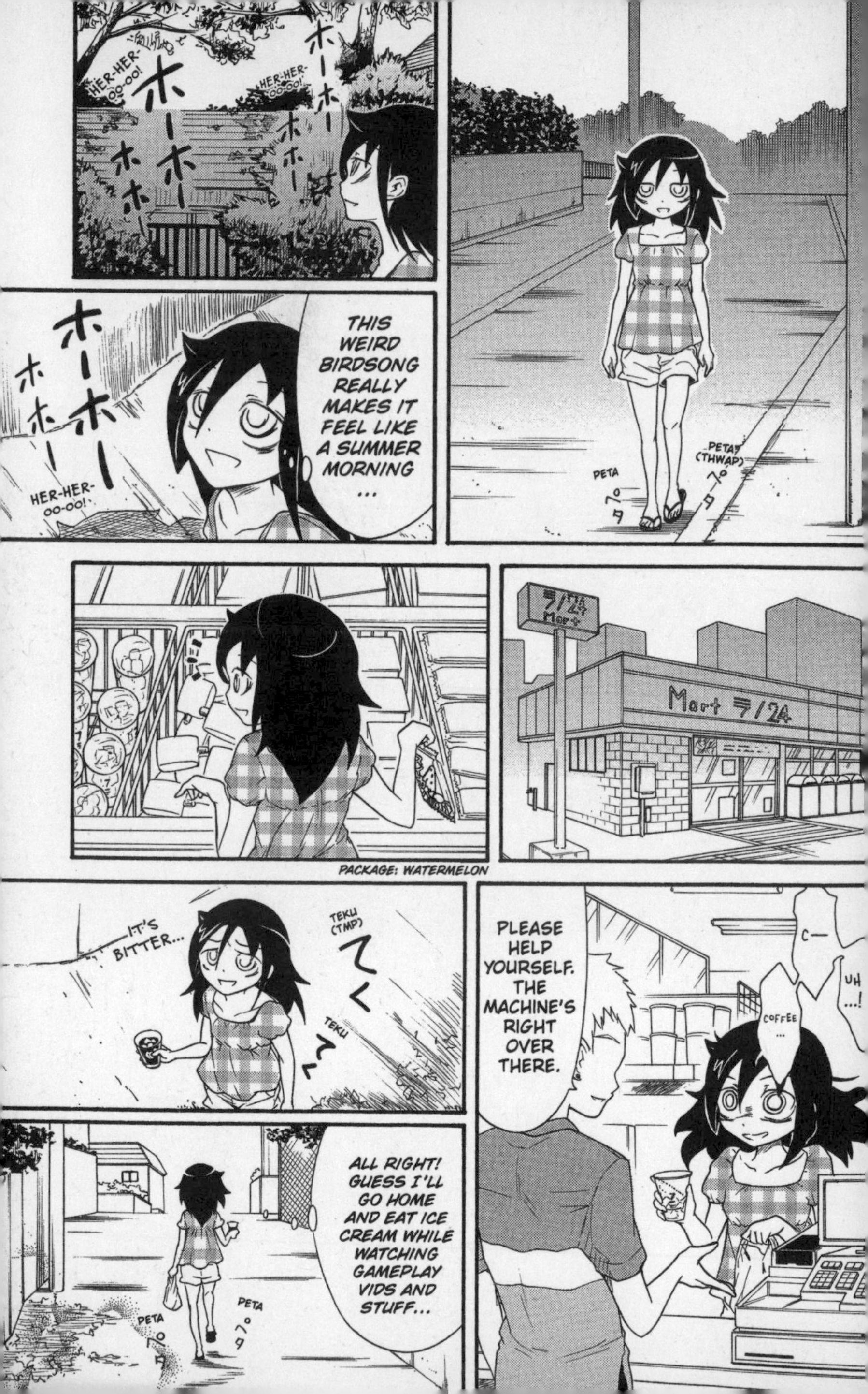

PETA (THWAP)
ペタ
PETA
ペタ
HER-HER-OO-OO!
ホーホーホーホー
HER-HER-OO-OO!
ホーホーホーホー
THIS WEIRD BIRDSONG REALLY MAKES IT FEEL LIKE A SUMMER MORNING ...
ホーホーホーホー
HER-HER-OO-OO!
ラ/24 Mart
Mart ラ/24
PACKAGE: WATERMELON
C—
UH ...!
COFFEE ...
PLEASE HELP YOURSELF. THE MACHINE'S RIGHT OVER THERE.
IT'S BITTER...
TEKU (TMP)
テク
TEKU
テク
ALL RIGHT! GUESS I'LL GO HOME AND EAT ICE CREAM WHILE WATCHING GAMEPLAY VIDS AND STUFF...
PETA
ペタ
PETA
ペタ

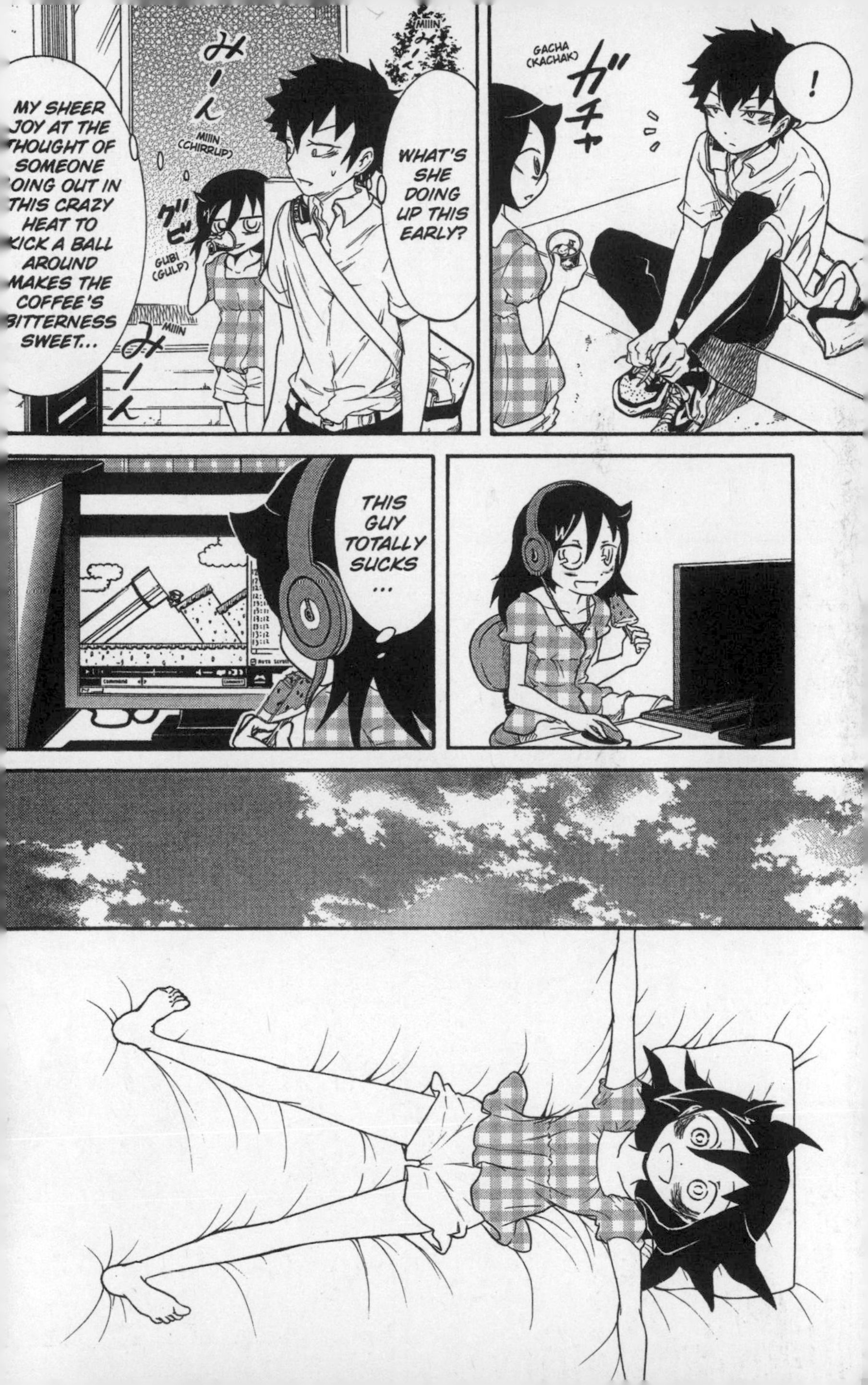

GACHA (KACHAK)
ガチャ
!
MIIN
みーん
WHAT'S SHE DOING UP THIS EARLY?
みーん
MIIN (CHIRRUP)
MY SHEER JOY AT THE THOUGHT OF SOMEONE GOING OUT IN THIS CRAZY HEAT TO KICK A BALL AROUND MAKES THE COFFEE'S BITTERNESS SWEET...
グビ
GUBI (GULP)
MIIN
みーん
THIS GUY TOTALLY SUCKS ...

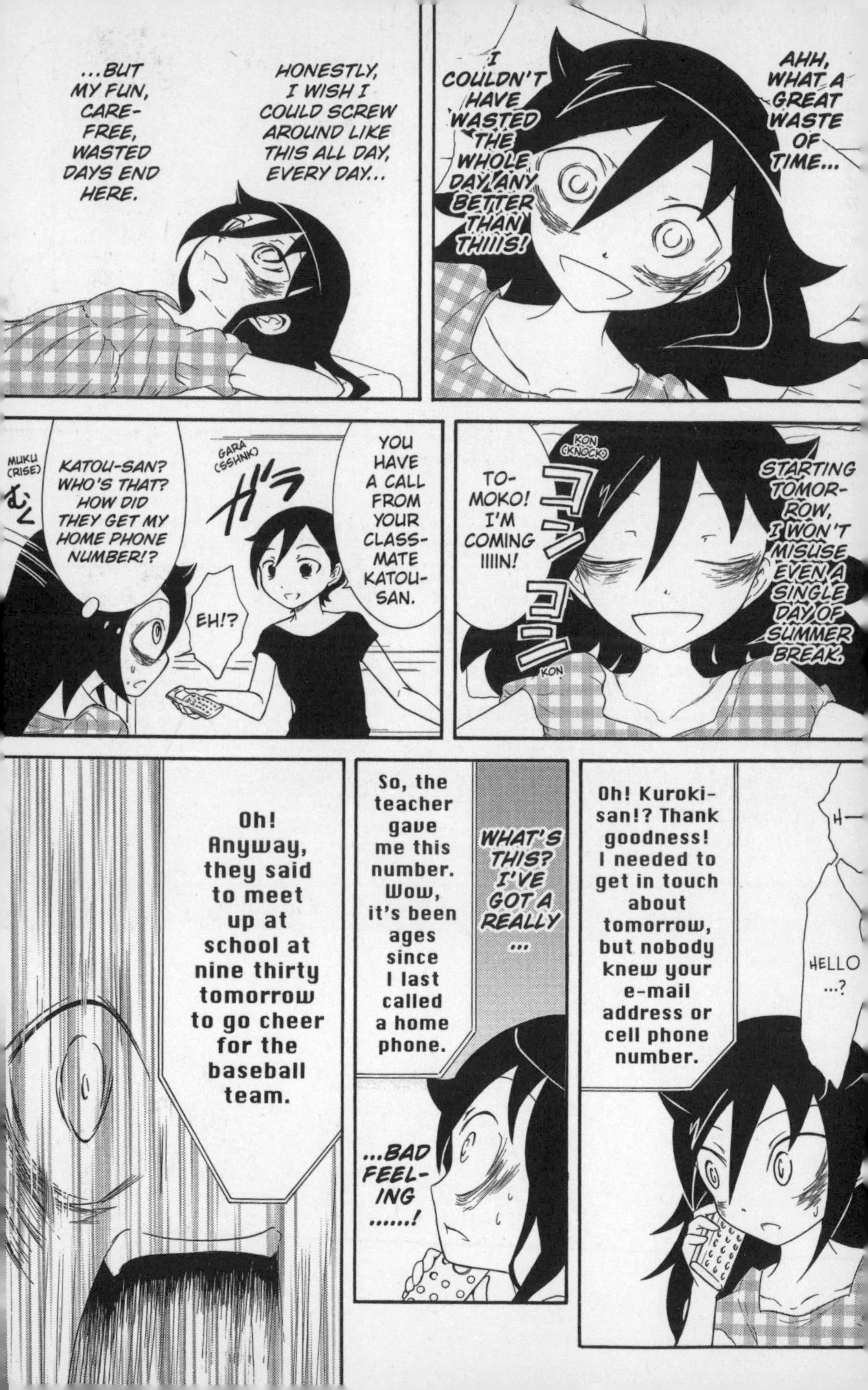

AHH, WHAT A GREAT WASTE OF TIME...
I COULDN'T HAVE WASTED THE WHOLE DAY ANY BETTER THAN THIIIS!
HONESTLY, I WISH I COULD SCREW AROUND LIKE THIS ALL DAY, EVERY DAY...
...BUT MY FUN, CAREFREE, WASTED DAYS END HERE.
STARTING TOMORROW, I WON'T MISUSE EVEN A SINGLE DAY OF SUMMER BREAK.
KON (KNOCK)
KON
TO-MOKO! I'M COMING IIIIN!
GARA (SSHNK)
ガラ
YOU HAVE A CALL FROM YOUR CLASSMATE KATOU-SAN.
EH!?
MUKU (RISE)
むく
KATOU-SAN? WHO'S THAT? HOW DID THEY GET MY HOME PHONE NUMBER!?
H—
HELLO ...?
Oh! Kuroki-san!? Thank goodness! I needed to get in touch about tomorrow, but nobody knew your e-mail address or cell phone number.
So, the teacher gave me this number. Wow, it's been ages since I last called a home phone.
WHAT'S THIS? I'VE GOT A REALLY ...
...BAD FEELING ......!
Oh! Anyway, they said to meet up at school at nine thirty tomorrow to go cheer for the baseball team.

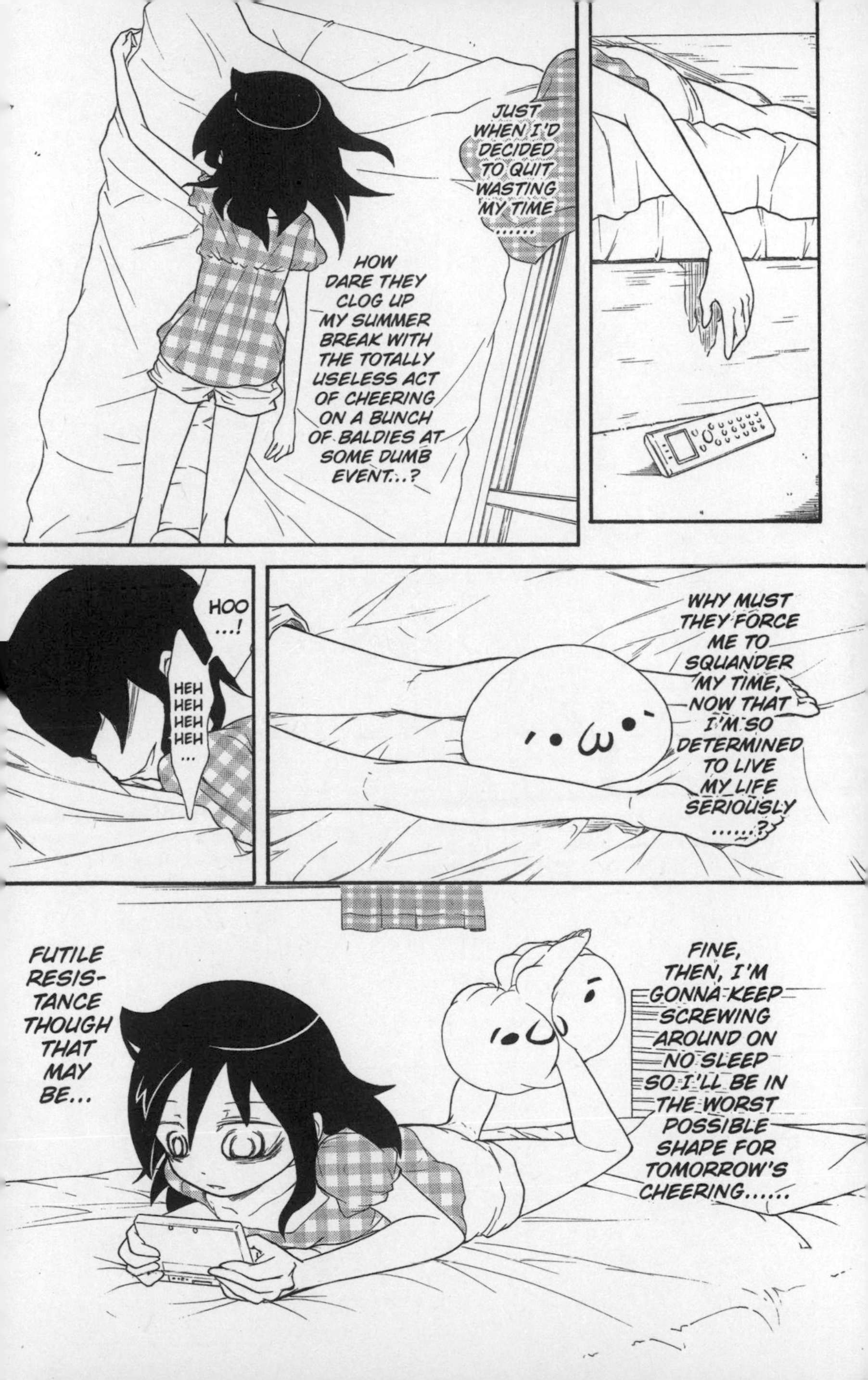
JUST WHEN I'D DECIDED TO QUIT WASTING MY TIME ......
HOW DARE THEY CLOG UP MY SUMMER BREAK WITH THE TOTALLY USELESS ACT OF CHEERING ON A BUNCH OF BALDIES AT SOME DUMB EVENT...?
WHY MUST THEY FORCE ME TO SQUANDER MY TIME, NOW THAT I'M SO DETERMINED TO LIVE MY LIFE SERIOUSLY ......?
HOO ...!
HEH HEH HEH HEH ...
FINE, THEN, I'M GONNA KEEP SCREWING AROUND ON NO SLEEP SO I'LL BE IN THE WORST POSSIBLE SHAPE FOR TOMORROW'S CHEERING......
FUTILE RESIS-TANCE THOUGH THAT MAY BE...

No Matter How I Look at It, It's You Guys' Fault I'm Not Popular!

FAIL 59: I'M NOT POPULAR, SO I'LL CHEER THEM ON.

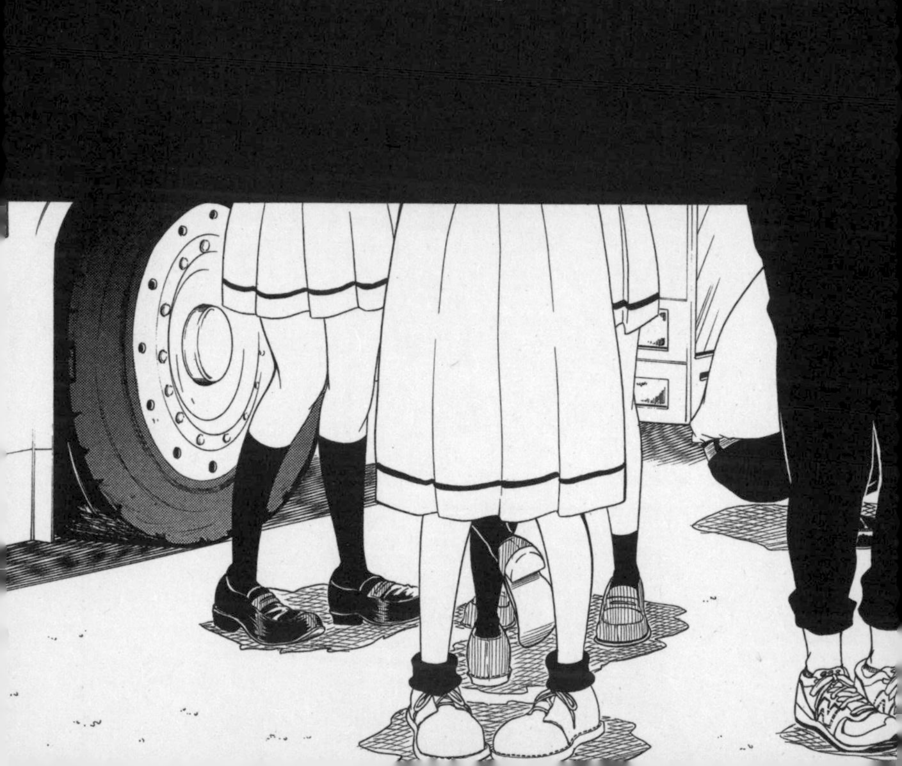

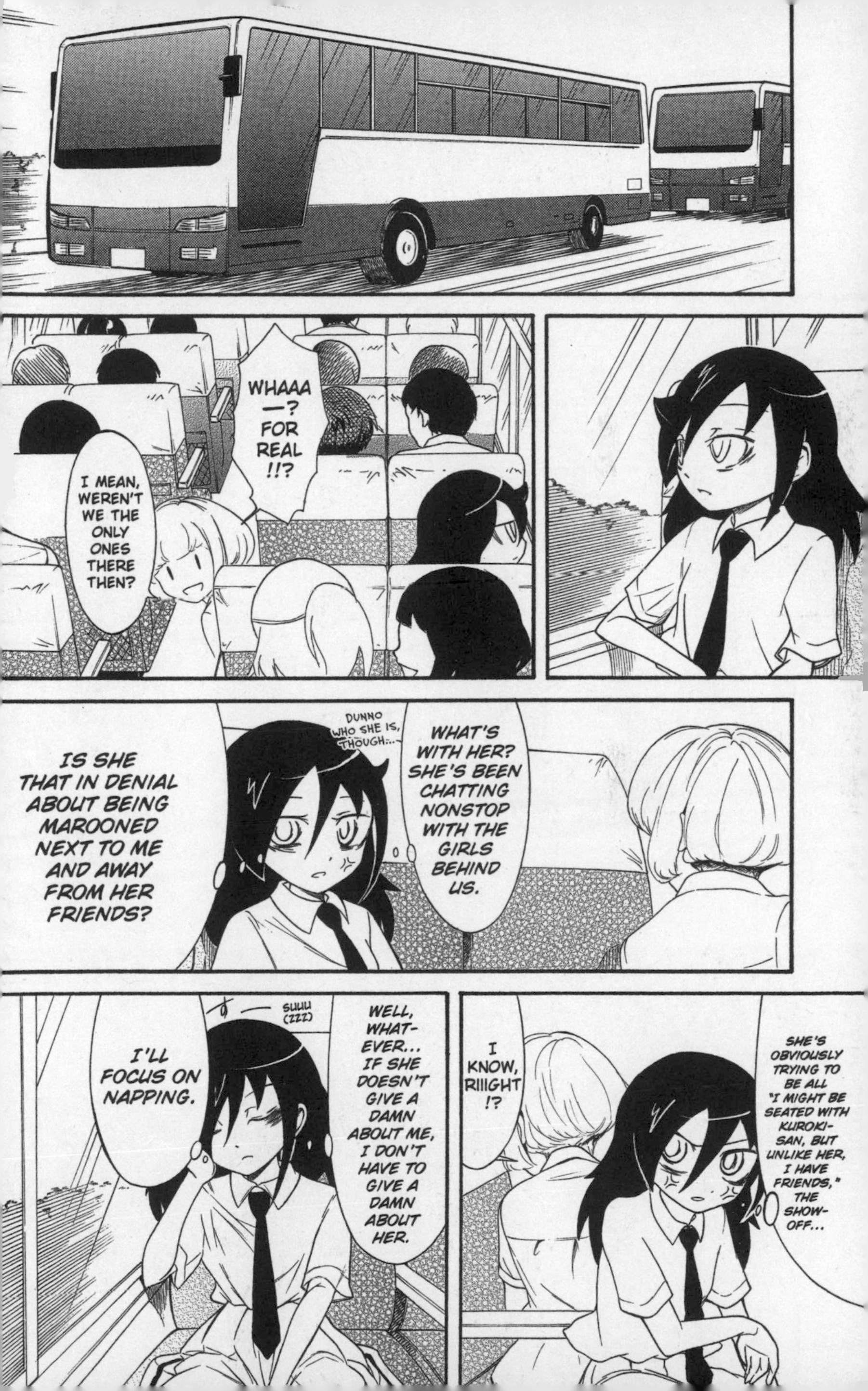
WHAAA—? FOR REAL!!?
I MEAN, WEREN'T WE THE ONLY ONES THERE THEN?
WHAT'S WITH HER? SHE'S BEEN CHATTING NONSTOP WITH THE GIRLS BEHIND US.
DUNNO WHO SHE IS, THOUGH...
IS SHE THAT IN DENIAL ABOUT BEING MAROONED NEXT TO ME AND AWAY FROM HER FRIENDS?
SHE'S OBVIOUSLY TRYING TO BE ALL "I MIGHT BE SEATED WITH KUROKI-SAN, BUT UNLIKE HER, I HAVE FRIENDS," THE SHOW-OFF...
I KNOW, RIIIGHT!?
WELL, WHAT-EVER... IF SHE DOESN'T GIVE A DAMN ABOUT ME, I DON'T HAVE TO GIVE A DAMN ABOUT HER.
SUUU (ZZZ)
I'LL FOCUS ON NAPPING.

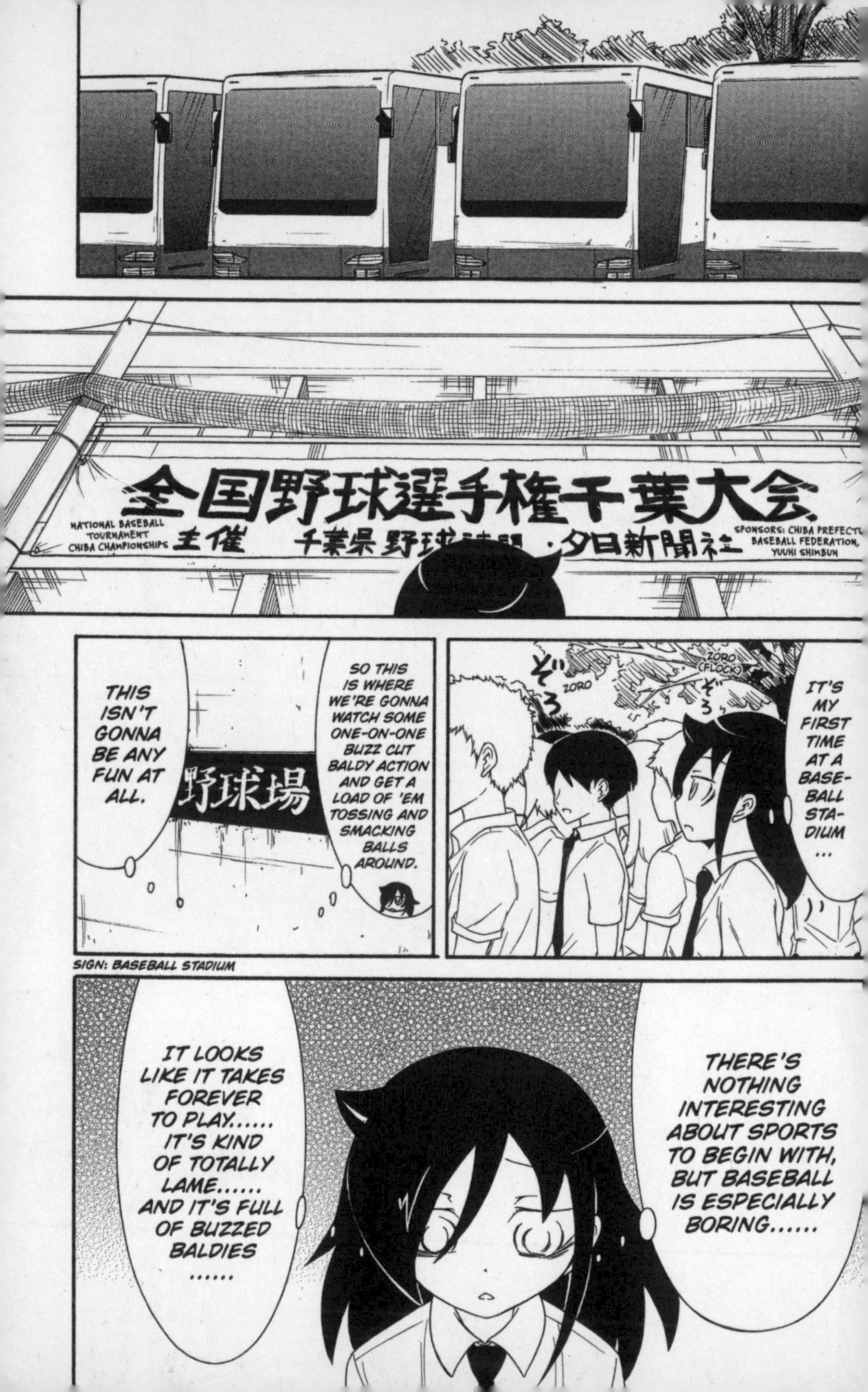

全国野球選手権千葉大会
NATIONAL BASEBALL TOURNAMENT CHIBA CHAMPIONSHIPS
主催
千葉県 野球
・夕日新聞社
SPONSORS: CHIBA PREFECTU BASEBALL FEDERATION, YUUHI SHIMBUN
ぞろ ZORO
ぞろ ZORO (FLOCK)
IT'S MY FIRST TIME AT A BASE-BALL STA-DIUM...
SO THIS IS WHERE WE'RE GONNA WATCH SOME ONE-ON-ONE BUZZ CUT BALDY ACTION AND GET A LOAD OF 'EM TOSSING AND SMACKING BALLS AROUND.
野球場
THIS ISN'T GONNA BE ANY FUN AT ALL.
SIGN: BASEBALL STADIUM
THERE'S NOTHING INTERESTING ABOUT SPORTS TO BEGIN WITH, BUT BASEBALL IS ESPECIALLY BORING......
IT LOOKS LIKE IT TAKES FOREVER TO PLAY...... IT'S KIND OF TOTALLY LAME...... AND IT'S FULL OF BUZZED BALDIES ......

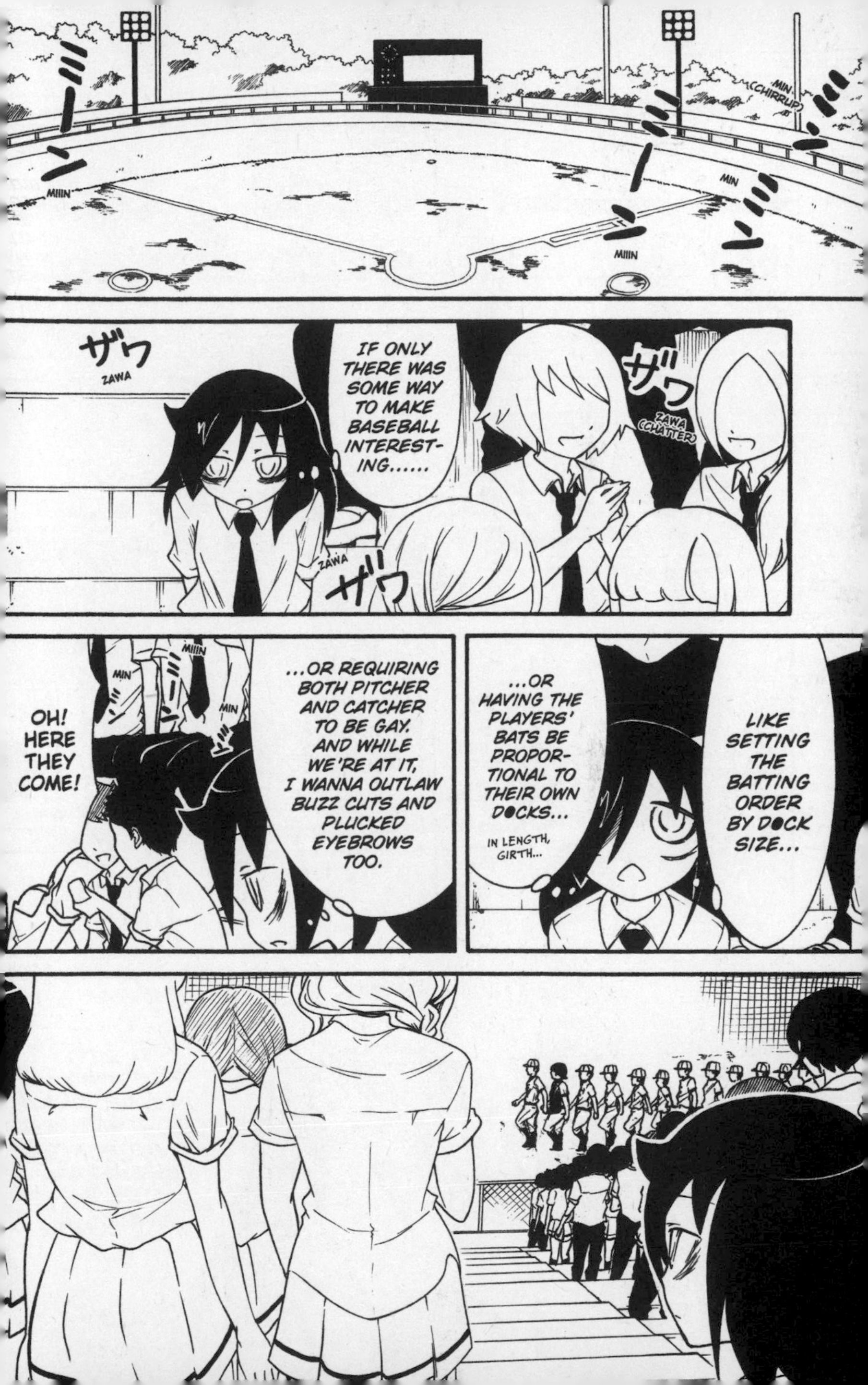

ミーン
MIN (CHIRRUP)
ミーン
MIN
MIIIN
ミーン
MIIIN
ザワ
ZAWA (CHATTER)
IF ONLY THERE WAS SOME WAY TO MAKE BASEBALL INTEREST-ING......
ザワ
ZAWA
ZAWA
ザワ
LIKE SETTING THE BATTING ORDER BY D●CK SIZE...
...OR HAVING THE PLAYERS' BATS BE PROPOR-TIONAL TO THEIR OWN D●CKS...
IN LENGTH, GIRTH...
...OR REQUIRING BOTH PITCHER AND CATCHER TO BE GAY. AND WHILE WE'RE AT IT, I WANNA OUTLAW BUZZ CUTS AND PLUCKED EYEBROWS TOO.
MIIIN
MIN
MIN
OH! HERE THEY COME!

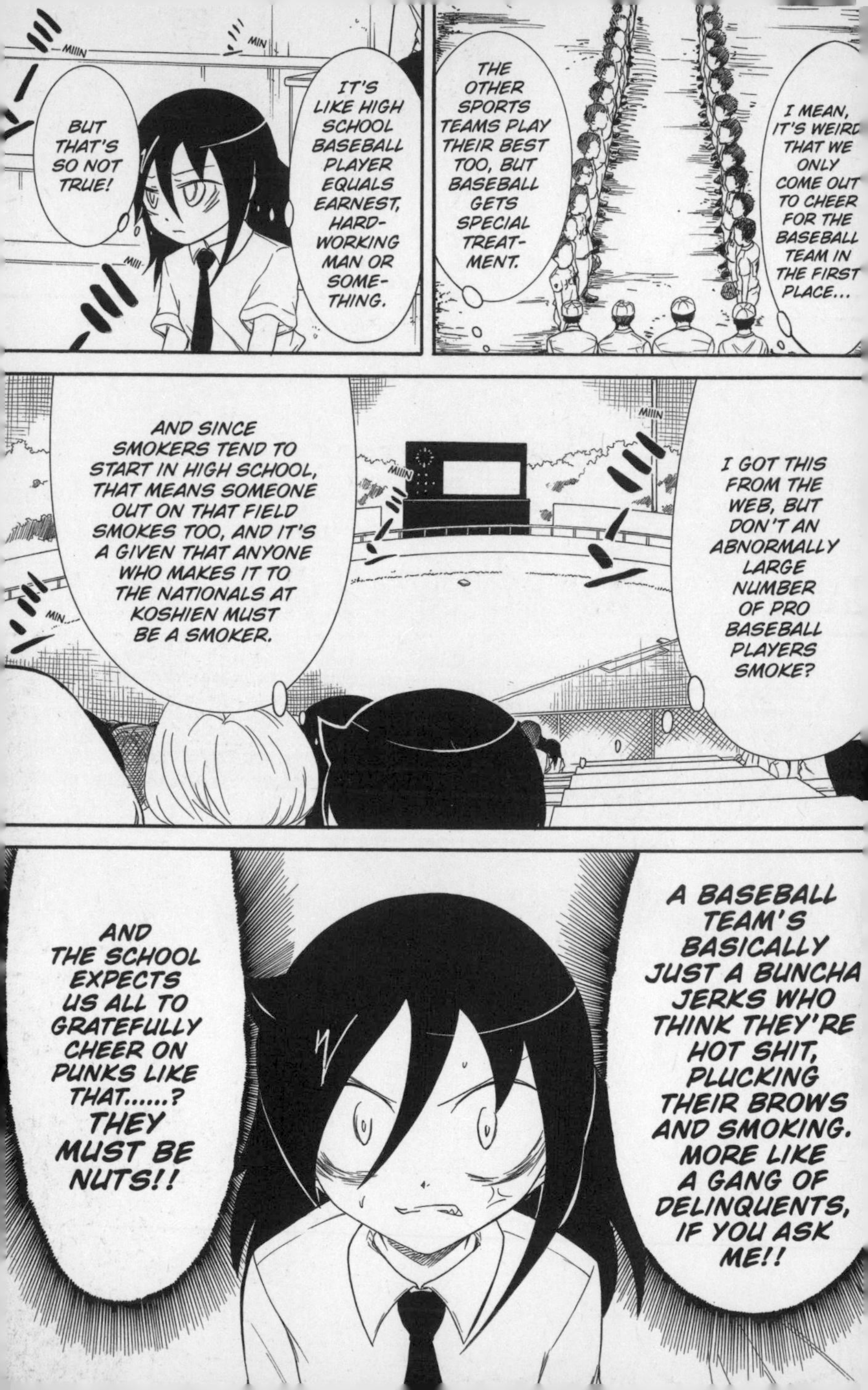
I MEAN, IT'S WEIRD THAT WE ONLY COME OUT TO CHEER FOR THE BASEBALL TEAM IN THE FIRST PLACE...
THE OTHER SPORTS TEAMS PLAY THEIR BEST TOO, BUT BASEBALL GETS SPECIAL TREATMENT.
MIN
MIIIN
IT'S LIKE HIGH SCHOOL BASEBALL PLAYER EQUALS EARNEST, HARD-WORKING MAN OR SOMETHING.
BUT THAT'S SO NOT TRUE!
MIII-
MIIIN
I GOT THIS FROM THE WEB, BUT DON'T AN ABNORMALLY LARGE NUMBER OF PRO BASEBALL PLAYERS SMOKE?
MIIIN
AND SINCE SMOKERS TEND TO START IN HIGH SCHOOL, THAT MEANS SOMEONE OUT ON THAT FIELD SMOKES TOO, AND IT'S A GIVEN THAT ANYONE WHO MAKES IT TO THE NATIONALS AT KOSHIEN MUST BE A SMOKER.
MIN...
A BASEBALL TEAM'S BASICALLY JUST A BUNCHA JERKS WHO THINK THEY'RE HOT SHIT, PLUCKING THEIR BROWS AND SMOKING. MORE LIKE A GANG OF DELINQUENTS, IF YOU ASK ME!!
AND THE SCHOOL EXPECTS US ALL TO GRATEFULLY CHEER ON PUNKS LIKE THAT......? THEY MUST BE NUTS!!

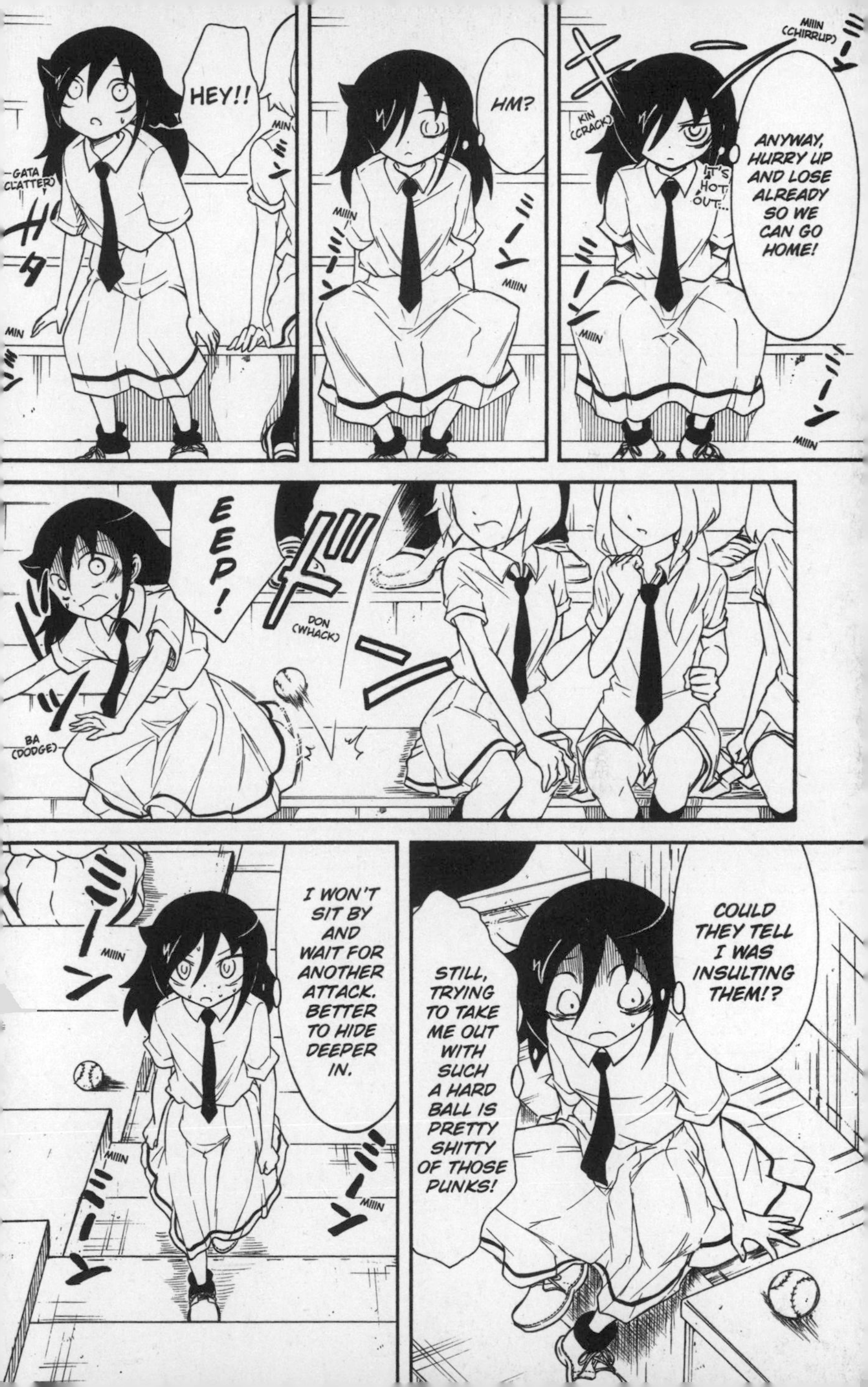
MIIIN (CHIRRUP)
ANYWAY, HURRY UP AND LOSE ALREADY SO WE CAN GO HOME!
KIN (CRACK)
IT'S HOT OUT...
MIIIN
MIIIN
HM?
MIIIN
MIIIN
HEY!!
MIN
GATA (CLATTER)
MIN
EEP!
DON (WHACK)
BA (DODGE)
COULD THEY TELL I WAS INSULTING THEM!?
STILL, TRYING TO TAKE ME OUT WITH SUCH A HARD BALL IS PRETTY SHITTY OF THOSE PUNKS!
I WON'T SIT BY AND WAIT FOR ANOTHER ATTACK. BETTER TO HIDE DEEPER IN.
MIIIN
MIIIN
MIIIN

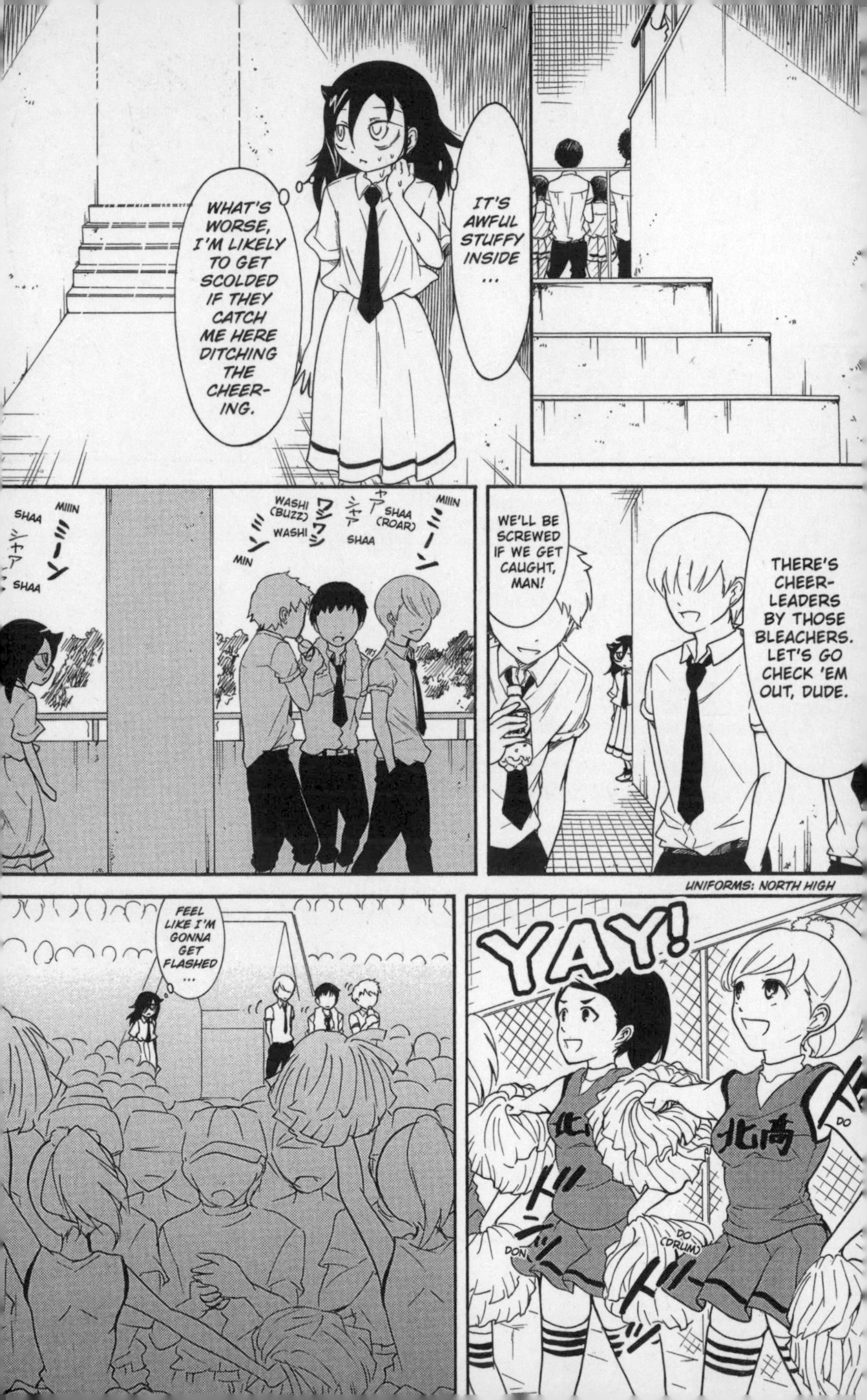

IT'S AWFUL STUFFY INSIDE ...
WHAT'S WORSE, I'M LIKELY TO GET SCOLDED IF THEY CATCH ME HERE DITCHING THE CHEER-ING.
THERE'S CHEER-LEADERS BY THOSE BLEACHERS. LET'S GO CHECK 'EM OUT, DUDE.
WE'LL BE SCREWED IF WE GET CAUGHT, MAN!
MIIIN ミーン
SHAA (ROAR) シャア SHAA
WASHI (BUZZ) ワシワシ WASHI
MIN ミン
MIIIN ミーン
SHAA シャア SHAA
UNIFORMS: NORTH HIGH
YAY!
DO
DO (DRUM)
DON
FEEL LIKE I'M GONNA GET FLASHED ...

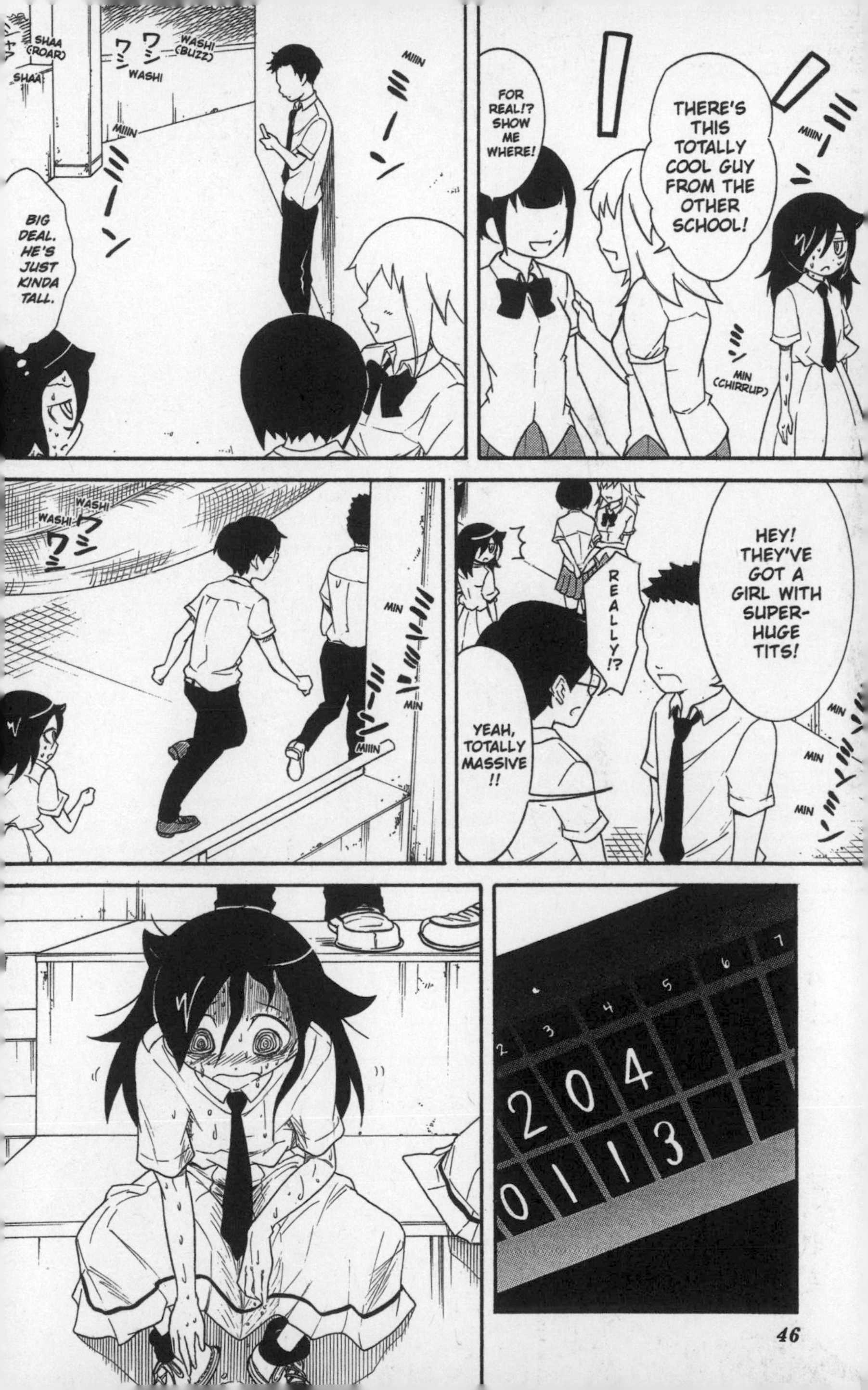
THERE'S THIS TOTALLY COOL GUY FROM THE OTHER SCHOOL!
MIIN
FOR REAL!? SHOW ME WHERE!
MIN (CHIRRUP)
MIIN
SHAA (ROAR)
SHAA
WASHI (BUZZ)
WASHI
MIIN
BIG DEAL. HE'S JUST KINDA TALL.
HEY! THEY'VE GOT A GIRL WITH SUPER-HUGE TITS!
REALLY!?
YEAH, TOTALLY MASSIVE!!
MIN
MIN
MIN
WASHI
WASHI
MIN
MIN
MIIN
2 3 4 5 6 7
204
0113

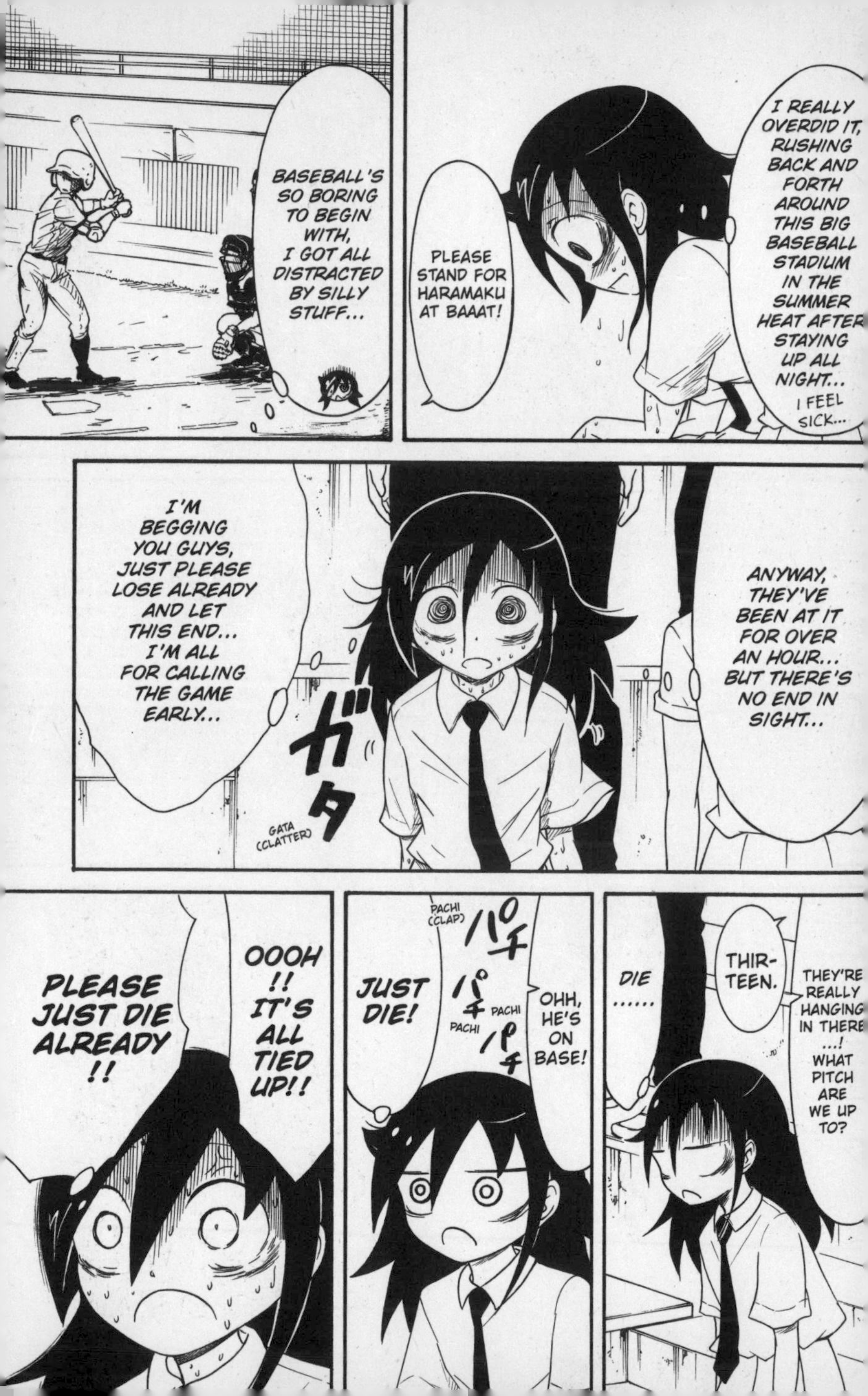
I REALLY OVERDID IT, RUSHING BACK AND FORTH AROUND THIS BIG BASEBALL STADIUM IN THE SUMMER HEAT AFTER STAYING UP ALL NIGHT... I FEEL SICK...
PLEASE STAND FOR HARAMAKU AT BAAAT!
BASEBALL'S SO BORING TO BEGIN WITH, I GOT ALL DISTRACTED BY SILLY STUFF...
ANYWAY, THEY'VE BEEN AT IT FOR OVER AN HOUR... BUT THERE'S NO END IN SIGHT...
ガタ
GATA (CLATTER)
I'M BEGGING YOU GUYS, JUST PLEASE LOSE ALREADY AND LET THIS END... I'M ALL FOR CALLING THE GAME EARLY...
THEY'RE REALLY HANGING IN THERE ...! WHAT PITCH ARE WE UP TO?
THIR-TEEN.
DIE ......
OHH, HE'S ON BASE!
パチ
PACHI (CLAP)
パチ
PACHI
パチ
PACHI
JUST DIE!
OOOH!! IT'S ALL TIED UP!!
PLEASE JUST DIE ALREADY!!

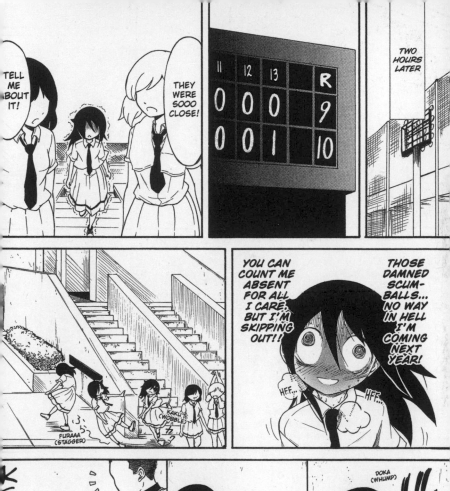

TELL ME 'BOUT IT!

THEY WERE SOOO CLOSE!

11	12	13		R
0	0	0		9
0	0	1		10

TWO HOURS LATER

YOU CAN COUNT ME ABSENT FOR ALL I CARE, BUT I'M SKIPPING OUT!!

THOSE DAMNED SCUMBALLS... NO WAY IN HELL I'M COMING NEXT YEAR!

HFF...

HFF...

FURAAA (STAGGER)

KAKUN (WOBBLE)

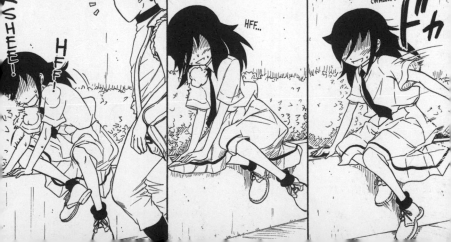

KSHEE!

HFF

HFF...

DOKA (WHUMP)

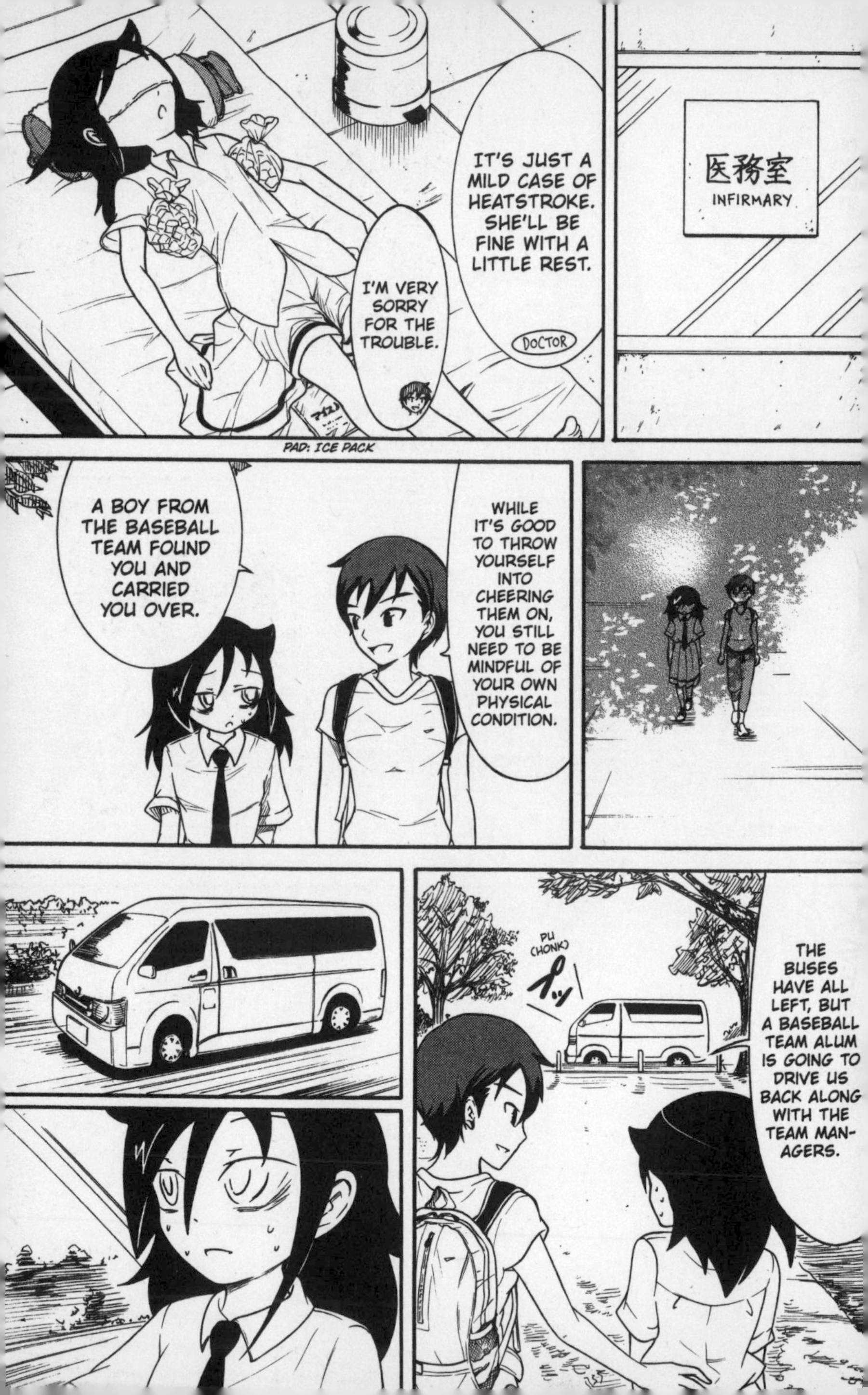
医務室
INFIRMARY
DOCTOR
IT'S JUST A MILD CASE OF HEATSTROKE. SHE'LL BE FINE WITH A LITTLE REST.
I'M VERY SORRY FOR THE TROUBLE.
PAD: ICE PACK
WHILE IT'S GOOD TO THROW YOURSELF INTO CHEERING THEM ON, YOU STILL NEED TO BE MINDFUL OF YOUR OWN PHYSICAL CONDITION.
A BOY FROM THE BASEBALL TEAM FOUND YOU AND CARRIED YOU OVER.
THE BUSES HAVE ALL LEFT, BUT A BASEBALL TEAM ALUM IS GOING TO DRIVE US BACK ALONG WITH THE TEAM MAN-AGERS.
PU (HONK)

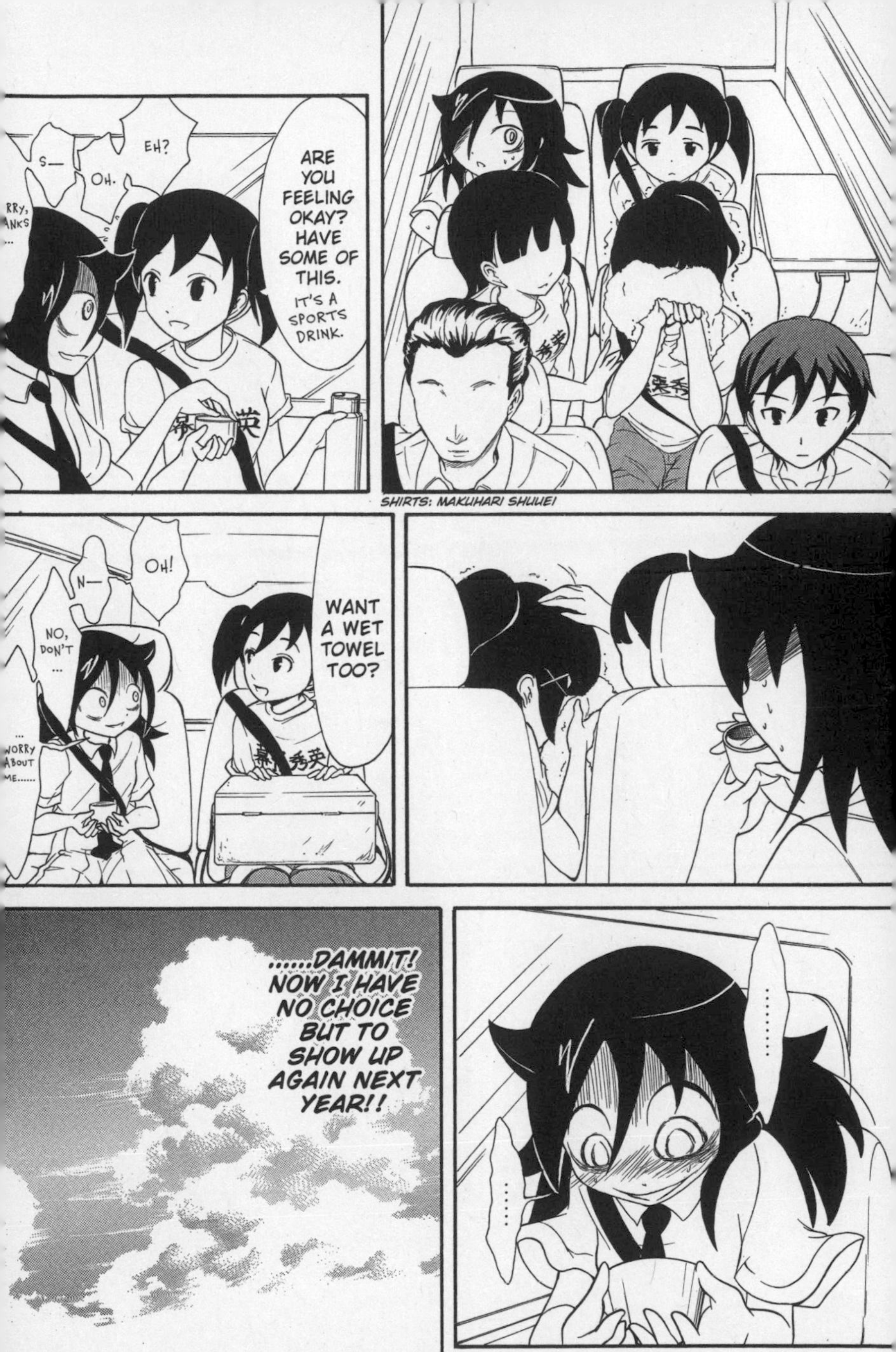
SHIRTS: MAKUHARI SHUUEI
ARE YOU FEELING OKAY? HAVE SOME OF THIS. IT'S A SPORTS DRINK.
EH?
OH.
S—
RRY, ANKS ...
WANT A WET TOWEL TOO?
OH!
N—
NO, DON'T ...
... WORRY ABOUT ME......
......
......
......DAMMIT! NOW I HAVE NO CHOICE BUT TO SHOW UP AGAIN NEXT YEAR!!

NoMatter How I
Look at It, It's You
Guys' Fault I'm Not
Popular!

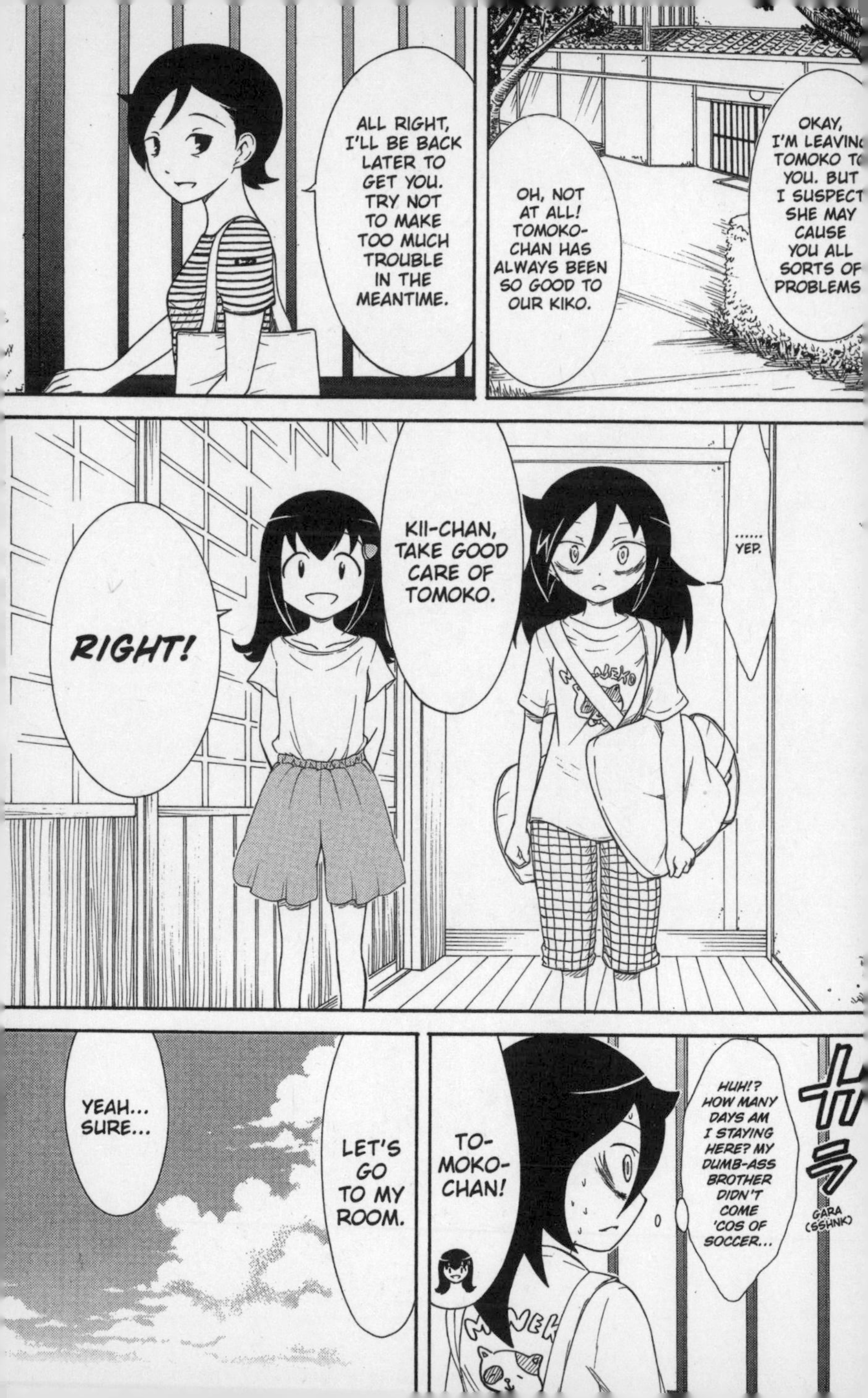
OKAY, I'M LEAVING TOMOKO TO YOU. BUT I SUSPECT SHE MAY CAUSE YOU ALL SORTS OF PROBLEMS
OH, NOT AT ALL! TOMOKO-CHAN HAS ALWAYS BEEN SO GOOD TO OUR KIKO.
ALL RIGHT, I'LL BE BACK LATER TO GET YOU. TRY NOT TO MAKE TOO MUCH TROUBLE IN THE MEANTIME.
......YEP.
KII-CHAN, TAKE GOOD CARE OF TOMOKO.
RIGHT!
ガラ
GARA (SSHNK)
HUH!? HOW MANY DAYS AM I STAYING HERE? MY DUMB-ASS BROTHER DIDN'T COME 'COS OF SOCCER...
TO-MOKO-CHAN!
LET'S GO TO MY ROOM.
YEAH... SURE...

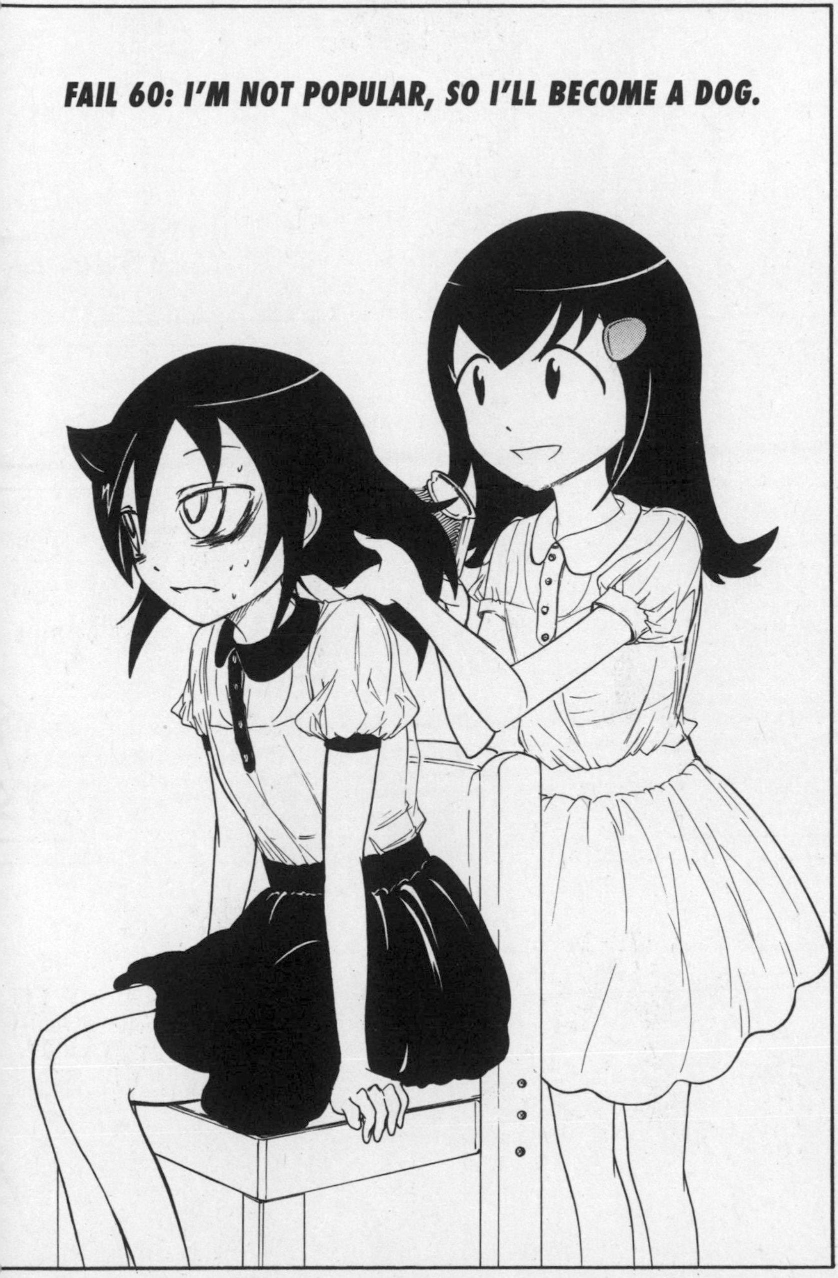
FAIL 60: I'M NOT POPULAR, SO I'LL BECOME A DOG.

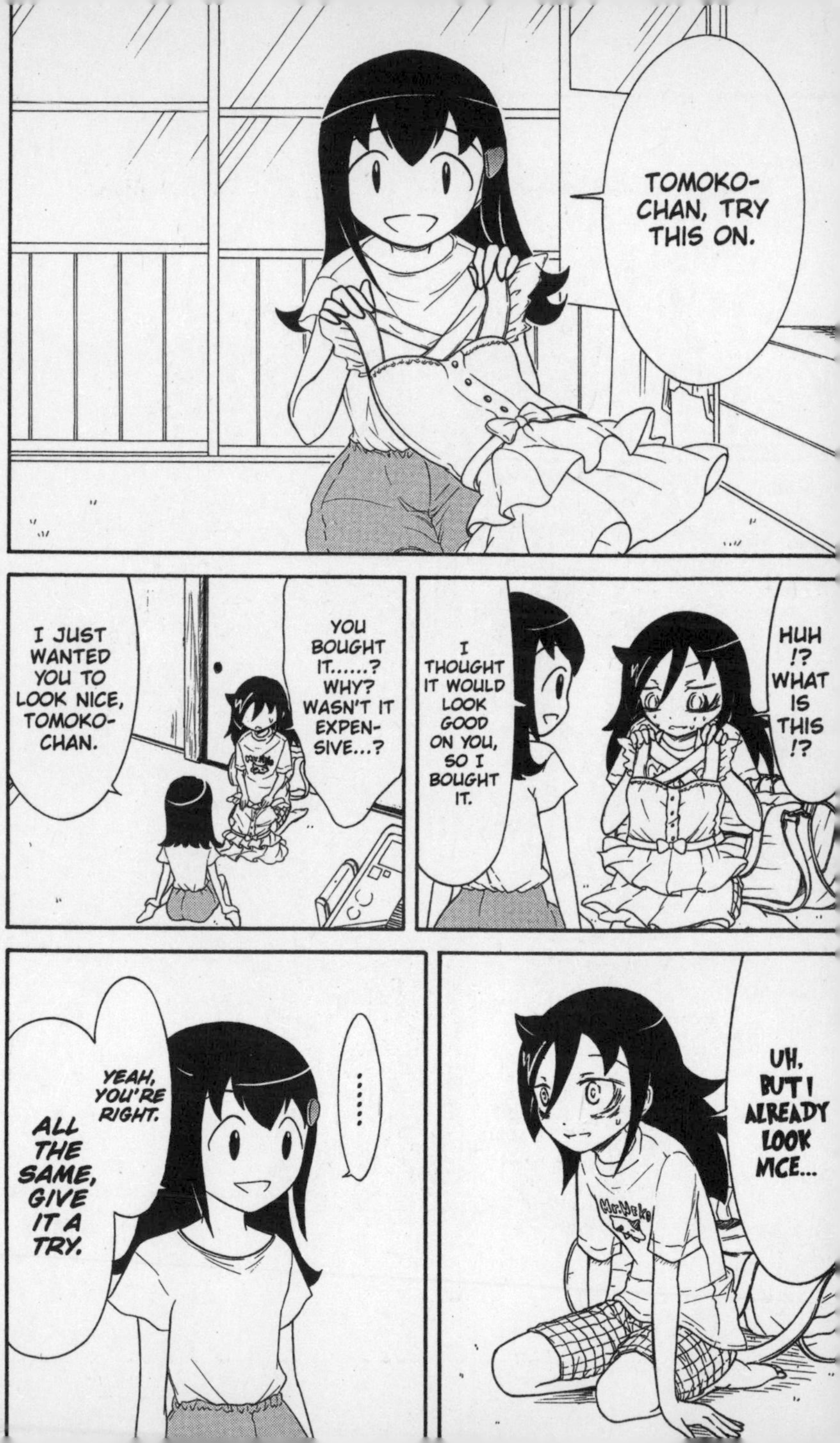
TOMOKO-CHAN, TRY THIS ON.
HUH!? WHAT IS THIS!?
I THOUGHT IT WOULD LOOK GOOD ON YOU, SO I BOUGHT IT.
YOU BOUGHT IT......? WHY? WASN'T IT EXPENSIVE...?
I JUST WANTED YOU TO LOOK NICE, TOMOKO-CHAN.
UH, BUT I ALREADY LOOK NICE...
......
YEAH, YOU'RE RIGHT.
ALL THE SAME, GIVE IT A TRY.

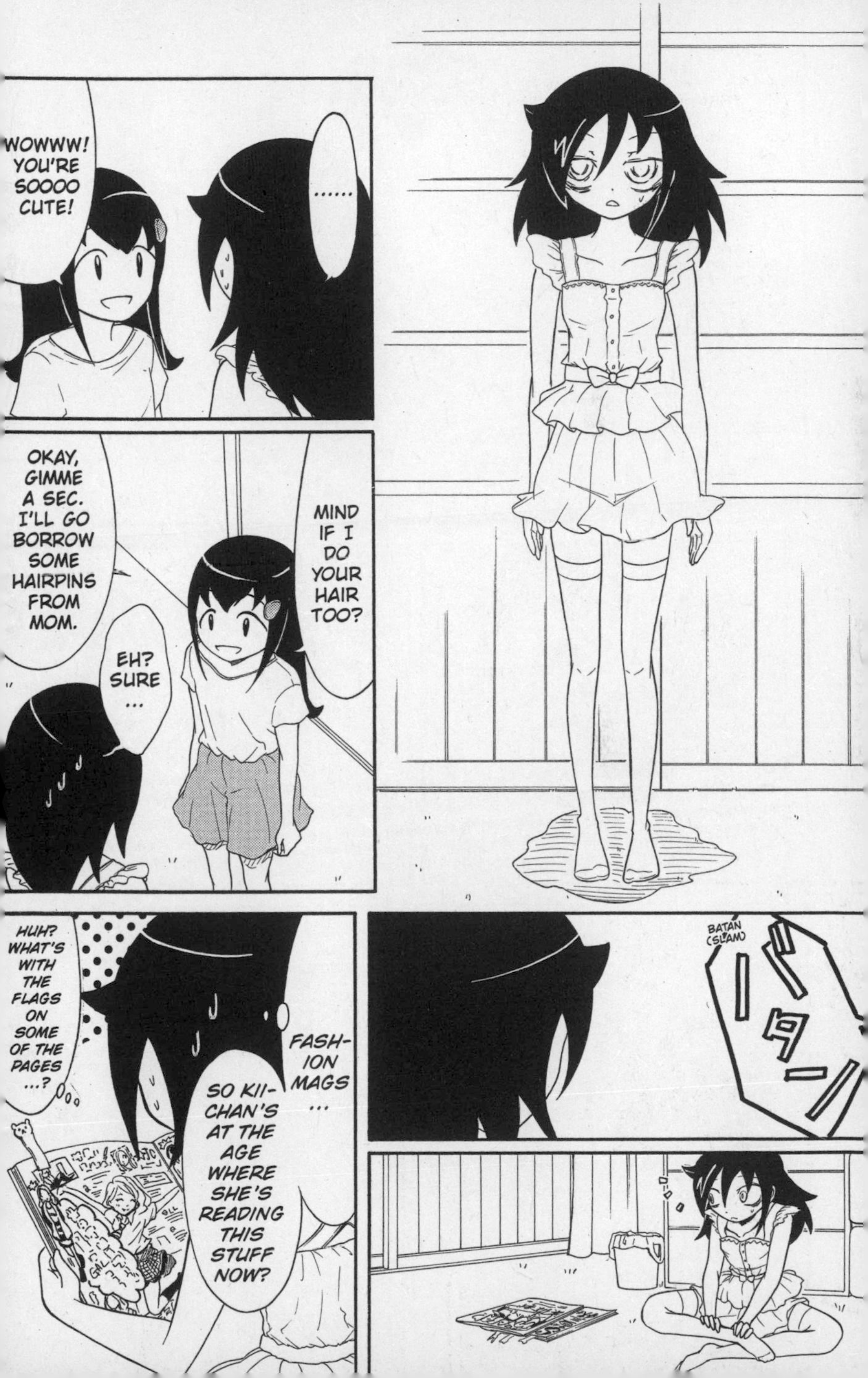
......
WOWWW! YOU'RE SOOOO CUTE!
MIND IF I DO YOUR HAIR TOO?
EH? SURE ...
OKAY, GIMME A SEC. I'LL GO BORROW SOME HAIRPINS FROM MOM.
BATAN (SLAM)
FASH-ION MAGS ...
SO KII-CHAN'S AT THE AGE WHERE SHE'S READING THIS STUFF NOW?
HUH? WHAT'S WITH THE FLAGS ON SOME OF THE PAGES ...?

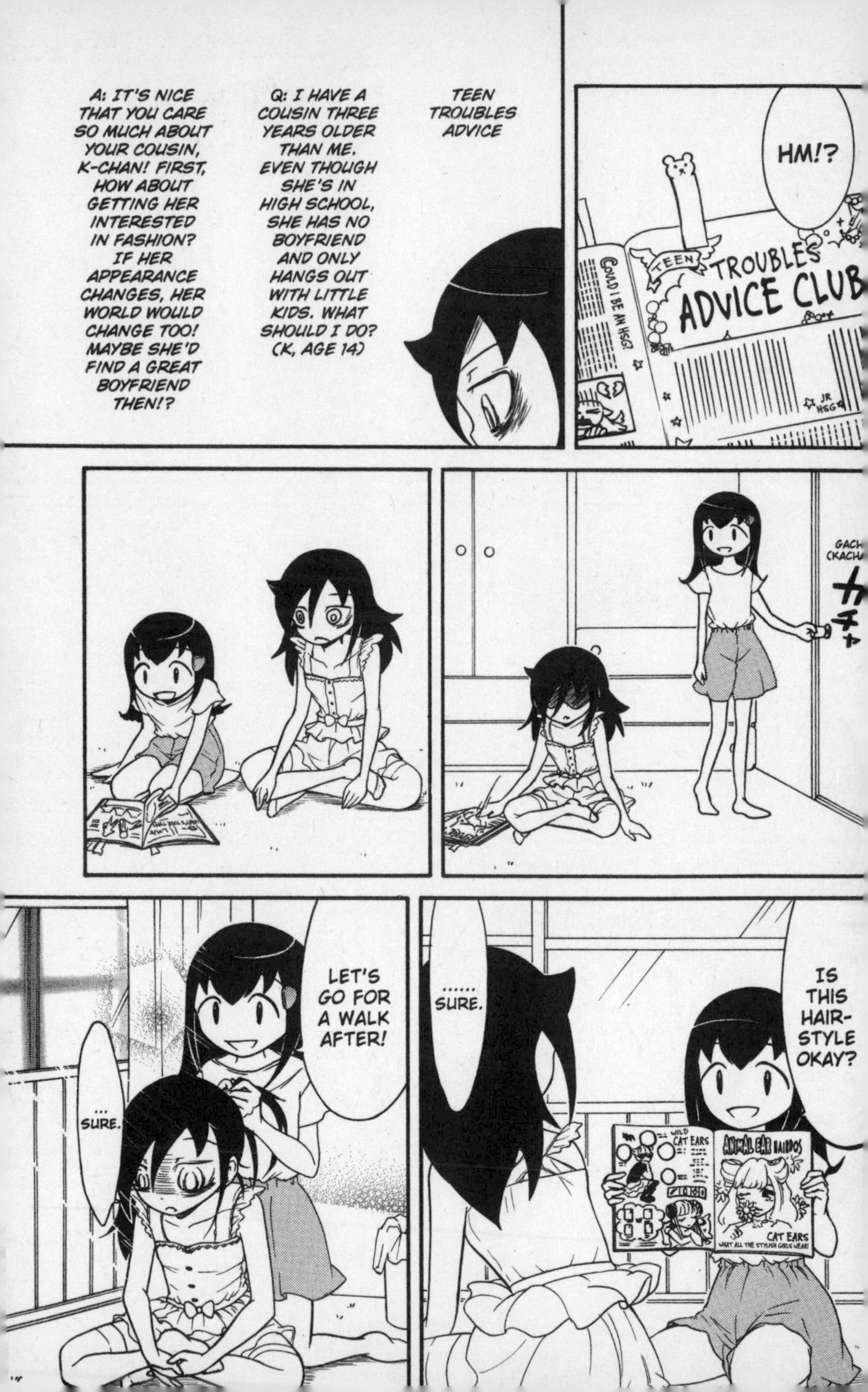
HM!?
TEEN TROUBLES ADVICE CLUB
COULD I BE AN HSG?
JR HSG
TEEN TROUBLES ADVICE
Q: I HAVE A COUSIN THREE YEARS OLDER THAN ME. EVEN THOUGH SHE'S IN HIGH SCHOOL, SHE HAS NO BOYFRIEND AND ONLY HANGS OUT WITH LITTLE KIDS. WHAT SHOULD I DO? (K, AGE 14)
A: IT'S NICE THAT YOU CARE SO MUCH ABOUT YOUR COUSIN, K-CHAN! FIRST, HOW ABOUT GETTING HER INTERESTED IN FASHION? IF HER APPEARANCE CHANGES, HER WORLD WOULD CHANGE TOO! MAYBE SHE'D FIND A GREAT BOYFRIEND THEN!?
GACH
(KACHA
IS THIS HAIR-STYLE OKAY?
ANIMAL EAR HAIRDOS
WILD CAT EARS
CAT EARS
WHAT ALL THE STYLISH GIRLS WEAR!
...... SURE.
LET'S GO FOR A WALK AFTER!
... SURE.

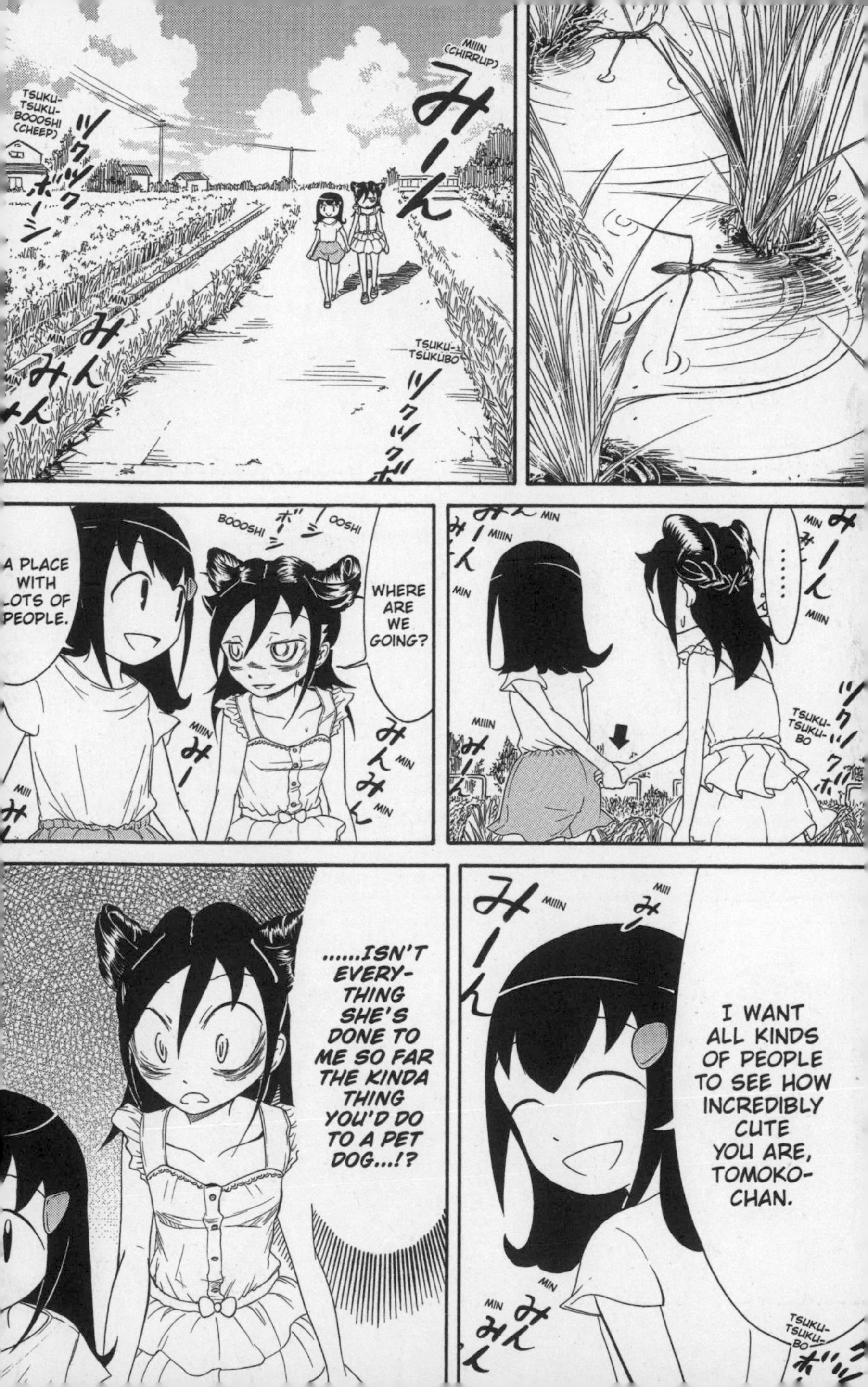
MIIIN (CHIRRUP)
TSUKU-TSUKU-BOOOSHI (CHEEP)
MIN
MIN
MIN
TSUKU-TSUKUBO
MIN
MIIIN
MIN
......
MIIIN
TSUKU-TSUKU-BO
MIIIN
BOOOSHI
OOSHI
WHERE ARE WE GOING?
A PLACE WITH LOTS OF PEOPLE.
MIIIN
MIN
MIN
MIII
MIIIN
MIII
I WANT ALL KINDS OF PEOPLE TO SEE HOW INCREDIBLY CUTE YOU ARE, TOMOKO-CHAN.
MIN
MIN
TSUKU-TSUKU-BO
......ISN'T EVERYTHING SHE'S DONE TO ME SO FAR THE KINDA THING YOU'D DO TO A PET DOG...!?

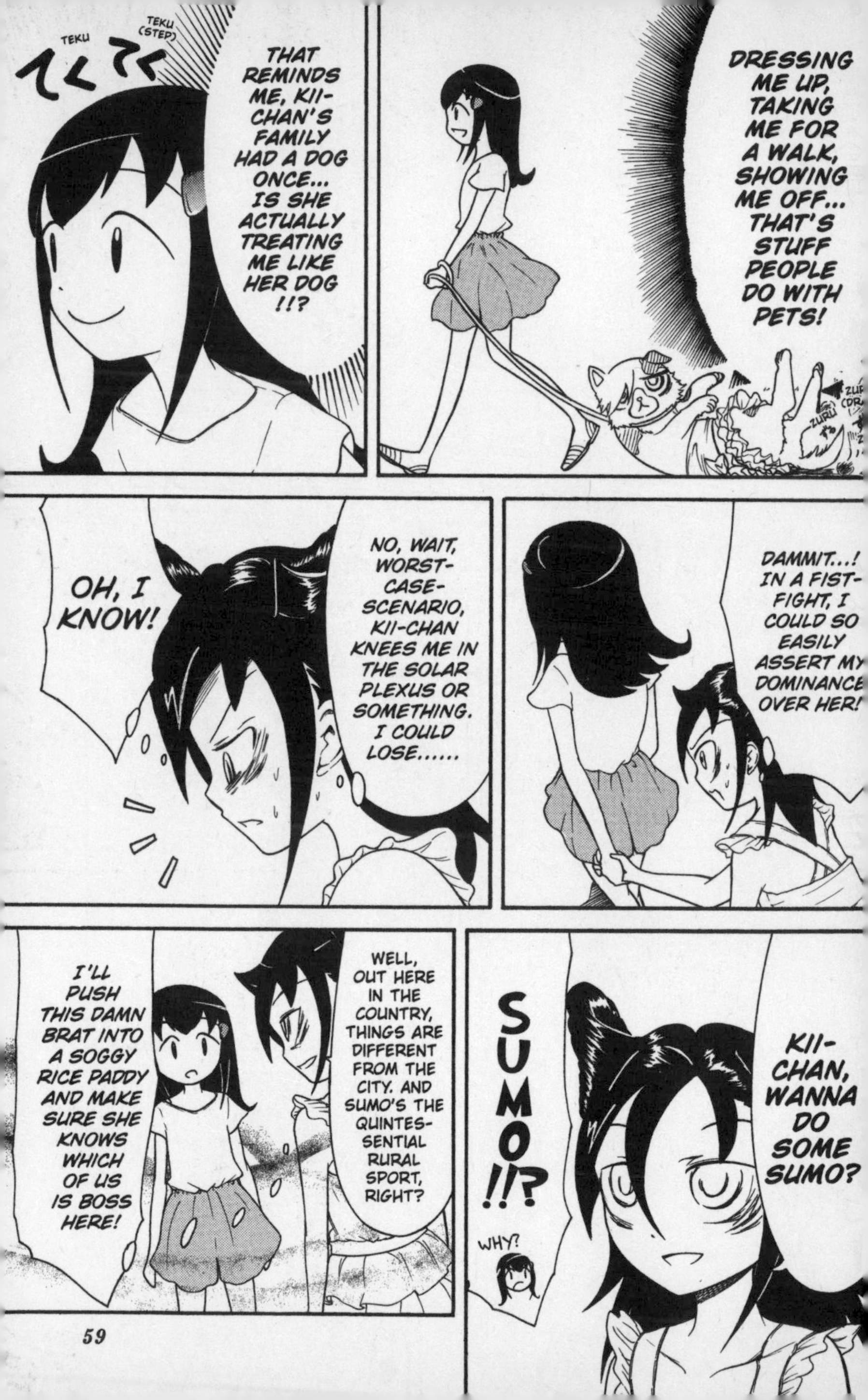

DRESSING ME UP, TAKING ME FOR A WALK, SHOWING ME OFF... THAT'S STUFF PEOPLE DO WITH PETS!
ZURU
TEKU
TEKU (STEP)
THAT REMINDS ME, KII-CHAN'S FAMILY HAD A DOG ONCE... IS SHE ACTUALLY TREATING ME LIKE HER DOG !!?
DAMMIT...! IN A FIST-FIGHT, I COULD SO EASILY ASSERT MY DOMINANCE OVER HER!
NO, WAIT, WORST-CASE-SCENARIO, KII-CHAN KNEES ME IN THE SOLAR PLEXUS OR SOMETHING. I COULD LOSE......
OH, I KNOW!
KII-CHAN, WANNA DO SOME SUMO?
SUMO!!?
WHY?
WELL, OUT HERE IN THE COUNTRY, THINGS ARE DIFFERENT FROM THE CITY. AND SUMO'S THE QUINTES-SENTIAL RURAL SPORT, RIGHT?
I'LL PUSH THIS DAMN BRAT INTO A SOGGY RICE PADDY AND MAKE SURE SHE KNOWS WHICH OF US IS BOSS HERE!

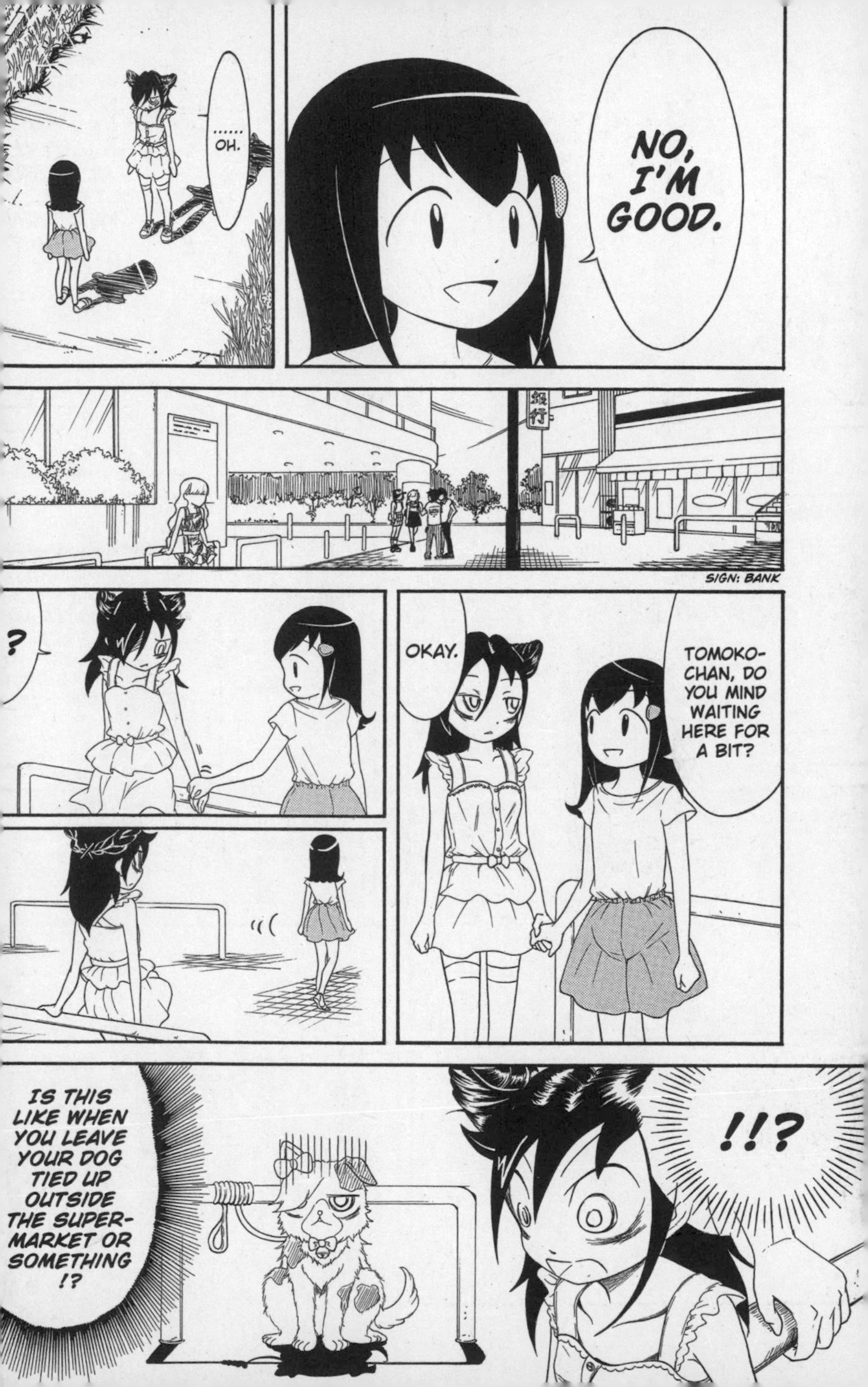
NO, I'M GOOD.
......OH.
SIGN: BANK
TOMOKO-CHAN, DO YOU MIND WAITING HERE FOR A BIT?
OKAY.
?
!!?
IS THIS LIKE WHEN YOU LEAVE YOUR DOG TIED UP OUTSIDE THE SUPER-MARKET OR SOMETHING!?

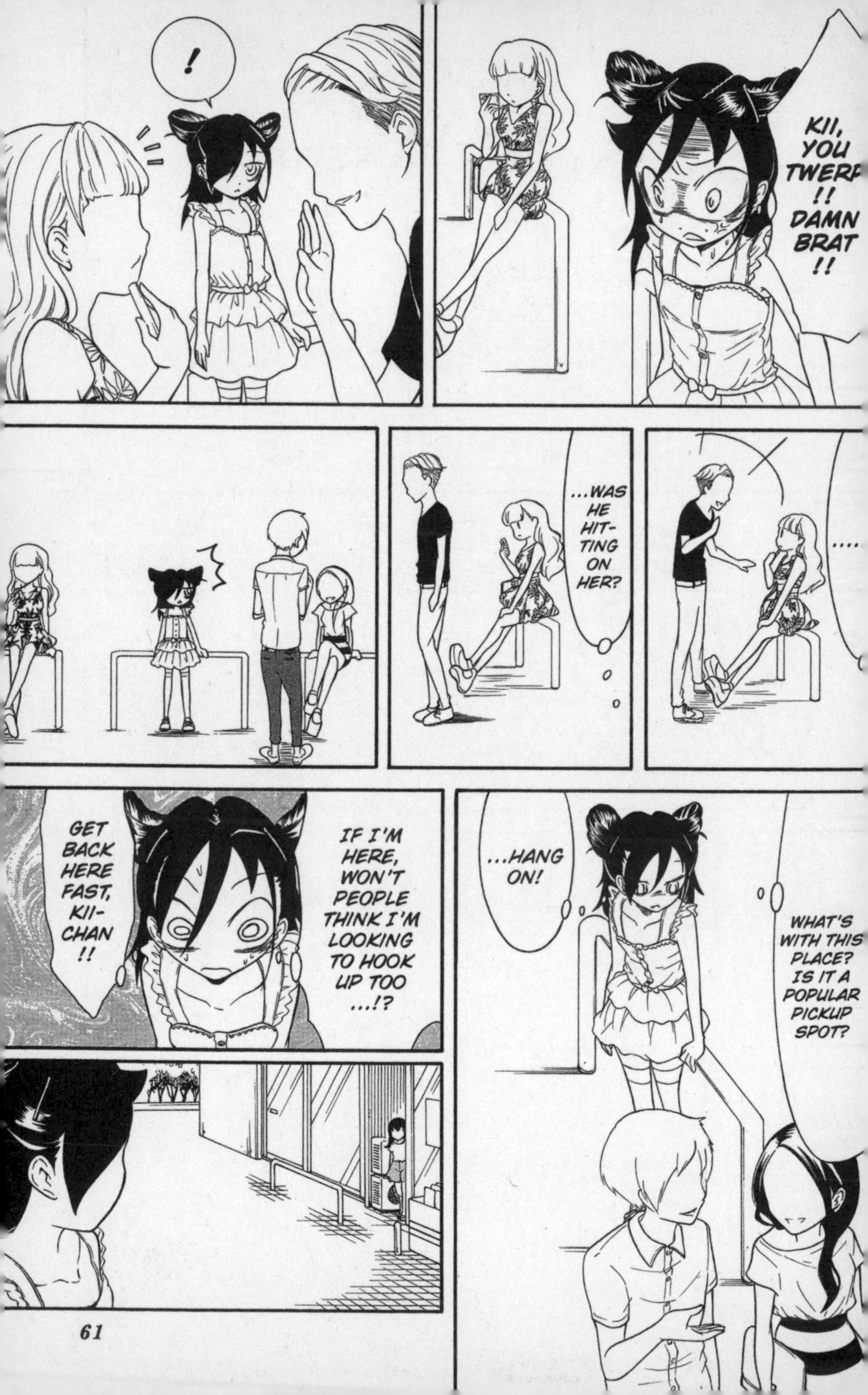
KII, YOU TWERP!! DAMN BRAT!!
!
....
...WAS HE HIT-TING ON HER?
...HANG ON!
WHAT'S WITH THIS PLACE? IS IT A POPULAR PICKUP SPOT?
IF I'M HERE, WON'T PEOPLE THINK I'M LOOKING TO HOOK UP TOO ...!?
GET BACK HERE FAST, KII-CHAN!!

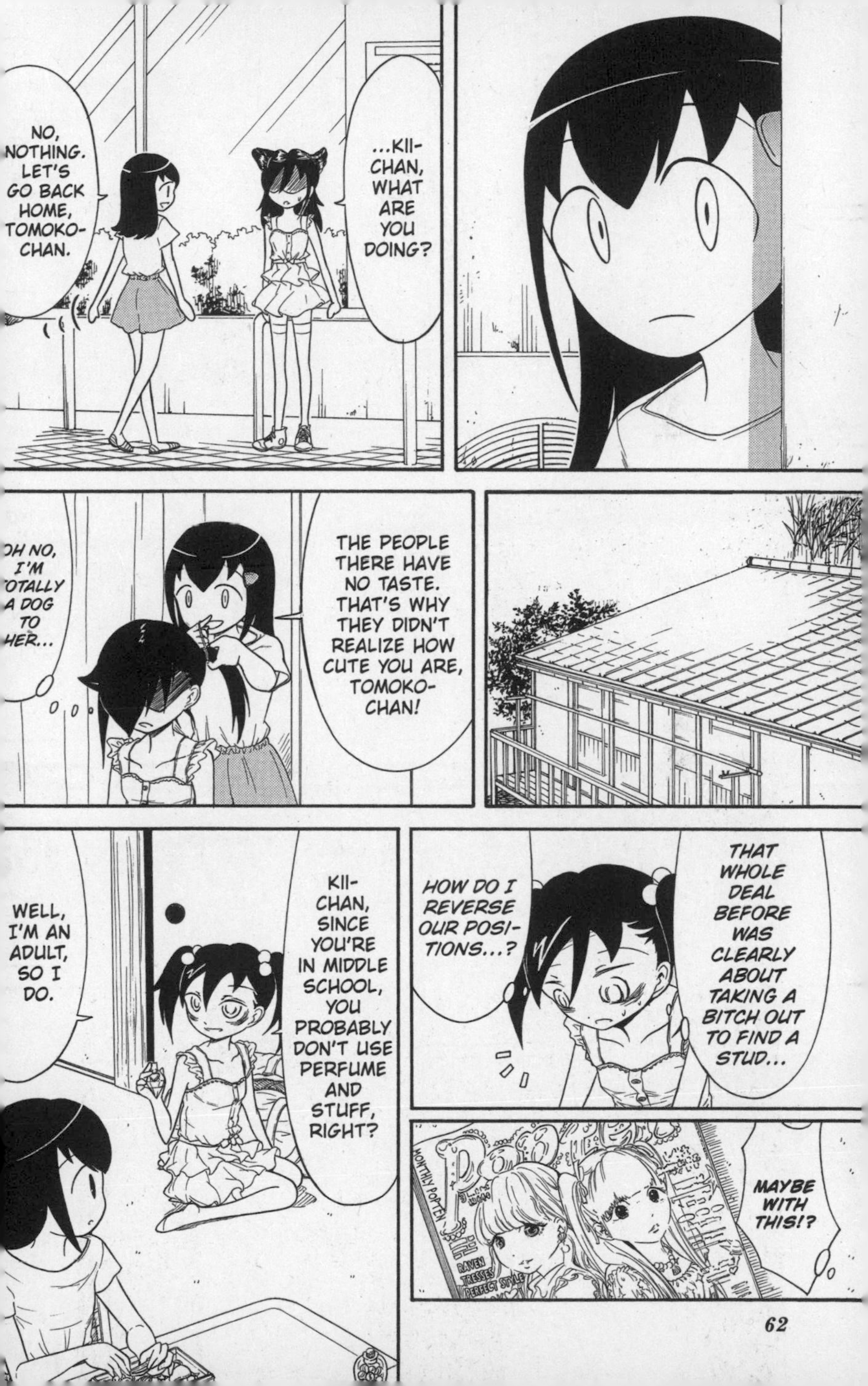
...KII-CHAN, WHAT ARE YOU DOING?
NO, NOTHING. LET'S GO BACK HOME, TOMOKO-CHAN.
THE PEOPLE THERE HAVE NO TASTE. THAT'S WHY THEY DIDN'T REALIZE HOW CUTE YOU ARE, TOMOKO-CHAN!
OH NO, I'M TOTALLY A DOG TO HER...
THAT WHOLE DEAL BEFORE WAS CLEARLY ABOUT TAKING A BITCH OUT TO FIND A STUD...
HOW DO I REVERSE OUR POSITIONS...?
MONTHLY POPTEEN
RAVEN TRESSES PERFECT STYLE
MAYBE WITH THIS!?
KII-CHAN, SINCE YOU'RE IN MIDDLE SCHOOL, YOU PROBABLY DON'T USE PERFUME AND STUFF, RIGHT?
WELL, I'M AN ADULT, SO I DO.

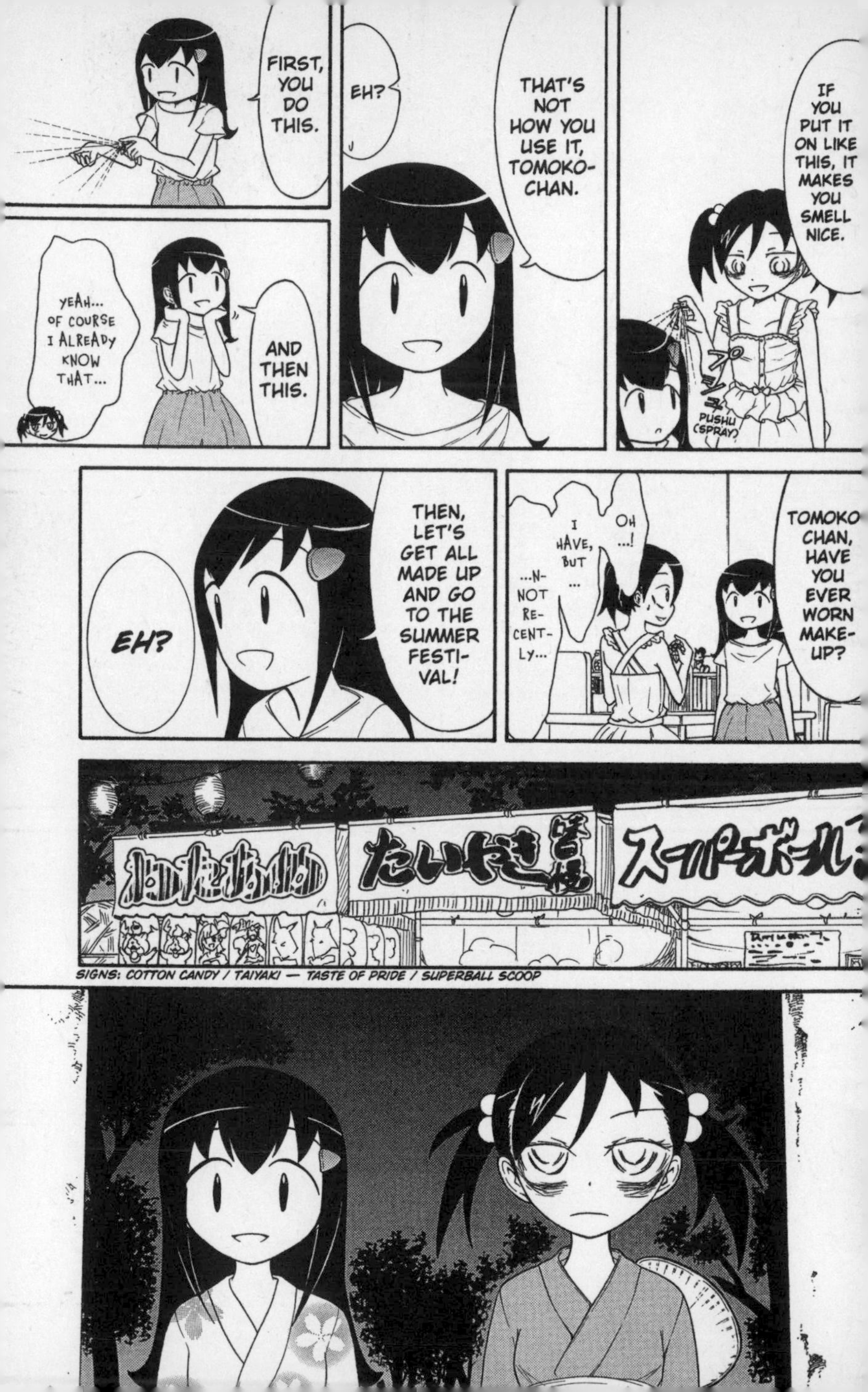
IF YOU PUT IT ON LIKE THIS, IT MAKES YOU SMELL NICE.
PUSHU (SPRAY)
THAT'S NOT HOW YOU USE IT, TOMOKO-CHAN.
EH?
FIRST, YOU DO THIS.
AND THEN THIS.
YEAH... OF COURSE I ALREADY KNOW THAT...
TOMOKO CHAN, HAVE YOU EVER WORN MAKE-UP?
OH ...!
I HAVE, BUT ...
...N-NOT RE-CENT-LY...
THEN, LET'S GET ALL MADE UP AND GO TO THE SUMMER FESTI-VAL!
EH?
SIGNS: COTTON CANDY / TAIYAKI — TASTE OF PRIDE / SUPERBALL SCOOP

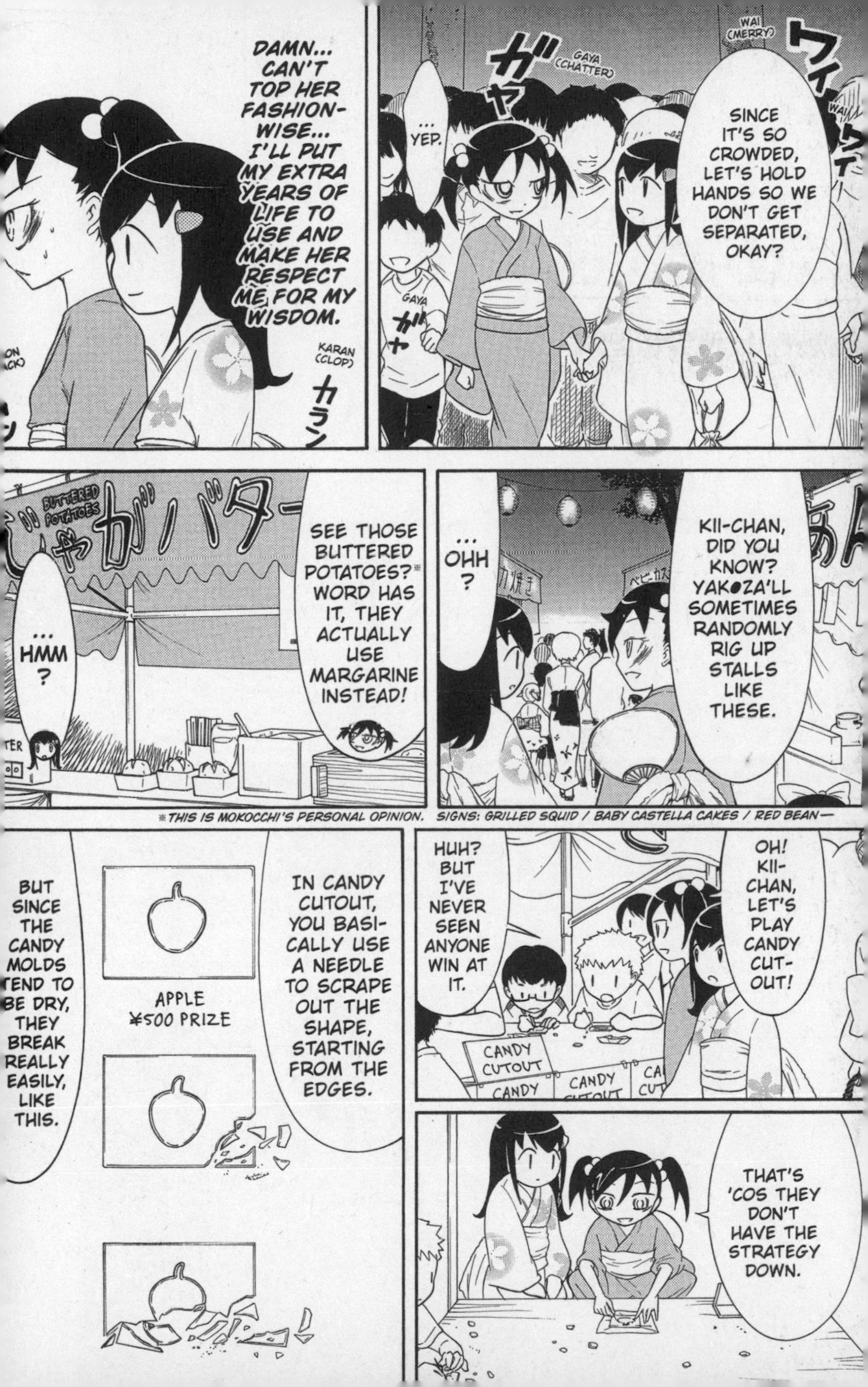
WAI (MERRY)
ワイ
WAI
ワイ
GAYA (CHATTER)
ガヤ
SINCE IT'S SO CROWDED, LET'S HOLD HANDS SO WE DON'T GET SEPARATED, OKAY?
... YEP.
GAYA
ガヤ
DAMN... CAN'T TOP HER FASHION-WISE... I'LL PUT MY EXTRA YEARS OF LIFE TO USE AND MAKE HER RESPECT ME FOR MY WISDOM.
KARAN (CLOP)
カラン
KII-CHAN, DID YOU KNOW? YAK●ZA'LL SOMETIMES RANDOMLY RIG UP STALLS LIKE THESE.
... OHH?
BUTTERED POTATOES
じゃがバター
SEE THOSE BUTTERED POTATOES?※ WORD HAS IT, THEY ACTUALLY USE MARGARINE INSTEAD!
... HMM?
※THIS IS MOKOCCHI'S PERSONAL OPINION.
SIGNS: GRILLED SQUID / BABY CASTELLA CAKES / RED BEAN—
OH! KII-CHAN, LET'S PLAY CANDY CUTOUT!
HUH? BUT I'VE NEVER SEEN ANYONE WIN AT IT.
CANDY CUTOUT
CANDY CUTOUT
THAT'S 'COS THEY DON'T HAVE THE STRATEGY DOWN.
IN CANDY CUTOUT, YOU BASICALLY USE A NEEDLE TO SCRAPE OUT THE SHAPE, STARTING FROM THE EDGES.
APPLE ¥500 PRIZE
BUT SINCE THE CANDY MOLDS TEND TO BE DRY, THEY BREAK REALLY EASILY, LIKE THIS.

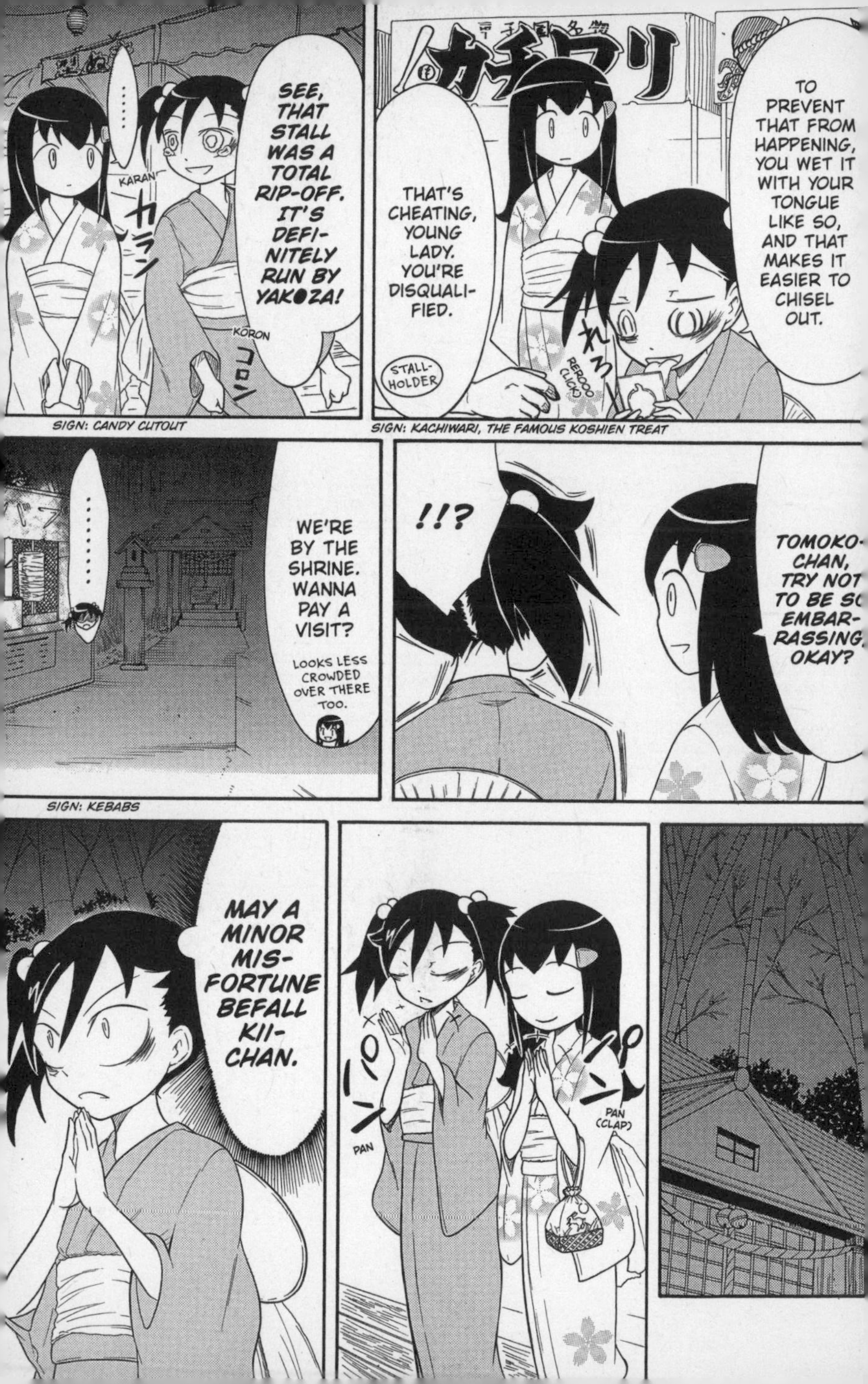
カチワリ
TO PREVENT THAT FROM HAPPENING, YOU WET IT WITH YOUR TONGUE LIKE SO, AND THAT MAKES IT EASIER TO CHISEL OUT.
れろ REROOO (CLICK)
THAT'S CHEATING, YOUNG LADY. YOU'RE DISQUALIFIED.
STALL-HOLDER
SEE, THAT STALL WAS A TOTAL RIP-OFF. IT'S DEFINITELY RUN BY YAKOZA!
......
カラン KARAN
コロン KORON
SIGN: CANDY CUTOUT
SIGN: KACHIWARI, THE FAMOUS KOSHIEN TREAT
TOMOKO-CHAN, TRY NOT TO BE SO EMBARRASSING, OKAY?
!!?
WE'RE BY THE SHRINE. WANNA PAY A VISIT?
LOOKS LESS CROWDED OVER THERE TOO.
......
SIGN: KEBABS
パン PAN (CLAP)
パン PAN
MAY A MINOR MISFORTUNE BEFALL KII-CHAN.

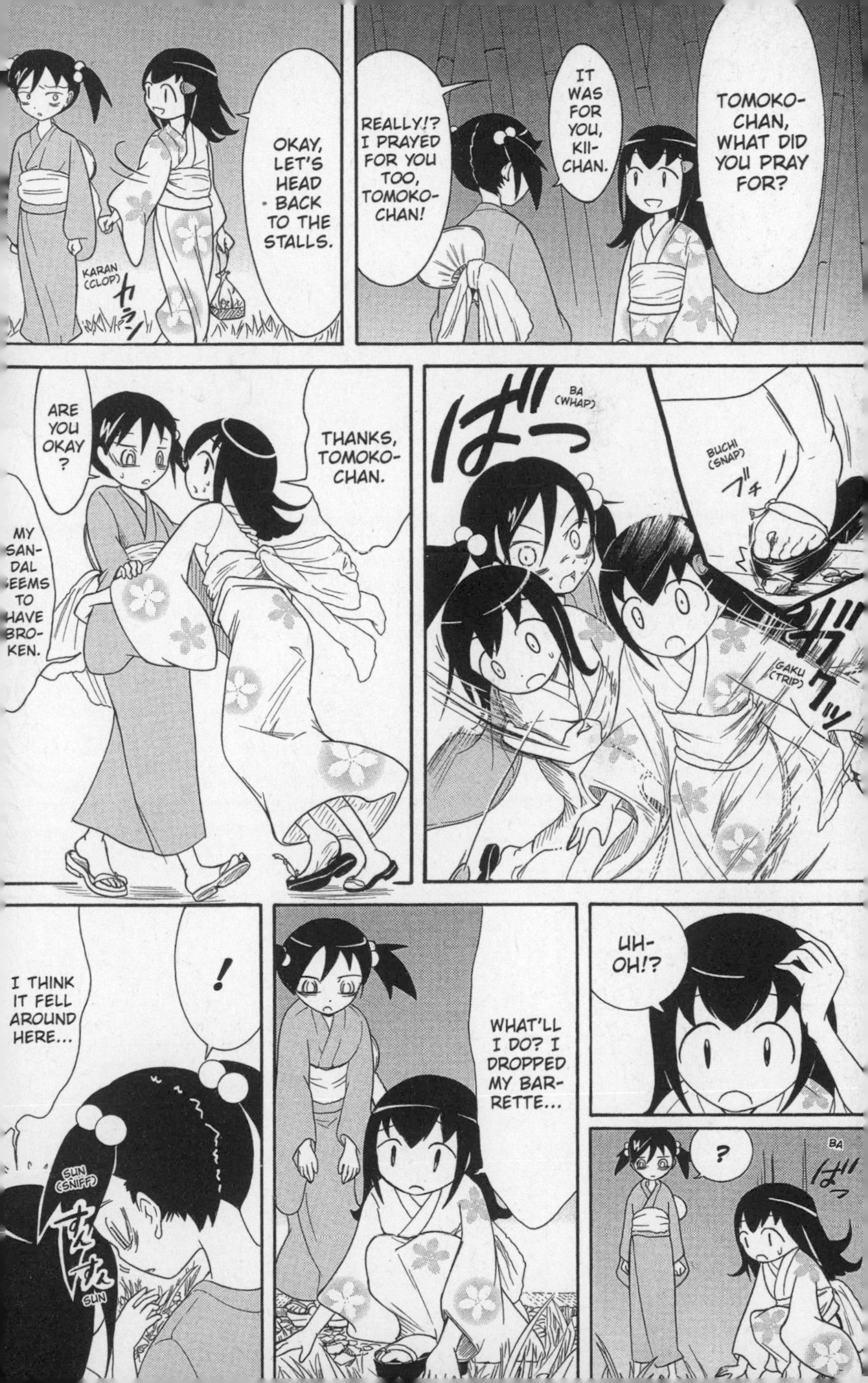
TOMOKO-CHAN, WHAT DID YOU PRAY FOR?
IT WAS FOR YOU, KII-CHAN.
REALLY!? I PRAYED FOR YOU TOO, TOMOKO-CHAN!
OKAY, LET'S HEAD BACK TO THE STALLS.
KARAN (CLOP)
カラン
BA (WHAP)
ばっ
BUCHI (SNAP)
ブチ
GAKU (TRIP)
ガクッ
THANKS, TOMOKO-CHAN.
ARE YOU OKAY?
MY SANDAL EEMS TO HAVE BROKEN.
UH-OH!?
?
BA
ばっ
WHAT'LL I DO? I DROPPED MY BARRETTE...
!
I THINK IT FELL AROUND HERE...
SUN (SNIFF)
すんすん
SUN

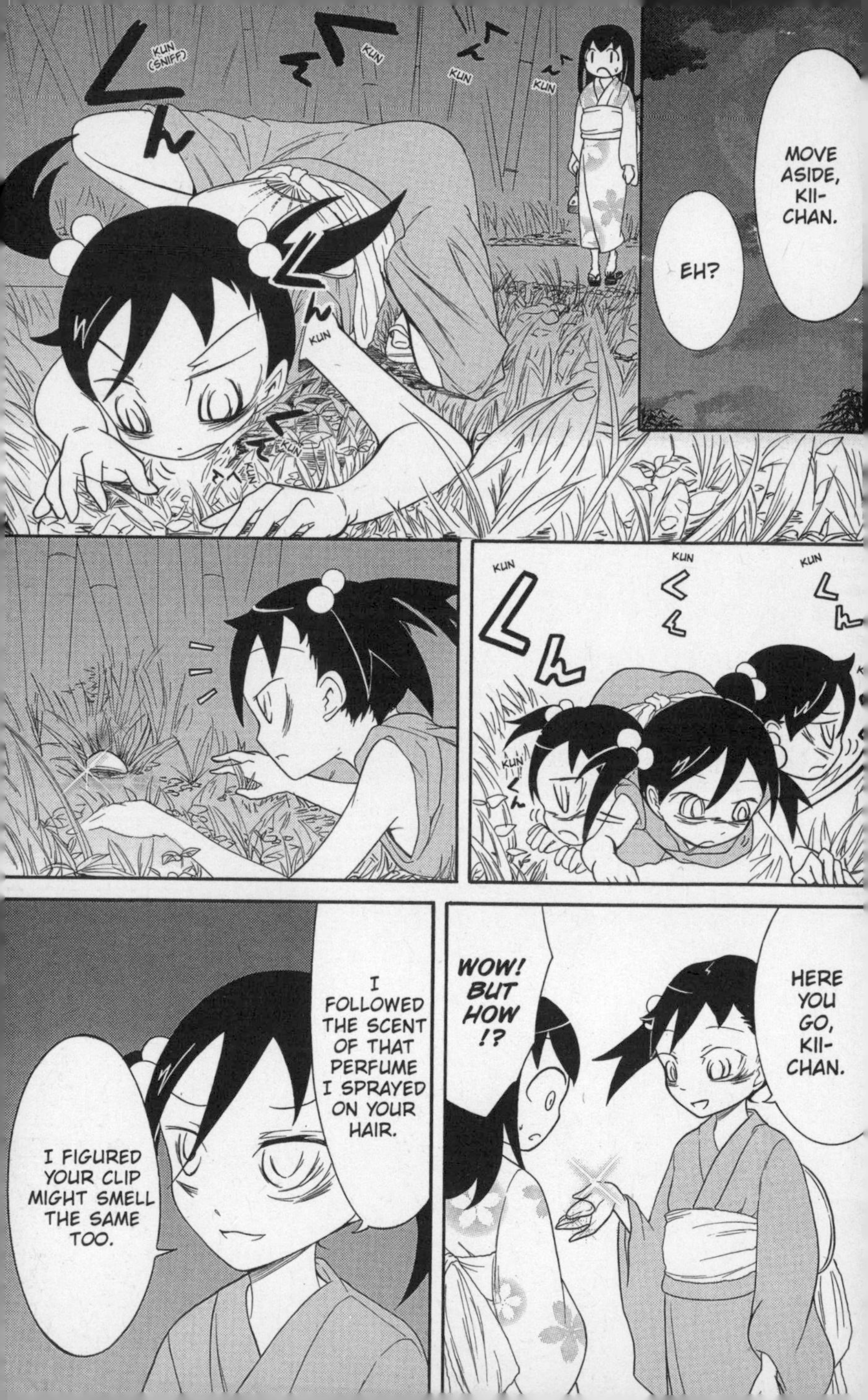

MOVE ASIDE, KII-CHAN.
EH?
KUN (SNIFF)
KUN
KUN
KUN
KUN
KUN
KUN
KUN
KUN
KUN
KUN
HERE YOU GO, KII-CHAN.
WOW! BUT HOW!?
I FOLLOWED THE SCENT OF THAT PERFUME I SPRAYED ON YOUR HAIR.
I FIGURED YOUR CLIP MIGHT SMELL THE SAME TOO.

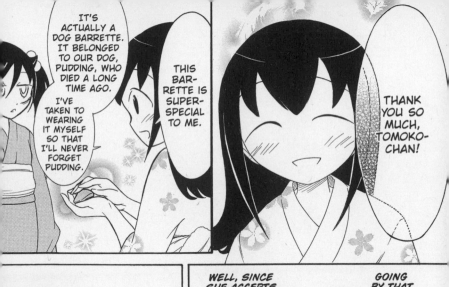

IT'S ACTUALLY A DOG BARRETTE. IT BELONGED TO OUR DOG, PUDDING, WHO DIED A LONG TIME AGO.

I'VE TAKEN TO WEARING IT MYSELF SO THAT I'LL NEVER FORGET PUDDING.

THIS BARRETTE IS SUPER-SPECIAL TO ME.

THANK YOU SO MUCH, TOMOKO-CHAN!

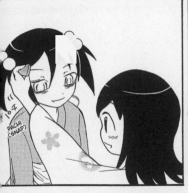

PACHI (SNAP)

WELL, SINCE SHE ACCEPTS MY SUPERIORITY NOW, GUESS I'LL OVERLOOK THE STUFF FROM BEFORE......

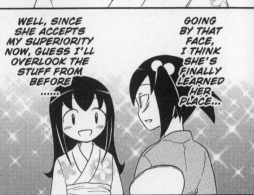

GOING BY THAT FACE, I THINK SHE'S FINALLY LEARNED HER PLACE...

NN!!?

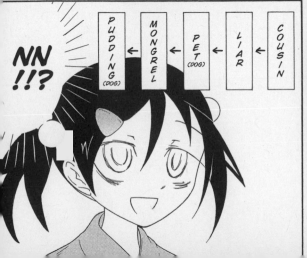

| PUDDING (DOG) | ← | MONGREL | ← | PET (DOG) | ← | LIAR | ← | COUSIN |

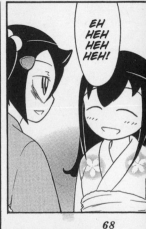

EH HEH HEH HEH!

68

No Matter How I Look at It, It's You Guys' Fault I'm Not Popular!

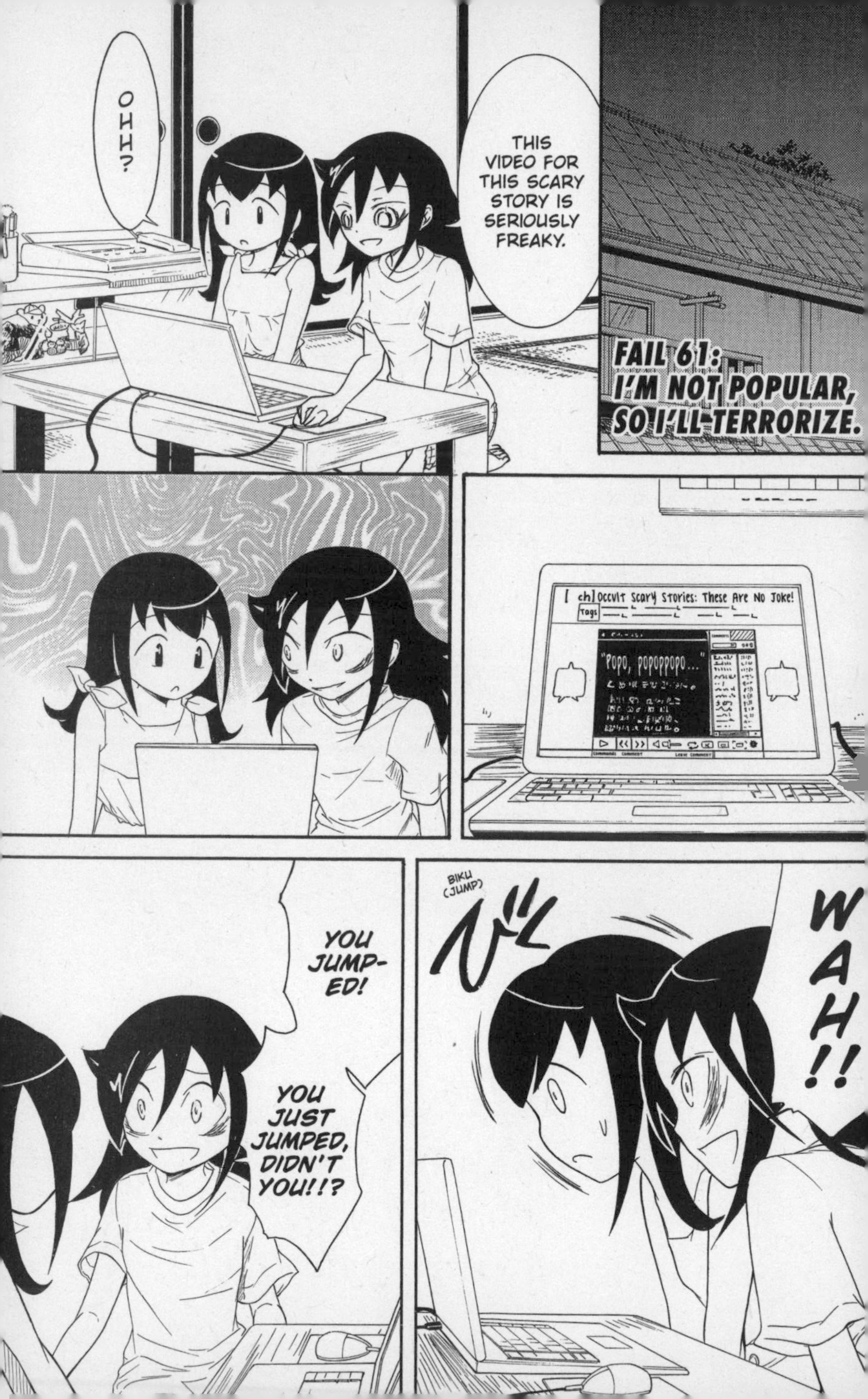
FAIL 61:
I'M NOT POPULAR, SO I'LL TERRORIZE.
THIS VIDEO FOR THIS SCARY STORY IS SERIOUSLY FREAKY.
OHH?
[ch] Occult Scary Stories: These Are No Joke!
Tags
"Popo, popoppopo..."
WAH!!
BIKU (JUMP)
YOU JUMPED!
YOU JUST JUMPED, DIDN'T YOU!!?

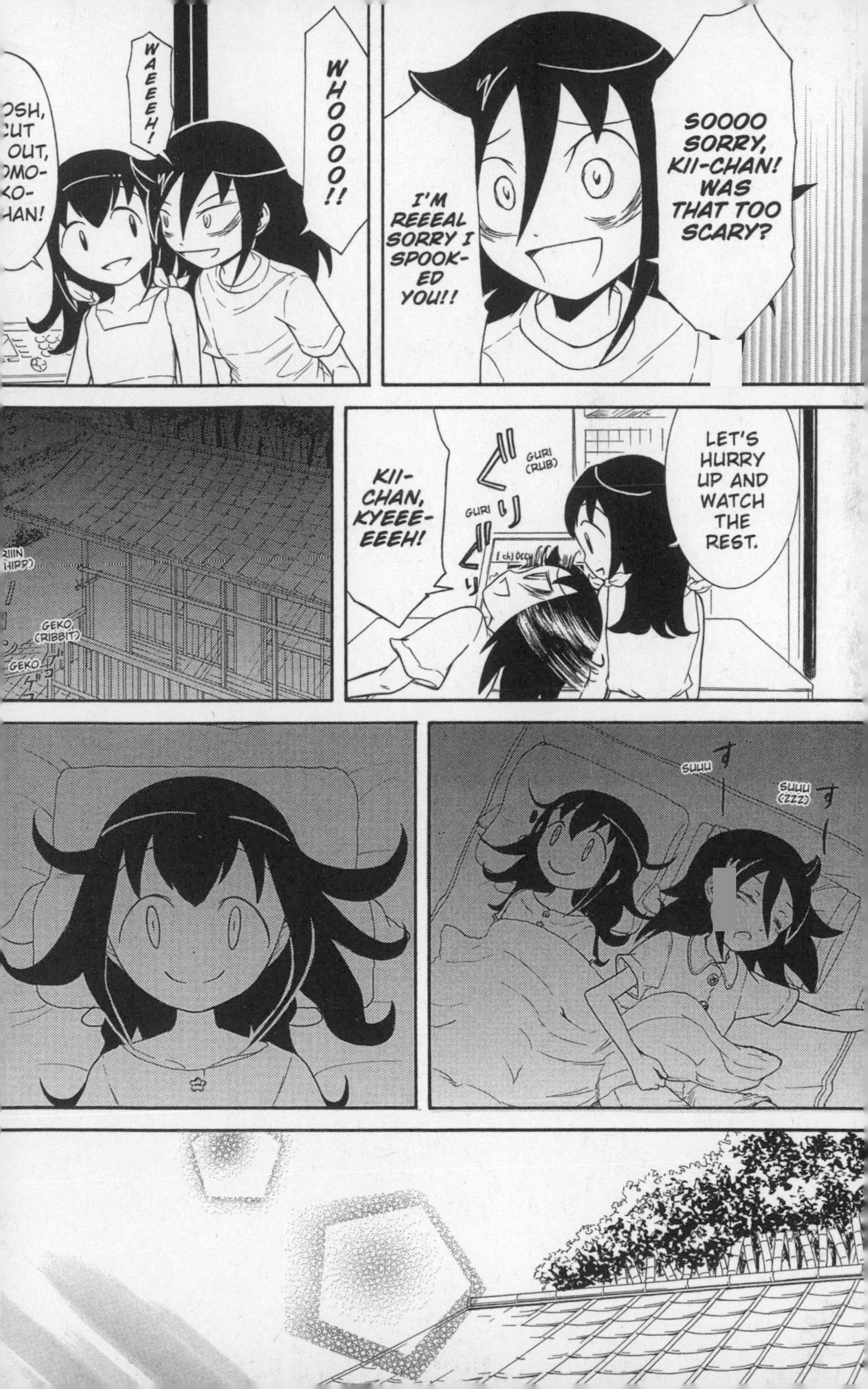
SOOOO SORRY, KII-CHAN! WAS THAT TOO SCARY?
I'M REEEAL SORRY I SPOOK-ED YOU!!
WHOOOOOO!!
WAEEEH!
OSH, CUT OUT, OMO-KO-HAN!
LET'S HURRY UP AND WATCH THE REST.
GURI (RUB)
GURI
KII-CHAN, KYEEE-EEEH!
RIIIN HIRP)
GEKO (RIBBIT)
GEKO
SUUU
SUUU (ZZZ)

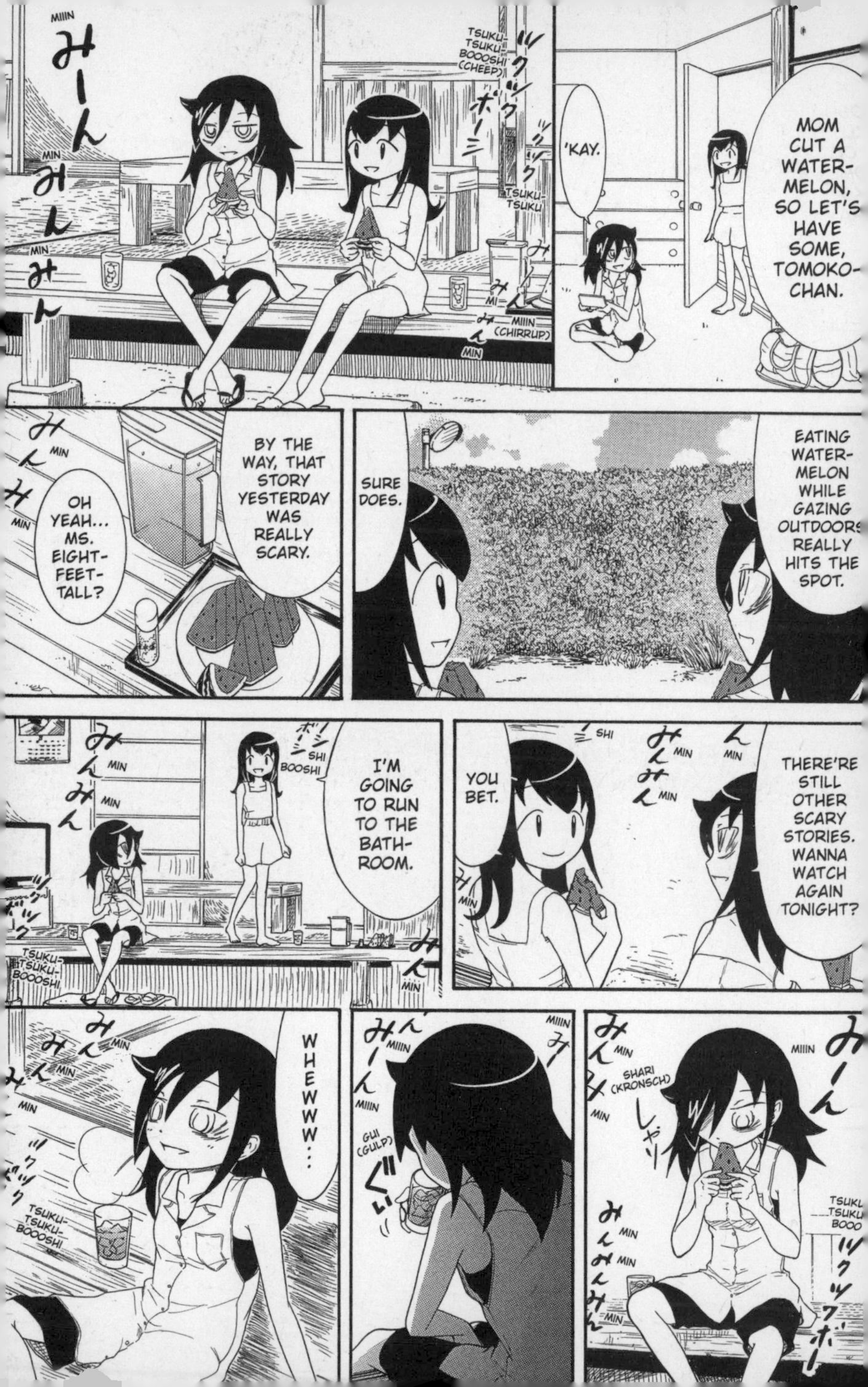
MOM CUT A WATERMELON, SO LET'S HAVE SOME, TOMOKO-CHAN.
'KAY.
TSUKU-TSUKU-BOOOSHI (CHEEP)
TSUKU-TSUKU
MIIIN
MIN
MIN
MI
MIN
MIIIN (CHIRRUP)
MIN
EATING WATERMELON WHILE GAZING OUTDOORS REALLY HITS THE SPOT.
SURE DOES.
BY THE WAY, THAT STORY YESTERDAY WAS REALLY SCARY.
OH YEAH... MS. EIGHT-FEET-TALL?
MIN
MIN
THERE'RE STILL OTHER SCARY STORIES. WANNA WATCH AGAIN TONIGHT?
MIN
MIN
MIN
SHI
YOU BET.
MIN
MIN
SHI BOOSHI
I'M GOING TO RUN TO THE BATHROOM.
MIN
MIN
TSUKU-TSUKU-BOOOSHI
MIIIN
SHARI (KRONSCH)
MIN
MIN
MIN
MIN
MIN
TSUKU-TSUKU-BOOO
MIIIN
MIIIN
MIIIN
GUI (GULP)
WHEWWW...
MIN
MIN
MIN
TSUKU-TSUKU-BOOOSHI

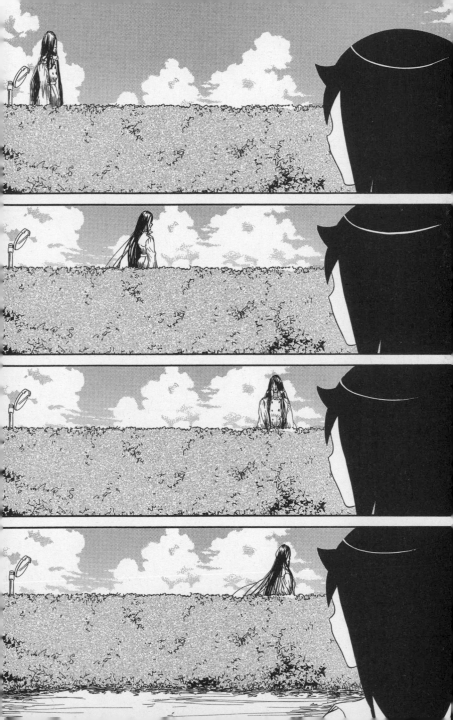

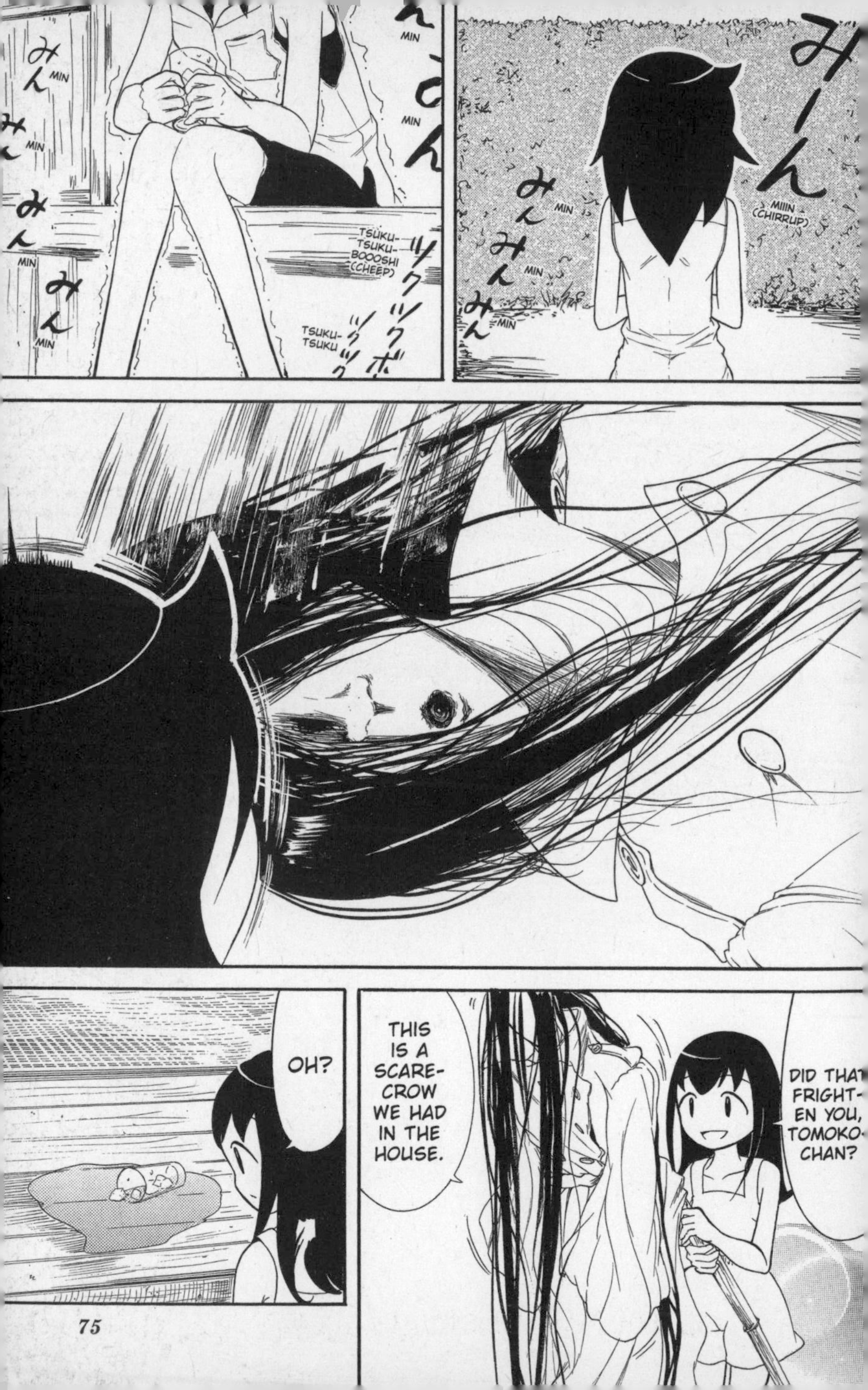
みーん
MIIIN (CHIRRUP)
みんみんみん
MIN
MIN
MIN
ツクツクボーシ
TSUKU-TSUKU-BOOOSHI (CHEEP)
ツクツク
TSUKU-TSUKU
MIN
MIN
みんみんみんみん
MIN
MIN
MIN
MIN
MIN
DID THAT FRIGHTEN YOU, TOMOKO-CHAN?
THIS IS A SCARECROW WE HAD IN THE HOUSE.
OH?

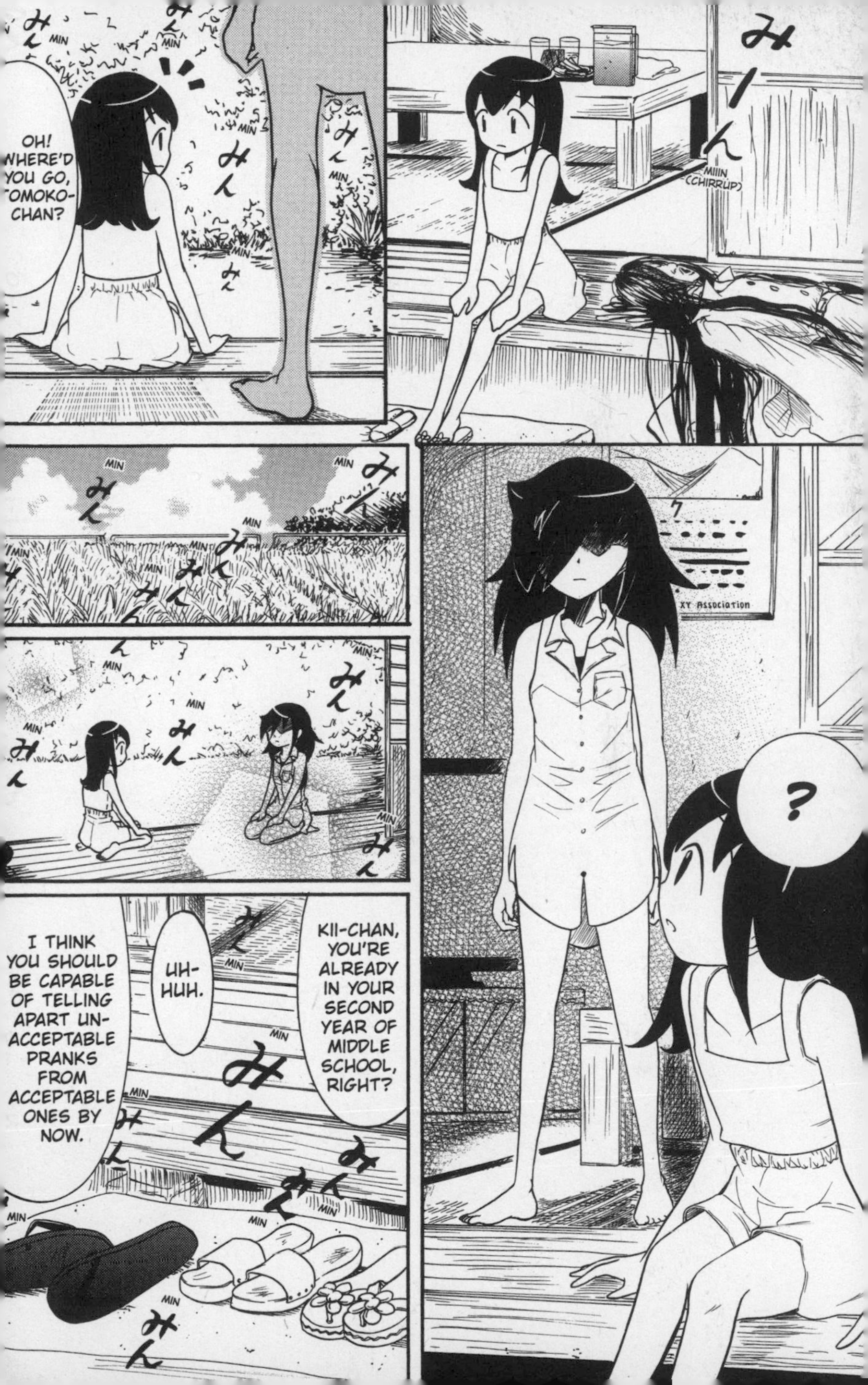

みーん
MIIN (CHIRRUP)
みんみん
MIN MIN
OH! WHERE'D YOU GO, TOMOKO-CHAN?
XY Association
?
みんみん
MIN MIN
みんみん
MIN MIN
KII-CHAN, YOU'RE ALREADY IN YOUR SECOND YEAR OF MIDDLE SCHOOL, RIGHT?
UH-HUH.
I THINK YOU SHOULD BE CAPABLE OF TELLING APART UN-ACCEPTABLE PRANKS FROM ACCEPTABLE ONES BY NOW.
みんみん
MIN MIN

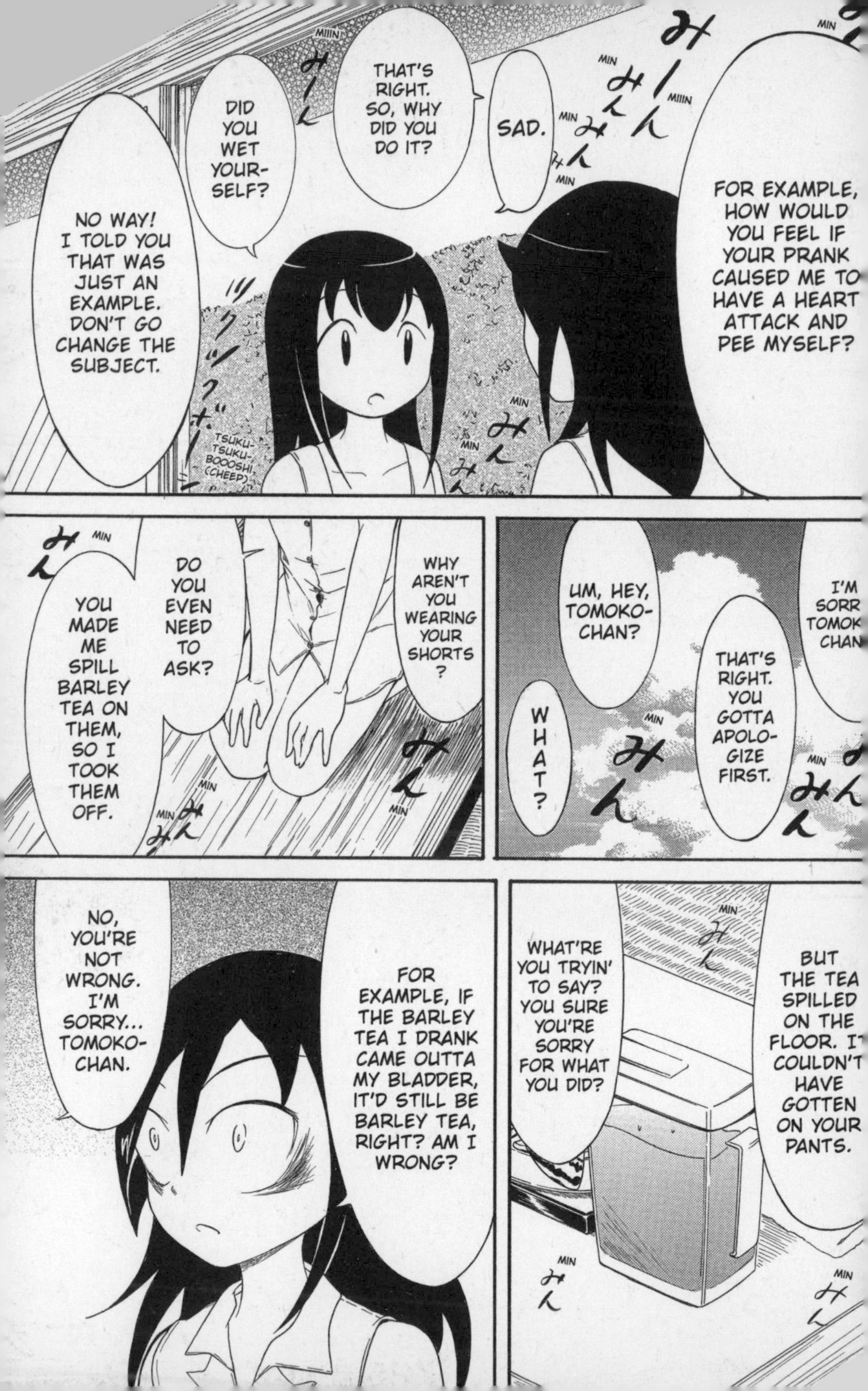
MIN
FOR EXAMPLE, HOW WOULD YOU FEEL IF YOUR PRANK CAUSED ME TO HAVE A HEART ATTACK AND PEE MYSELF?
MIN
MIIIN
MIN
MIN
SAD.
THAT'S RIGHT. SO, WHY DID YOU DO IT?
MIIIN
DID YOU WET YOURSELF?
NO WAY! I TOLD YOU THAT WAS JUST AN EXAMPLE. DON'T GO CHANGE THE SUBJECT.
MIN
MIN
TSUKU-TSUKU-BOOOSHI (CHEEP)
I'M SORR TOMOK CHAN
MIN
THAT'S RIGHT. YOU GOTTA APOLOGIZE FIRST.
UM, HEY, TOMOKO-CHAN?
MIN
WHAT?
WHY AREN'T YOU WEARING YOUR SHORTS?
MIN
DO YOU EVEN NEED TO ASK?
MIN
YOU MADE ME SPILL BARLEY TEA ON THEM, SO I TOOK THEM OFF.
MIN
MIN
BUT THE TEA SPILLED ON THE FLOOR. I COULDN'T HAVE GOTTEN ON YOUR PANTS.
MIN
WHAT'RE YOU TRYIN' TO SAY? YOU SURE YOU'RE SORRY FOR WHAT YOU DID?
MIN
FOR EXAMPLE, IF THE BARLEY TEA I DRANK CAME OUTTA MY BLADDER, IT'D STILL BE BARLEY TEA, RIGHT? AM I WRONG?
NO, YOU'RE NOT WRONG. I'M SORRY... TOMOKO-CHAN.

No Matter How I Look at It, It's You Guys' Fault I'm Not Popular!

FAIL 62: I'M NOT POPULAR, SO I'LL GO BACK HOME.

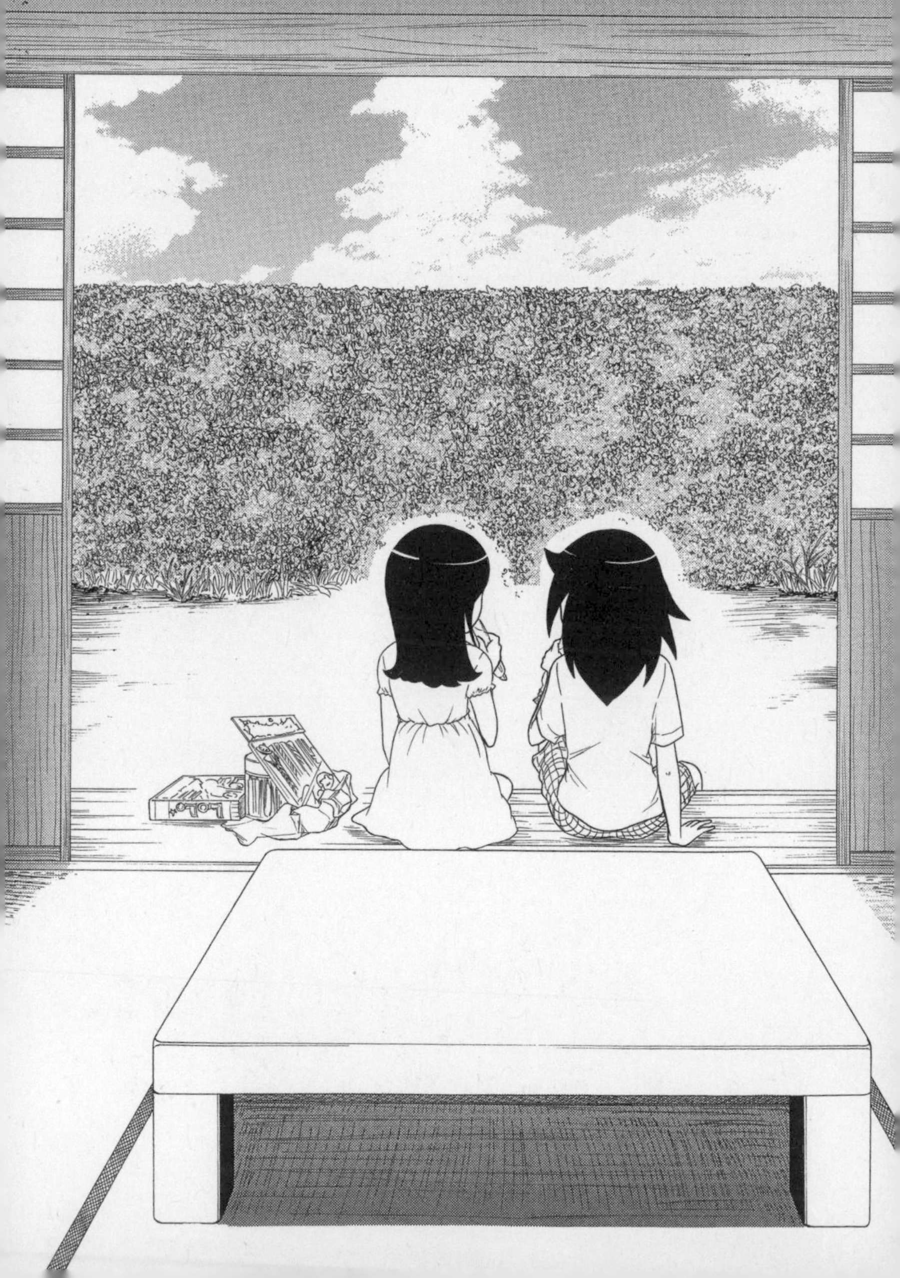

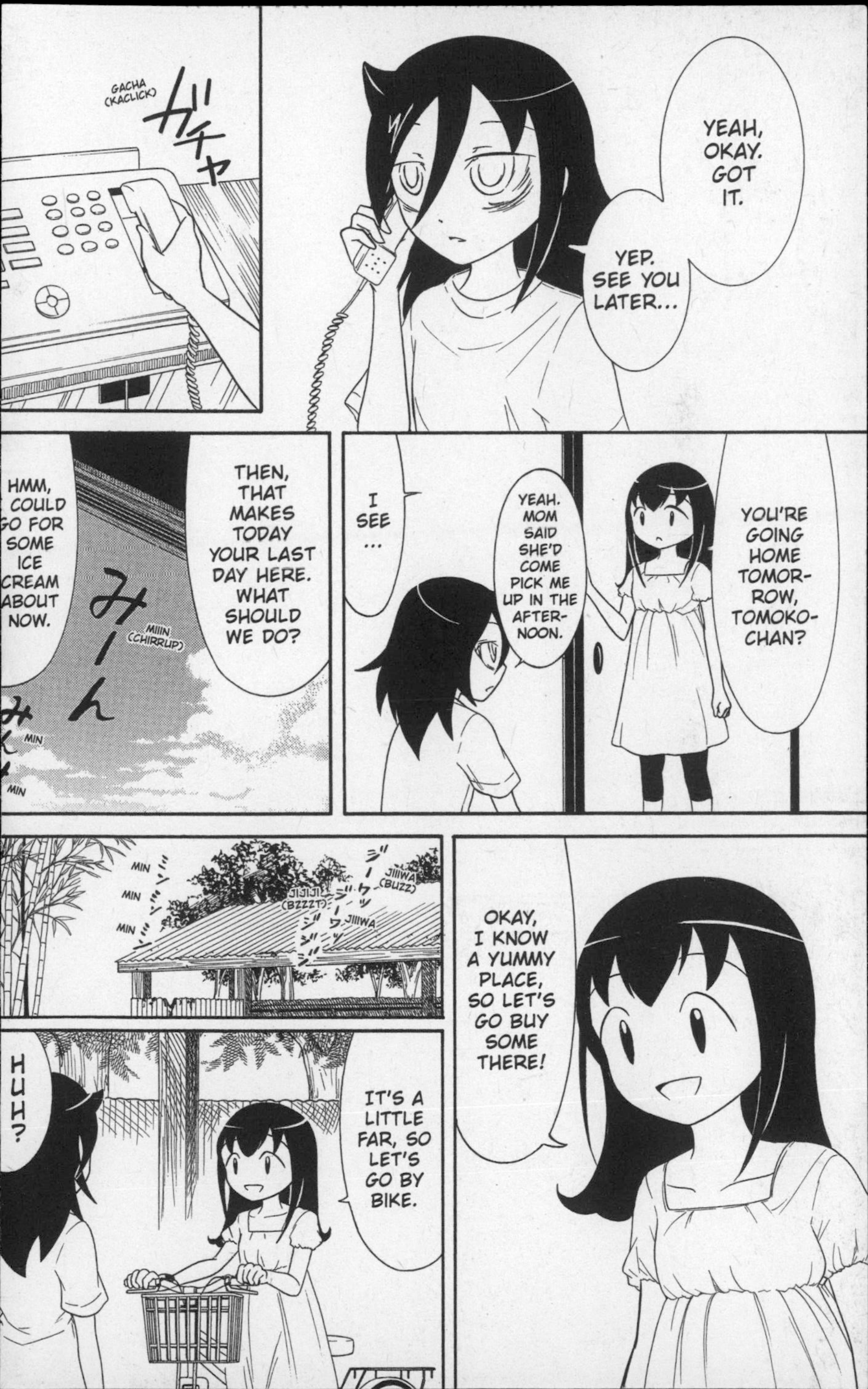
YEAH, OKAY. GOT IT.
YEP. SEE YOU LATER...
GACHA (KACLICK)
ガチャ
YOU'RE GOING HOME TOMOR-ROW, TOMOKO-CHAN?
YEAH. MOM SAID SHE'D COME PICK ME UP IN THE AFTER-NOON.
I SEE ...
THEN, THAT MAKES TODAY YOUR LAST DAY HERE. WHAT SHOULD WE DO?
HMM, COULD GO FOR SOME ICE CREAM ABOUT NOW.
みーん
MIIIN (CHIRRUP)
MIN
MIN
OKAY, I KNOW A YUMMY PLACE, SO LET'S GO BUY SOME THERE!
MIN
MIN
MIN
JIIIWA (BUZZ)
JIJIJI (BZZZT)
JIIIWA
IT'S A LITTLE FAR, SO LET'S GO BY BIKE.
HUH?

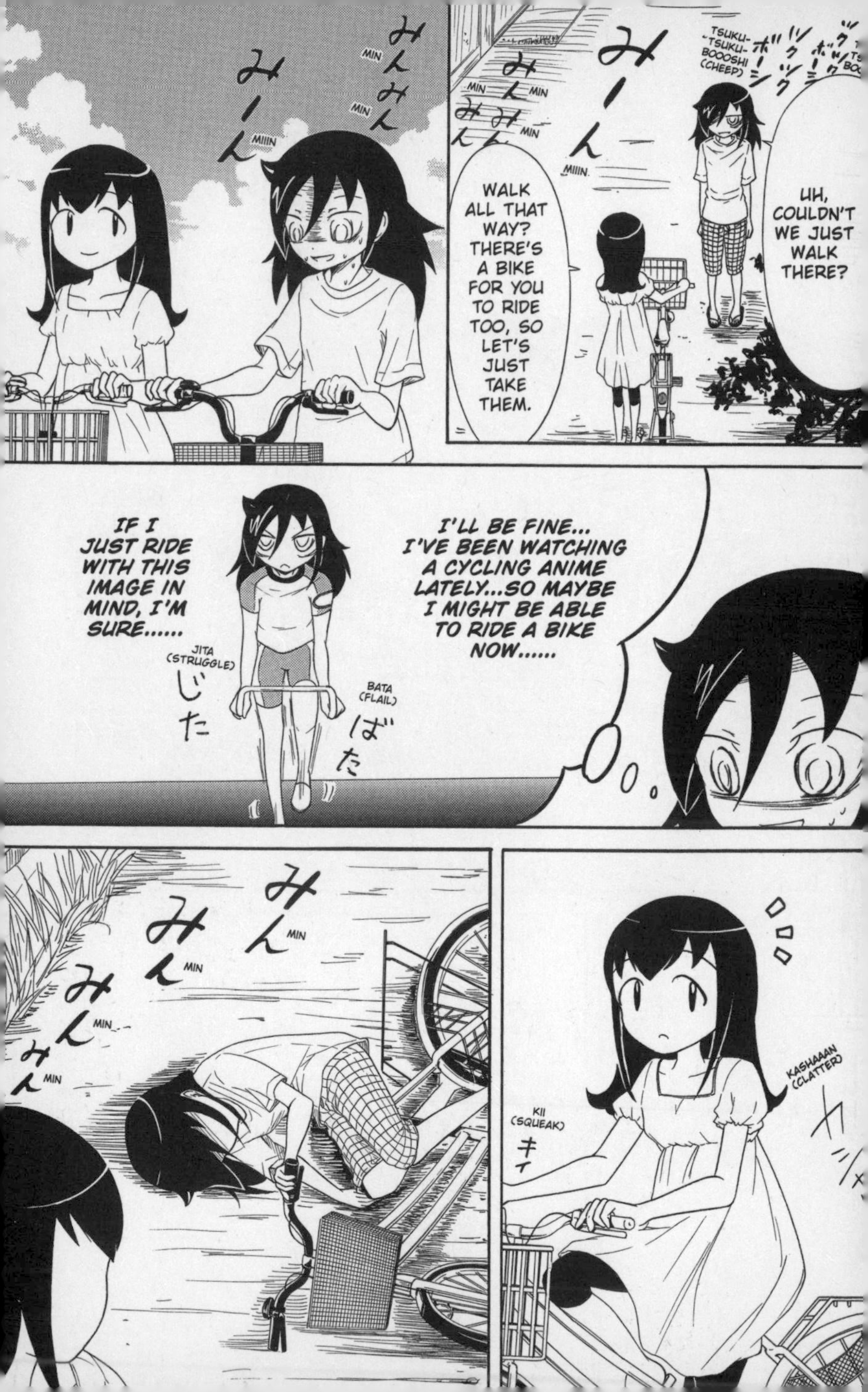
TSUKU-TSUKU-BOOOSHI (CHEEP)
UH, COULDN'T WE JUST WALK THERE?
みーん
MIIIN
みんみん
MIN MIN
WALK ALL THAT WAY? THERE'S A BIKE FOR YOU TO RIDE TOO, SO LET'S JUST TAKE THEM.
みんみん
MIN MIN
みーん
MIIIN
I'LL BE FINE... I'VE BEEN WATCHING A CYCLING ANIME LATELY...SO MAYBE I MIGHT BE ABLE TO RIDE A BIKE NOW......
IF I JUST RIDE WITH THIS IMAGE IN MIND, I'M SURE......
BATA (FLAIL)
ばた
JITA (STRUGGLE)
じた
KASHAAAN (CLATTER)
KII (SQUEAK)
キィ
みん MIN
みん MIN
みん MIN
みん MIN

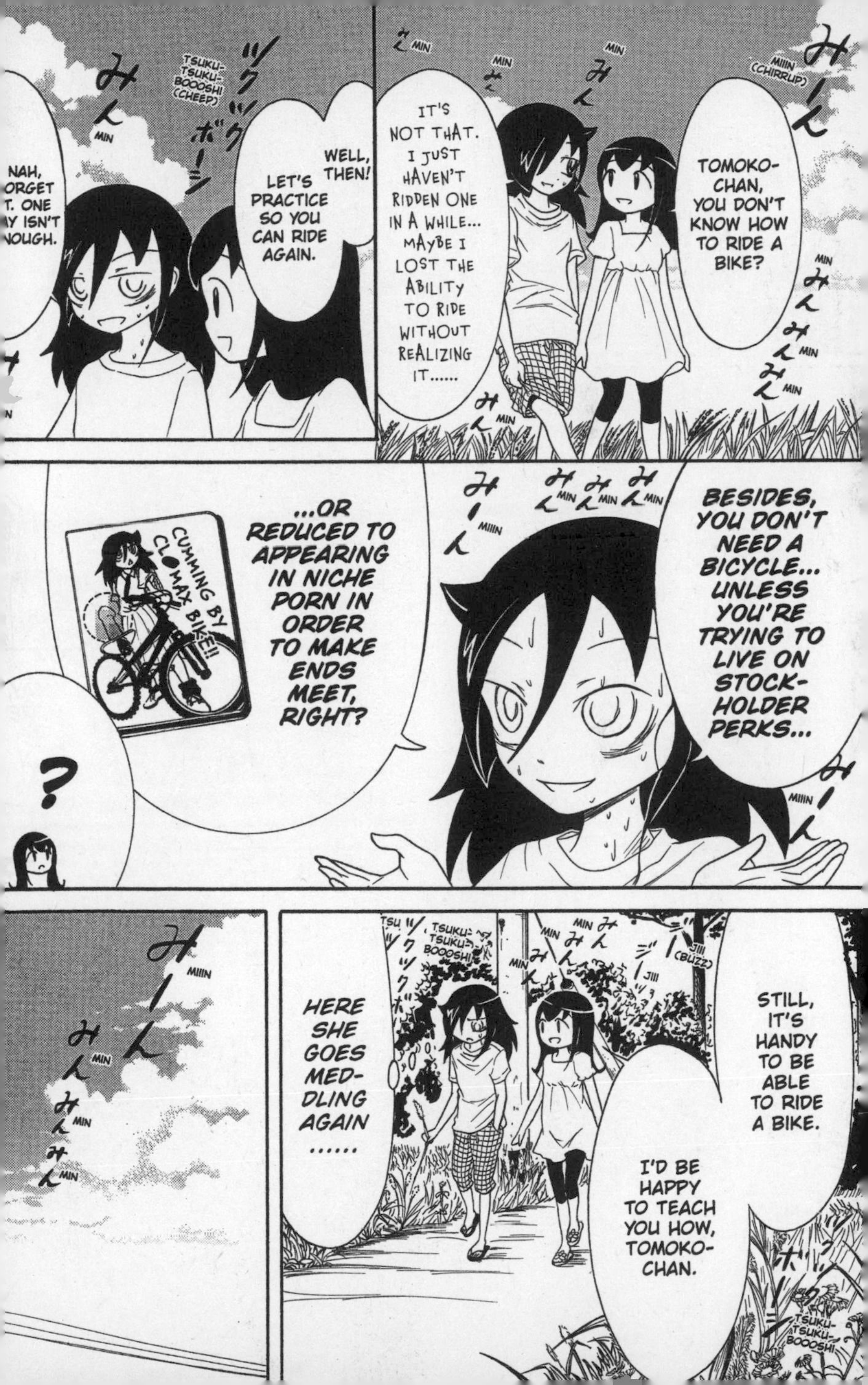
MIIIN (CHIRRUP)
TOMOKO-CHAN, YOU DON'T KNOW HOW TO RIDE A BIKE?
MIN MIN MIN
IT'S NOT THAT. I JUST HAVEN'T RIDDEN ONE IN A WHILE... MAYBE I LOST THE ABILITY TO RIDE WITHOUT REALIZING IT......
MIN MIN MIN
TSUKU-TSUKU-BOOOSHI (CHEEP)
WELL, THEN! LET'S PRACTICE SO YOU CAN RIDE AGAIN.
MIN
NAH, ORGET T. ONE AY ISN'T NOUGH.
MIN MIN MIN MIIIN
BESIDES, YOU DON'T NEED A BICYCLE... UNLESS YOU'RE TRYING TO LIVE ON STOCK-HOLDER PERKS...
MIIIN
...OR REDUCED TO APPEARING IN NICHE PORN IN ORDER TO MAKE ENDS MEET, RIGHT?
CUMMING BY CLIMAX BIKE!!
?
JIII (BUZZ)
JIII
STILL, IT'S HANDY TO BE ABLE TO RIDE A BIKE.
I'D BE HAPPY TO TEACH YOU HOW, TOMOKO-CHAN.
TSUKU-TSUKU-BOOOSHI
MIN MIN MIN
TSU TSUKU-TSUKU-BOOOSHI
HERE SHE GOES MEDDLING AGAIN ......
MIIIN
MIN
MIN
MIN

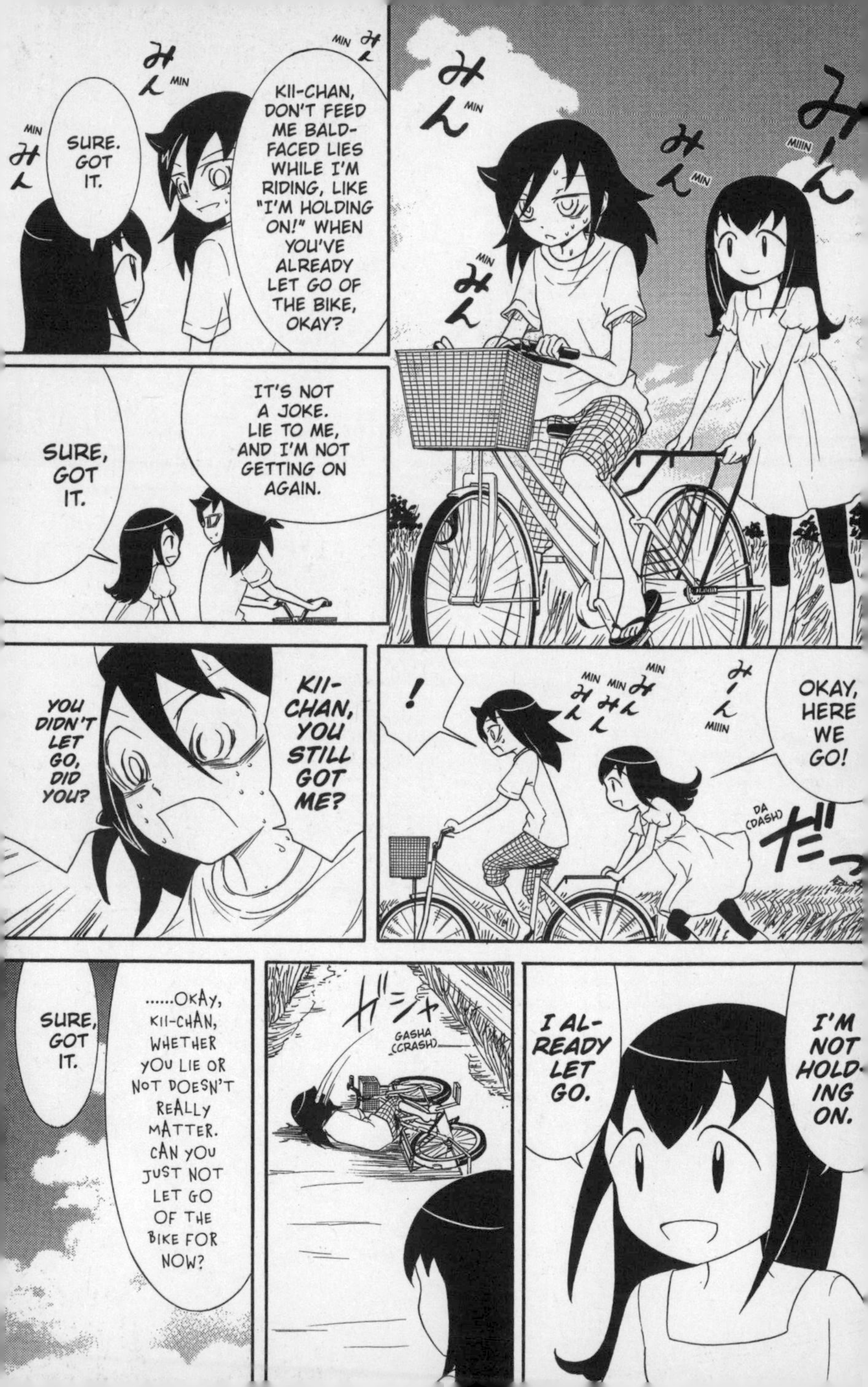
みーん MIIIN
みん MIN
みん MIN
みん MIN
KII-CHAN, DON'T FEED ME BALD-FACED LIES WHILE I'M RIDING, LIKE "I'M HOLDING ON!" WHEN YOU'VE ALREADY LET GO OF THE BIKE, OKAY?
SURE. GOT IT.
みん MIN
みん MIN
みん MIN
IT'S NOT A JOKE. LIE TO ME, AND I'M NOT GETTING ON AGAIN.
SURE, GOT IT.
OKAY, HERE WE GO!
みーん MIIIN
みん MIN
みん MIN
みん MIN
!
だっ DA (DASH)
KII-CHAN, YOU STILL GOT ME?
YOU DIDN'T LET GO, DID YOU?
I'M NOT HOLDING ON.
I ALREADY LET GO.
ガシャ GASHA (CRASH)
......OKAY, KII-CHAN, WHETHER YOU LIE OR NOT DOESN'T REALLY MATTER. CAN YOU JUST NOT LET GO OF THE BIKE FOR NOW?
SURE, GOT IT.

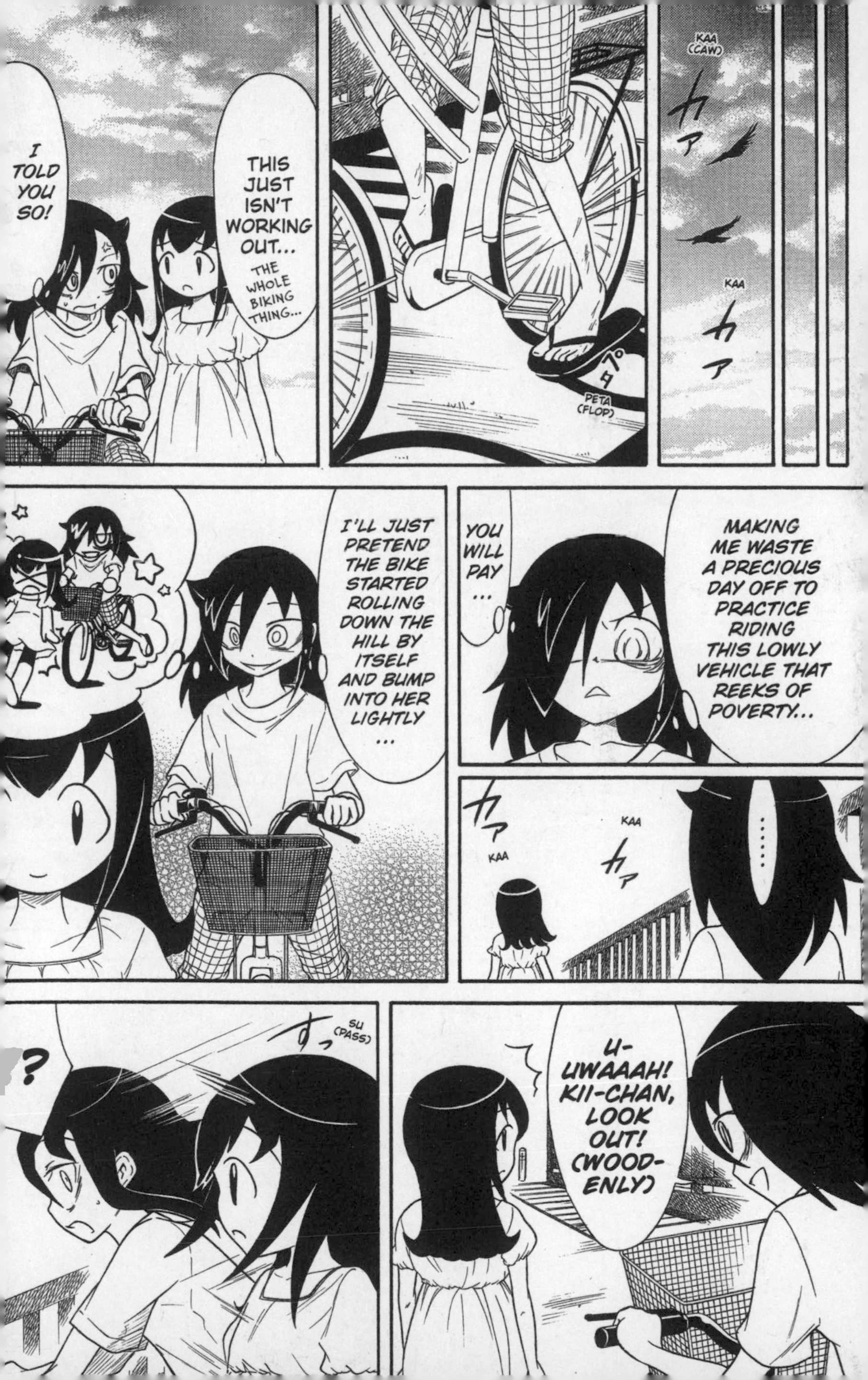
KAA (CAW)
カァ
KAA
カァ
ペタ
PETA (FLOP)
THIS JUST ISN'T WORKING OUT... THE WHOLE BIKING THING...
I TOLD YOU SO!
MAKING ME WASTE A PRECIOUS DAY OFF TO PRACTICE RIDING THIS LOWLY VEHICLE THAT REEKS OF POVERTY...
YOU WILL PAY ...
KAA
カァ
KAA
カァ
......
I'LL JUST PRETEND THE BIKE STARTED ROLLING DOWN THE HILL BY ITSELF AND BUMP INTO HER LIGHTLY ...
U-UWAAAH! KII-CHAN, LOOK OUT! (WOODENLY)
すっ
SU (PASS)
?

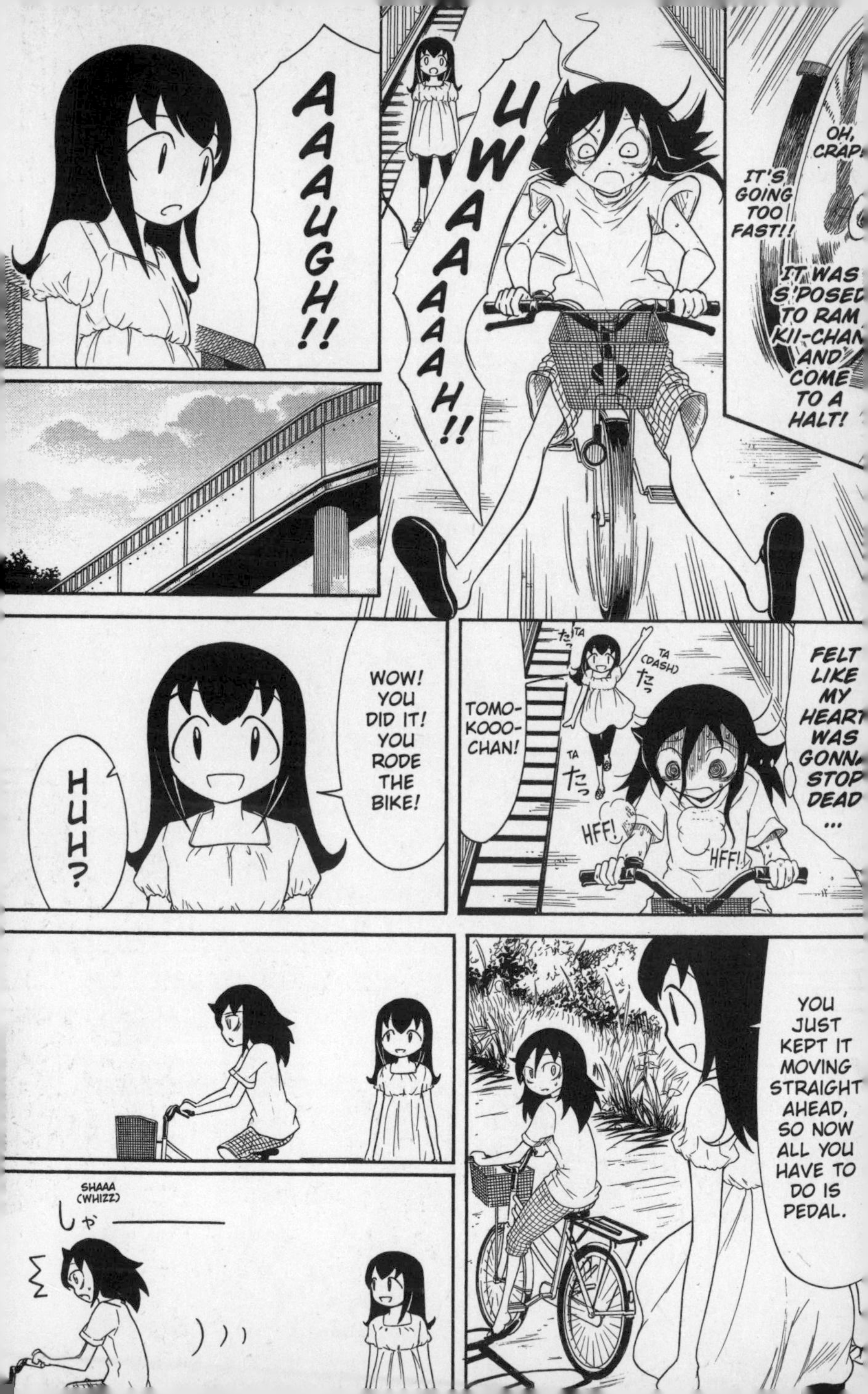

OH, CRAP!
IT'S GOING TOO FAST!!
IT WAS S'POSED TO RAM KII-CHAN AND COME TO A HALT!
UWAAAAAAAAH!!
AAAAUGH!!
FELT LIKE MY HEART WAS GONNA STOP DEAD...
TA たっ
TA (DASH) たっ
TA たっ
TOMO-KOOOO-CHAN!
HFF!
HFF!
WOW! YOU DID IT! YOU RODE THE BIKE!
HUH?
YOU JUST KEPT IT MOVING STRAIGHT AHEAD, SO NOW ALL YOU HAVE TO DO IS PEDAL.
SHAAA (WHIZZ)
しゃー

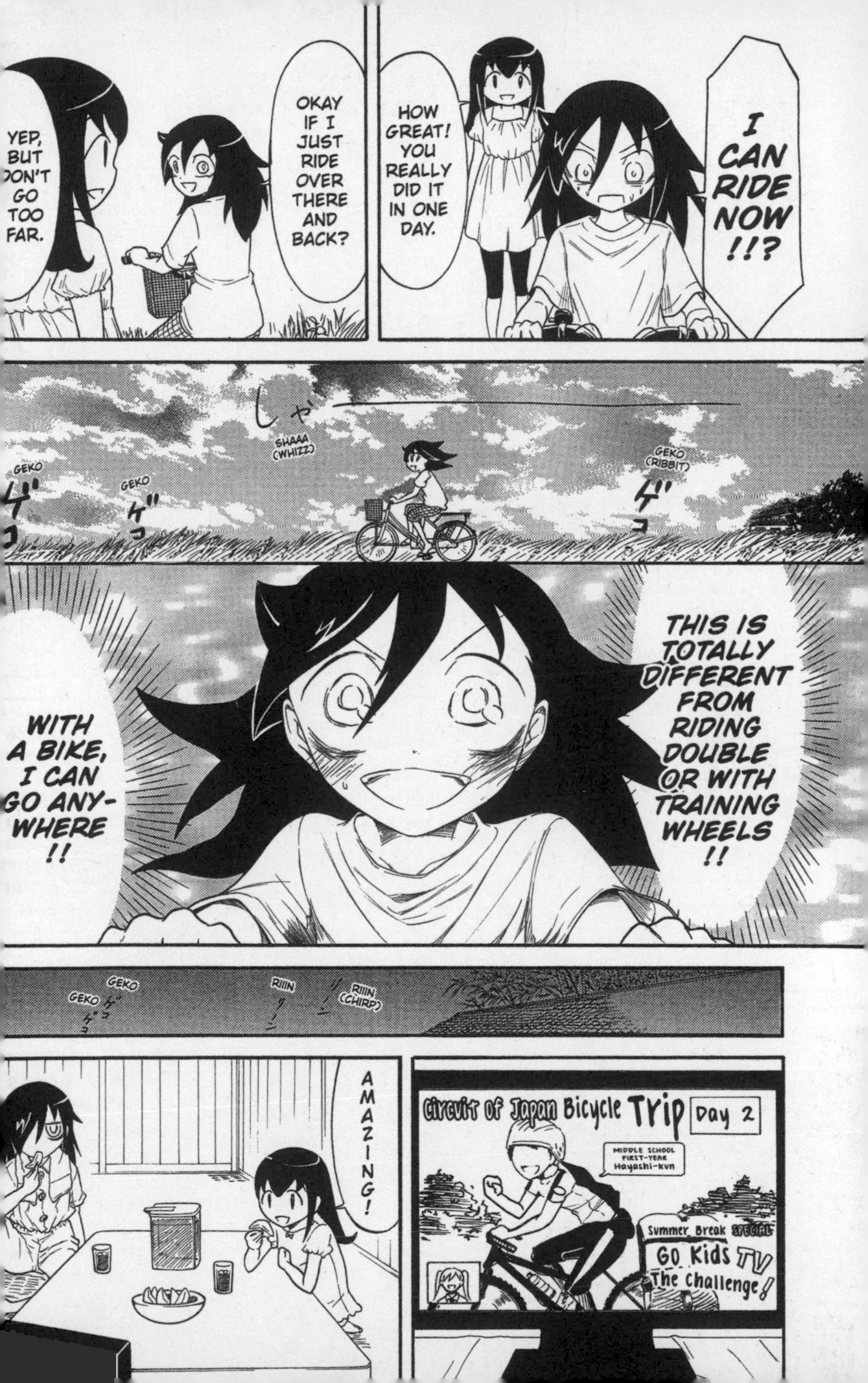
I CAN RIDE NOW!!?
HOW GREAT! YOU REALLY DID IT IN ONE DAY.
OKAY IF I JUST RIDE OVER THERE AND BACK?
YEP, BUT DON'T GO TOO FAR.
SHAAA (WHIZZ)
GEKO (RIBBIT)
GEKO
GEKO
THIS IS TOTALLY DIFFERENT FROM RIDING DOUBLE OR WITH TRAINING WHEELS!!
WITH A BIKE, I CAN GO ANYWHERE!!
RIIIN (CHIRP)
RIIIN
GEKO
GEKO
Circuit of Japan Bicycle Trip
Day 2
MIDDLE SCHOOL FIRST-YEAR Hayashi-kun
Summer Break SPECIAL
GO Kids TV The Challenge!
AMAZING!

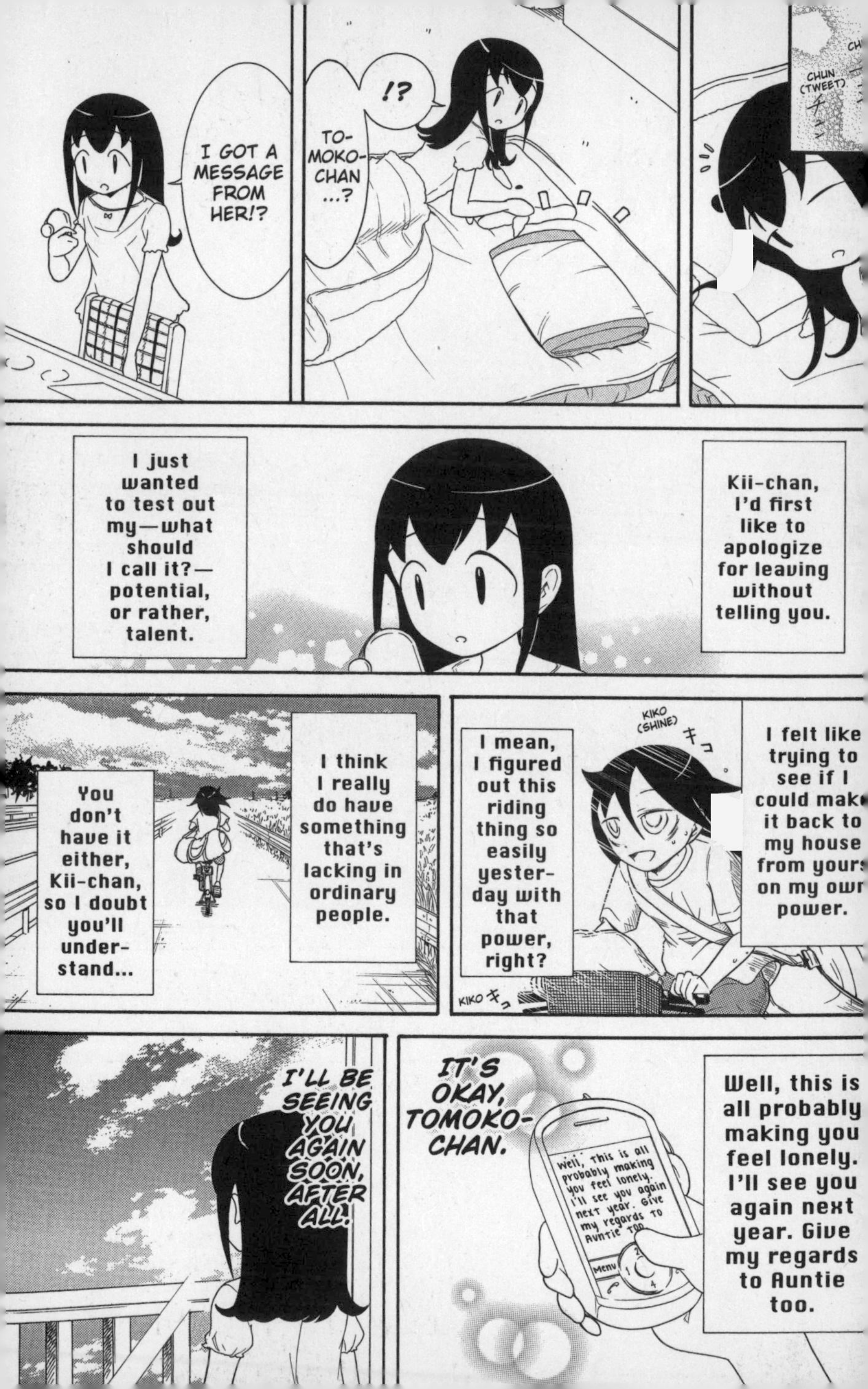
CHUN (TWEET)
!?
TO-MOKO-CHAN ...?
I GOT A MESSAGE FROM HER!?
Kii-chan, I'd first like to apologize for leaving without telling you.
I just wanted to test out my—what should I call it?—potential, or rather, talent.
I felt like trying to see if I could mak it back to my house from your on my ow power.
KIKO (SHINE)
I mean, I figured out this riding thing so easily yester-day with that power, right?
KIKO
I think I really do have something that's lacking in ordinary people.
You don't have it either, Kii-chan, so I doubt you'll under-stand...
Well, this is all probably making you feel lonely. I'll see you again next year. Give my regards to Auntie too.
Well, this is all probably making you feel lonely. I'll see you again next year. Give my regards to Auntie too.
Menu
IT'S OKAY, TOMOKO-CHAN.
I'LL BE SEEING YOU AGAIN SOON, AFTER ALL!

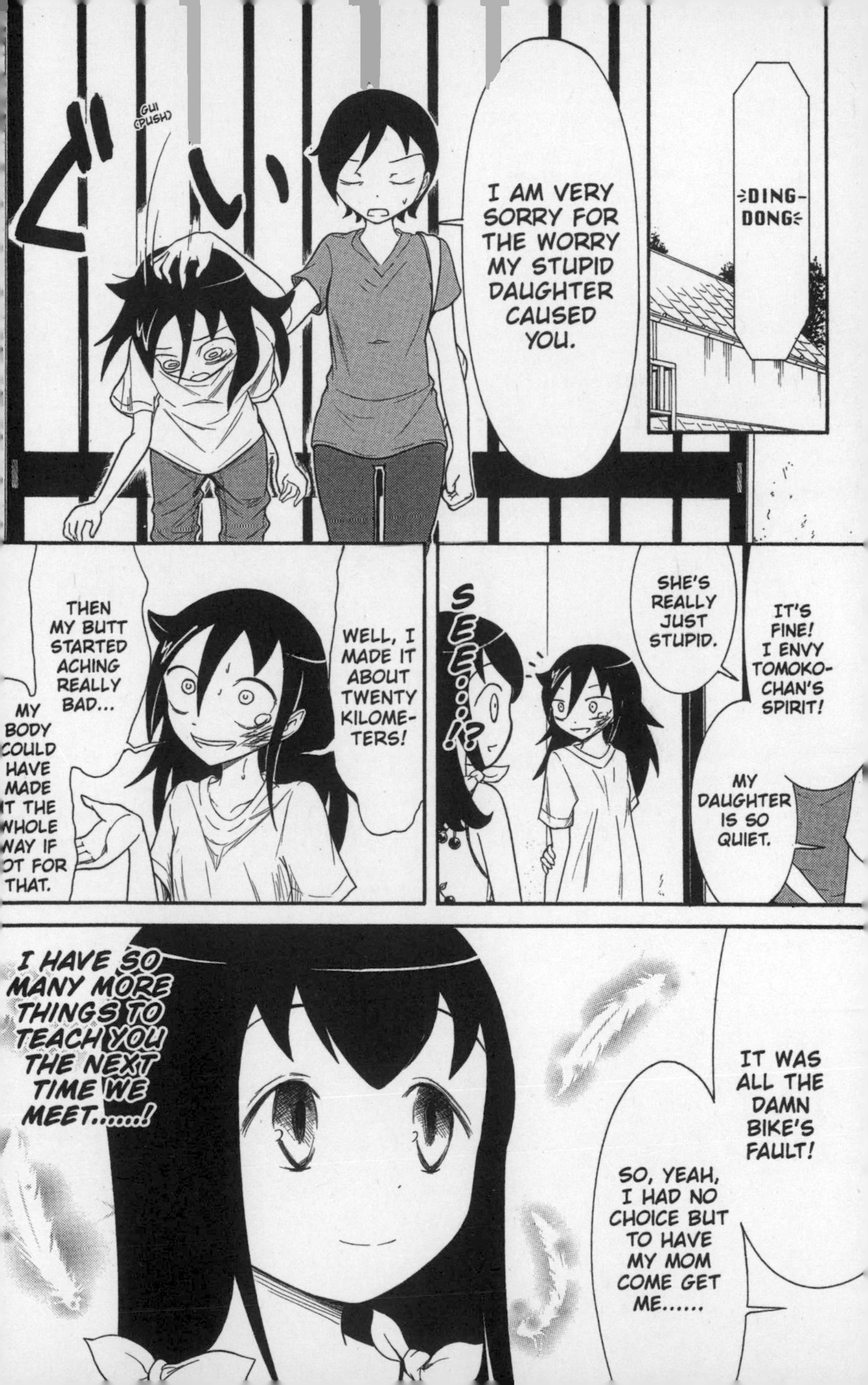

DING-DONG
GUI (PUSH)
I AM VERY SORRY FOR THE WORRY MY STUPID DAUGHTER CAUSED YOU.
IT'S FINE! I ENVY TOMOKO-CHAN'S SPIRIT!
MY DAUGHTER IS SO QUIET.
SHE'S REALLY JUST STUPID.
SEE...!?
WELL, I MADE IT ABOUT TWENTY KILOMETERS!
THEN MY BUTT STARTED ACHING REALLY BAD...
MY BODY COULD HAVE MADE IT THE WHOLE WAY IF NOT FOR THAT.
IT WAS ALL THE DAMN BIKE'S FAULT!
SO, YEAH, I HAD NO CHOICE BUT TO HAVE MY MOM COME GET ME......
I HAVE SO MANY MORE THINGS TO TEACH YOU THE NEXT TIME WE MEET......!

No Matter How I Look at It, It's You Guys' Fault I'm Not Popular!

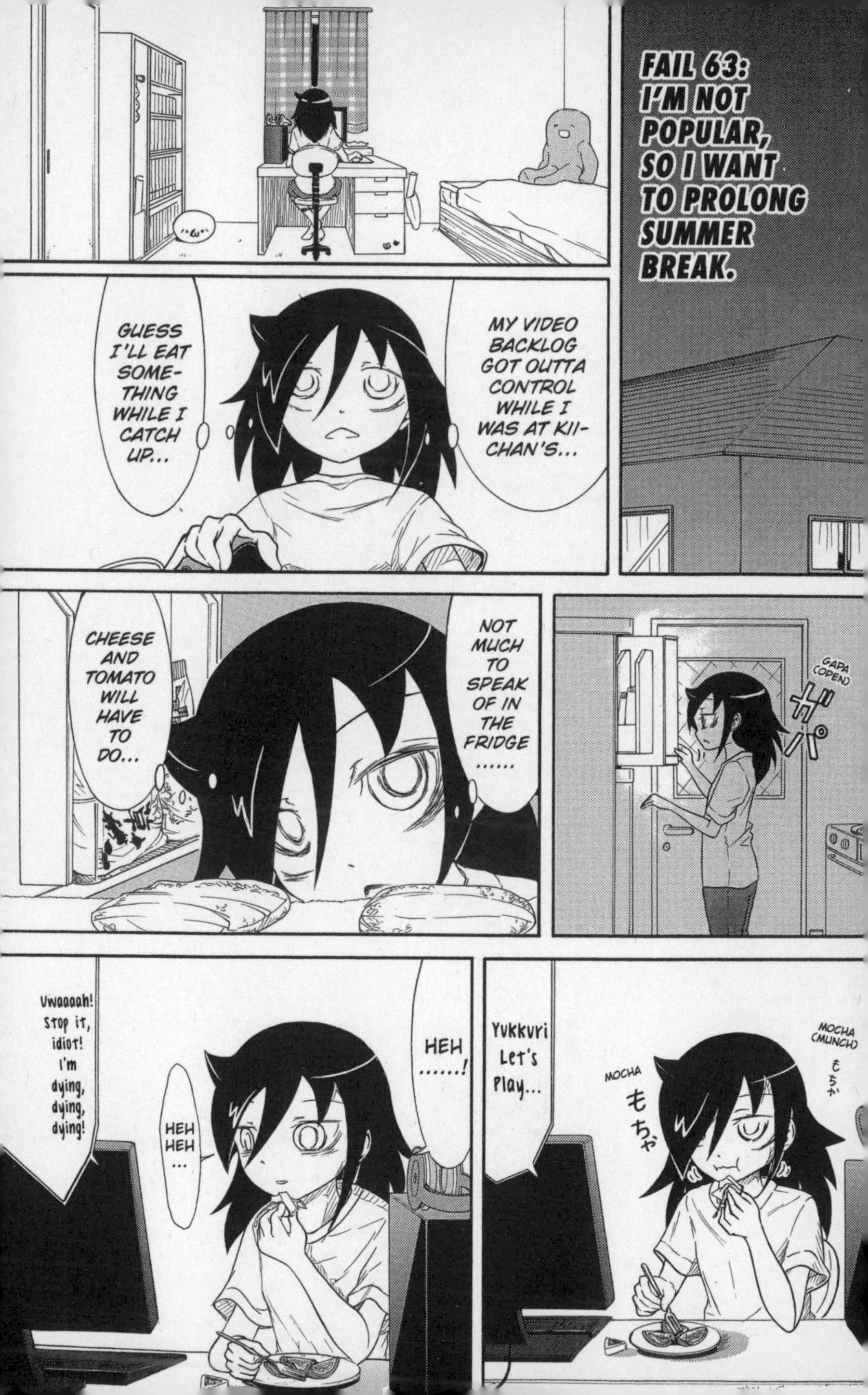
FAIL 63: I'M NOT POPULAR, SO I WANT TO PROLONG SUMMER BREAK.
MY VIDEO BACKLOG GOT OUTTA CONTROL WHILE I WAS AT KII-CHAN'S...
GUESS I'LL EAT SOME-THING WHILE I CATCH UP...
GAPA (OPEN)
ガパ
NOT MUCH TO SPEAK OF IN THE FRIDGE ......
CHEESE AND TOMATO WILL HAVE TO DO...
MOCHA (MUNCH)
もちゃ
MOCHA
もちゃ
Yukkuri Let's Play...
HEH ......!
HEH HEH ...
Uwaaaah! Stop it, idiot! I'm dying, dying, dying!

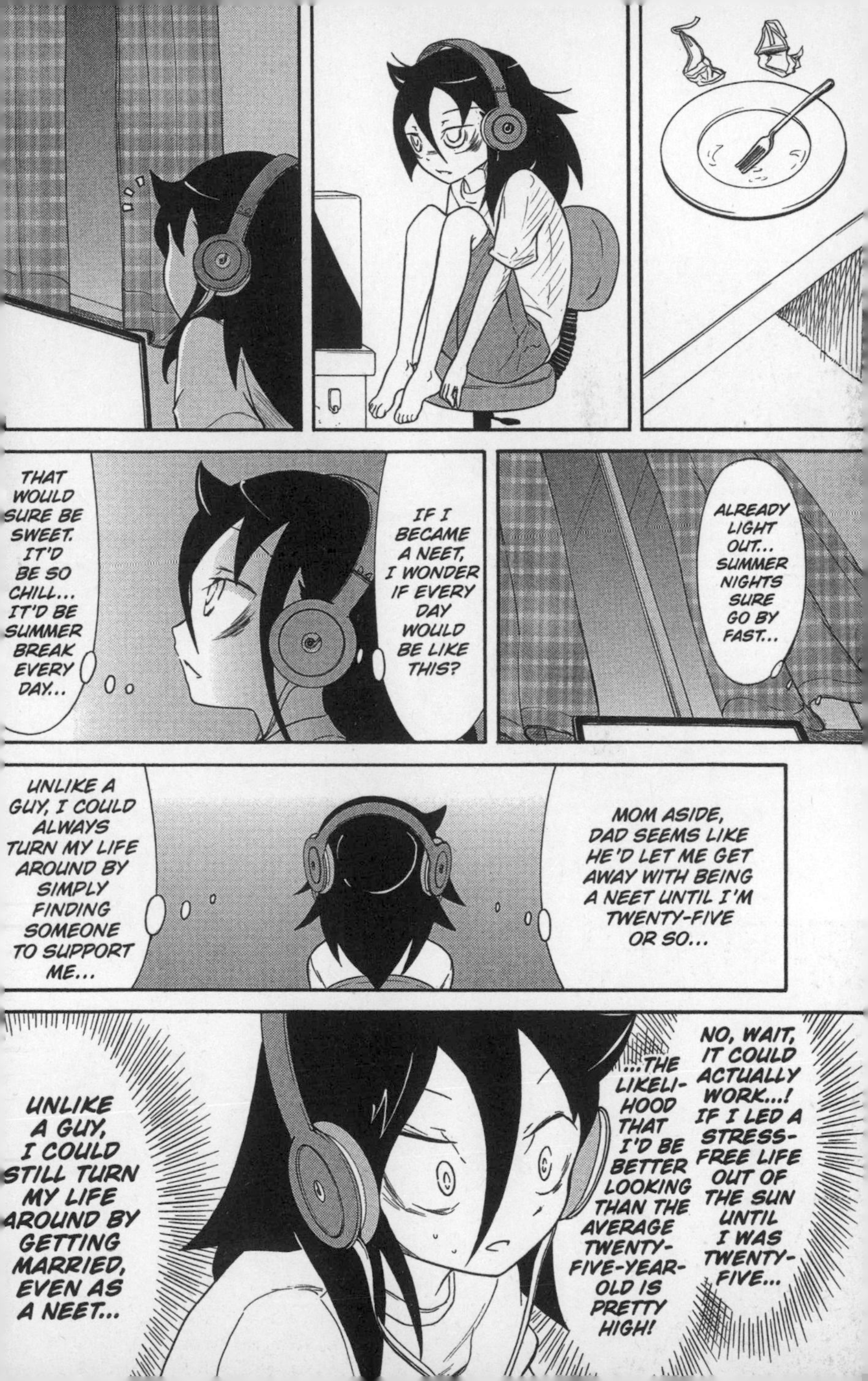
ALREADY LIGHT OUT... SUMMER NIGHTS SURE GO BY FAST...
IF I BECAME A NEET, I WONDER IF EVERY DAY WOULD BE LIKE THIS?
THAT WOULD SURE BE SWEET. IT'D BE SO CHILL... IT'D BE SUMMER BREAK EVERY DAY...
MOM ASIDE, DAD SEEMS LIKE HE'D LET ME GET AWAY WITH BEING A NEET UNTIL I'M TWENTY-FIVE OR SO...
UNLIKE A GUY, I COULD ALWAYS TURN MY LIFE AROUND BY SIMPLY FINDING SOMEONE TO SUPPORT ME...
NO, WAIT, IT COULD ACTUALLY WORK...! IF I LED A STRESS-FREE LIFE OUT OF THE SUN UNTIL I WAS TWENTY-FIVE...
...THE LIKELIHOOD THAT I'D BE BETTER LOOKING THAN THE AVERAGE TWENTY-FIVE-YEAR-OLD IS PRETTY HIGH!
UNLIKE A GUY, I COULD STILL TURN MY LIFE AROUND BY GETTING MARRIED, EVEN AS A NEET...

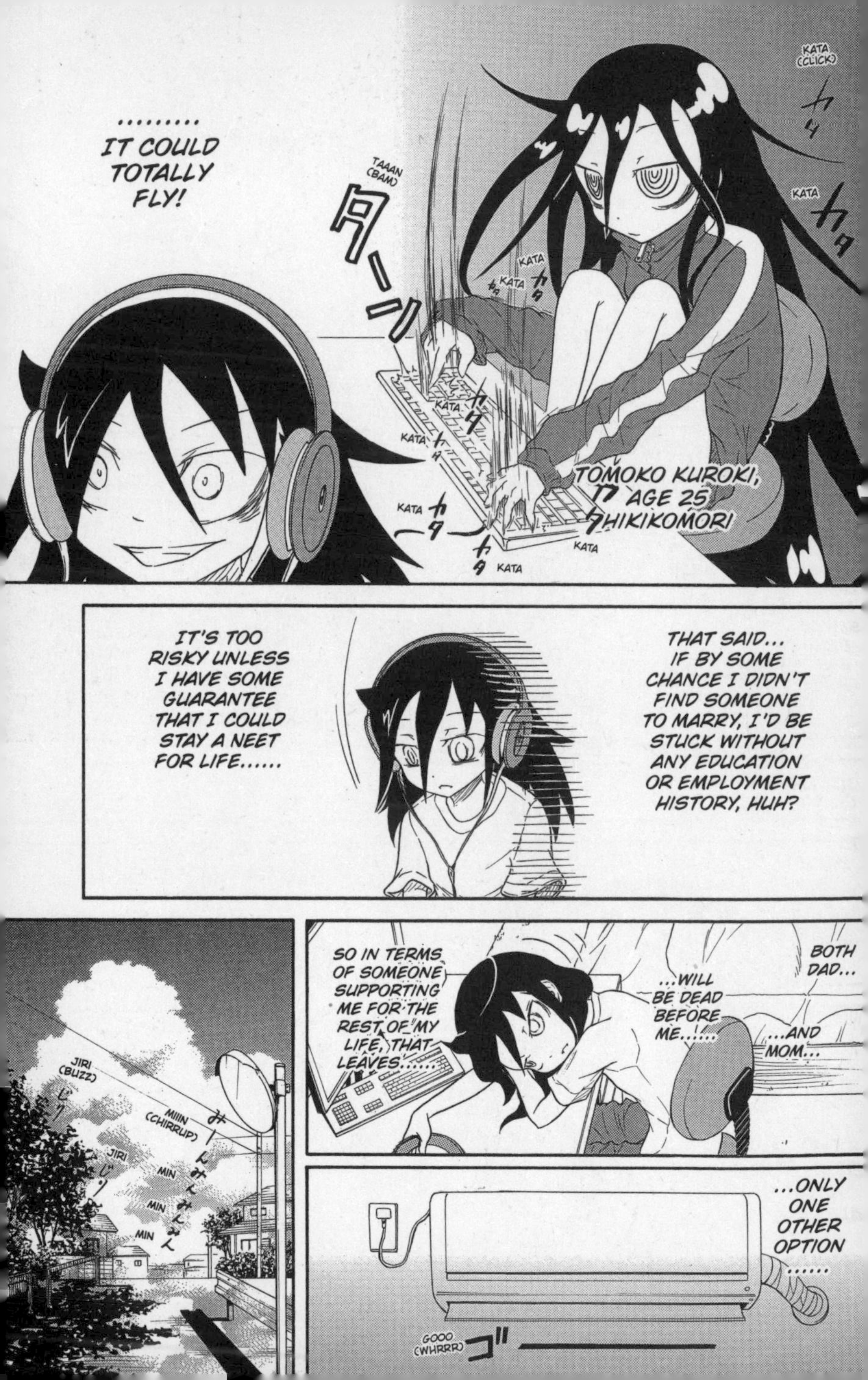
KATA (CLICK)
KATA
TAAAN (BAM)
KATA
KATA
KATA
KATA
KATA
KATA
KATA
TOMOKO KUROKI, AGE 25 HIKIKOMORI
....
IT COULD TOTALLY FLY!
THAT SAID... IF BY SOME CHANCE I DIDN'T FIND SOMEONE TO MARRY, I'D BE STUCK WITHOUT ANY EDUCATION OR EMPLOYMENT HISTORY, HUH?
IT'S TOO RISKY UNLESS I HAVE SOME GUARANTEE THAT I COULD STAY A NEET FOR LIFE......
BOTH DAD...
...AND MOM...
...WILL BE DEAD BEFORE ME...!...
SO IN TERMS OF SOMEONE SUPPORTING ME FOR THE REST OF MY LIFE, THAT LEAVES......
...ONLY ONE OTHER OPTION......
GOOO (WHRRR)
JIRI (BUZZ)
MIIIN (CHIRRUP)
JIRI
MIN
MIN
MIN

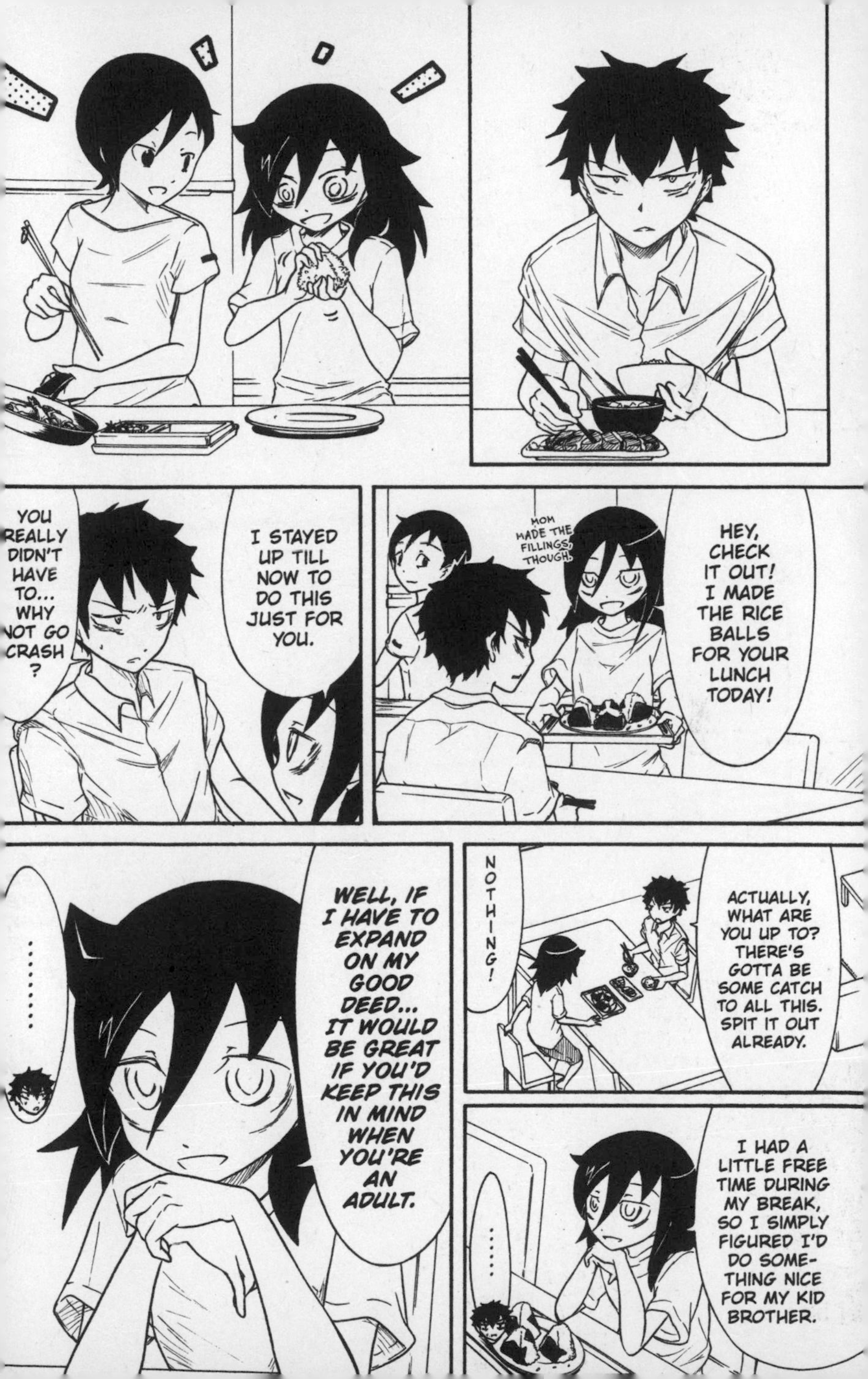
HEY, CHECK IT OUT! I MADE THE RICE BALLS FOR YOUR LUNCH TODAY!
MOM MADE THE FILLINGS, THOUGH.
I STAYED UP TILL NOW TO DO THIS JUST FOR YOU.
YOU REALLY DIDN'T HAVE TO... WHY NOT GO CRASH?
ACTUALLY, WHAT ARE YOU UP TO? THERE'S GOTTA BE SOME CATCH TO ALL THIS. SPIT IT OUT ALREADY.
NOTHING!
I HAD A LITTLE FREE TIME DURING MY BREAK, SO I SIMPLY FIGURED I'D DO SOME-THING NICE FOR MY KID BROTHER.
......
WELL, IF I HAVE TO EXPAND ON MY GOOD DEED... IT WOULD BE GREAT IF YOU'D KEEP THIS IN MIND WHEN YOU'RE AN ADULT.
....

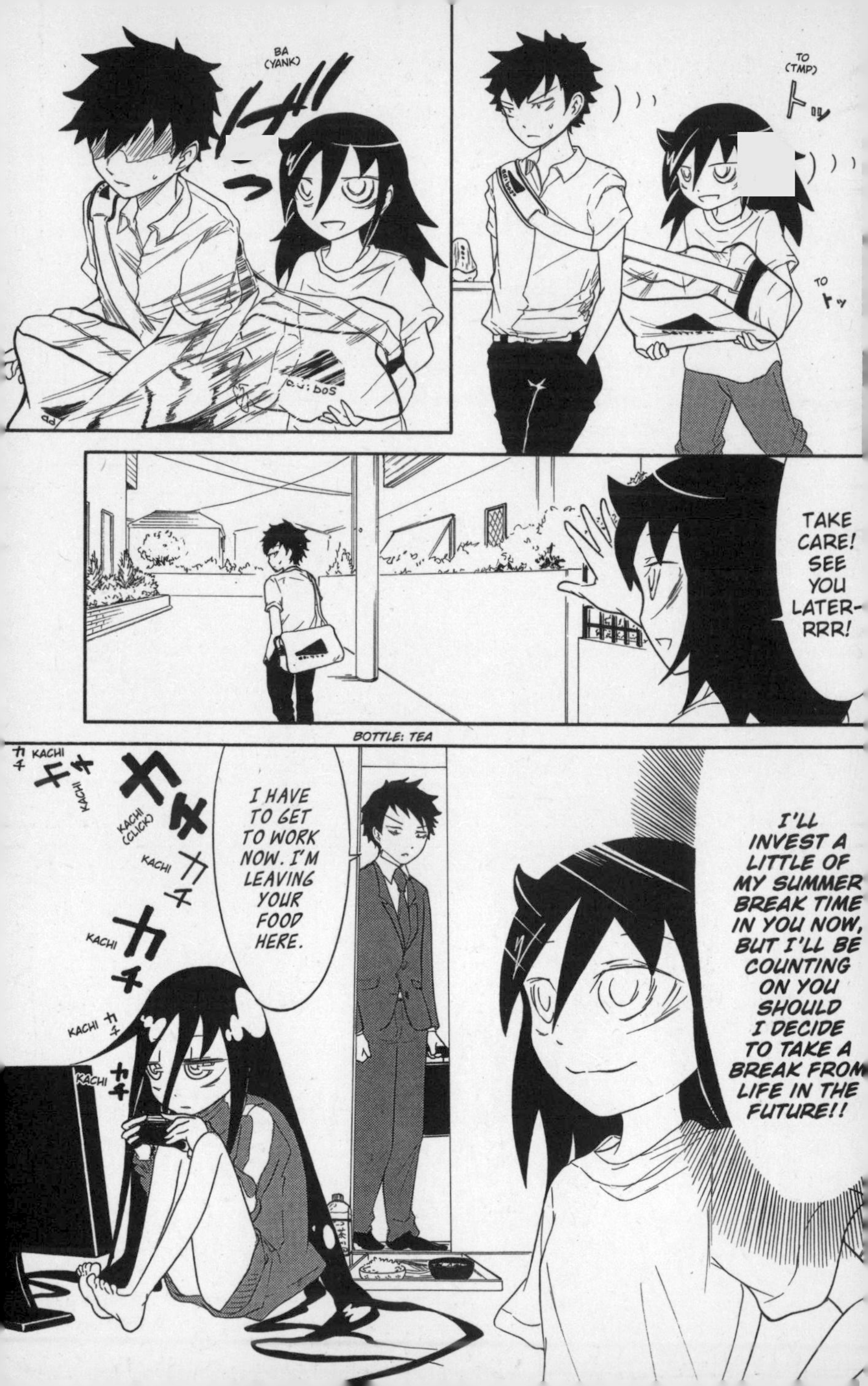
TO (TMP)
トッ
TO
トッ
BA (YANK)
TAKE CARE! SEE YOU LATER-RRR!
BOTTLE: TEA
I'LL INVEST A LITTLE OF MY SUMMER BREAK TIME IN YOU NOW, BUT I'LL BE COUNTING ON YOU SHOULD I DECIDE TO TAKE A BREAK FROM LIFE IN THE FUTURE!!
I HAVE TO GET TO WORK NOW. I'M LEAVING YOUR FOOD HERE.
KACHI
KACHI
KACHI (CLICK)
KACHI
KACHI
KACHI
KACHI

No Matter How I Look at It, It's You Guys' Fault I'm Not Popular!

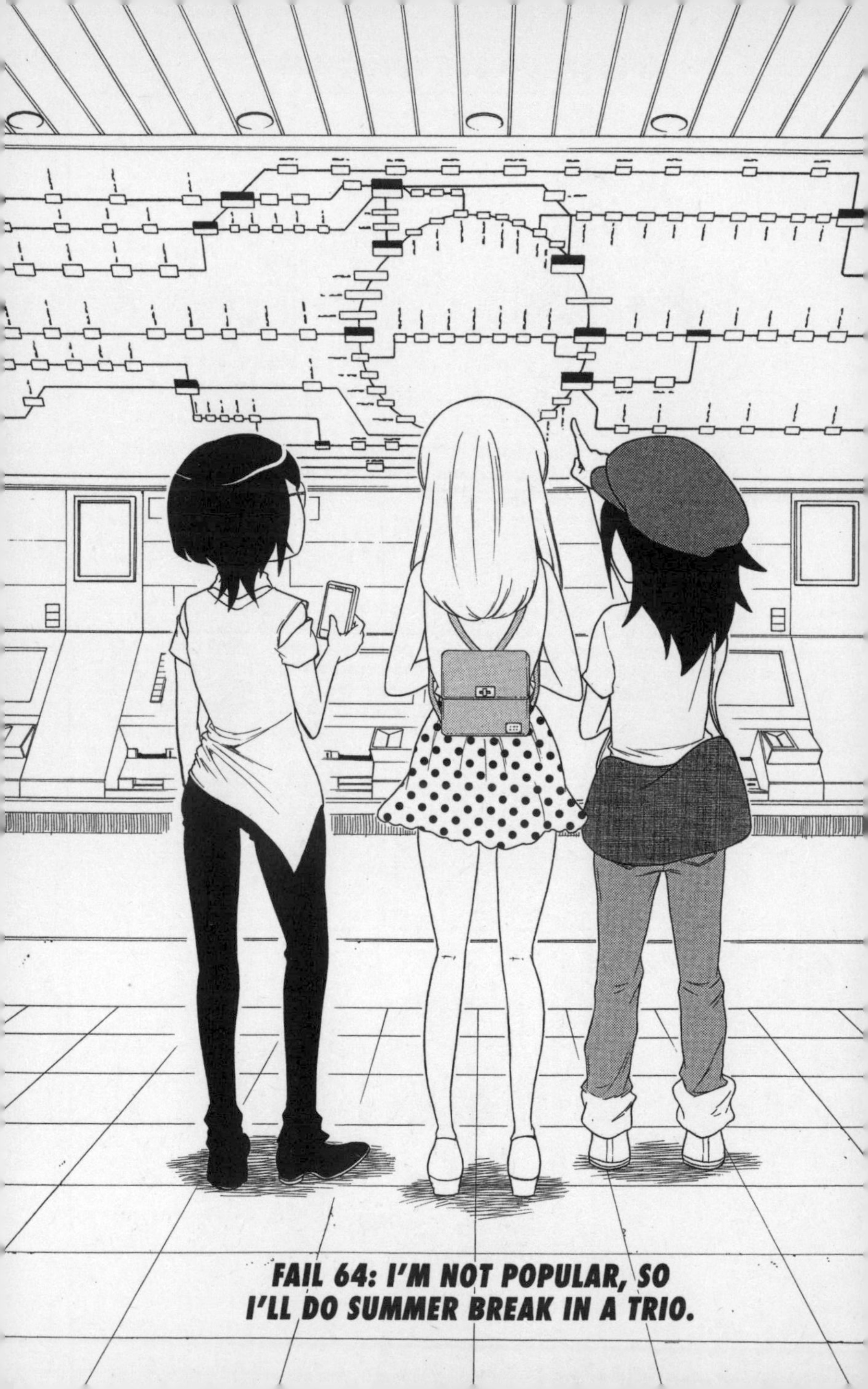

FAIL 64: I'M NOT POPULAR, SO I'LL DO SUMMER BREAK IN A TRIO.

AUGUST 4TH • BUG COLLECTING

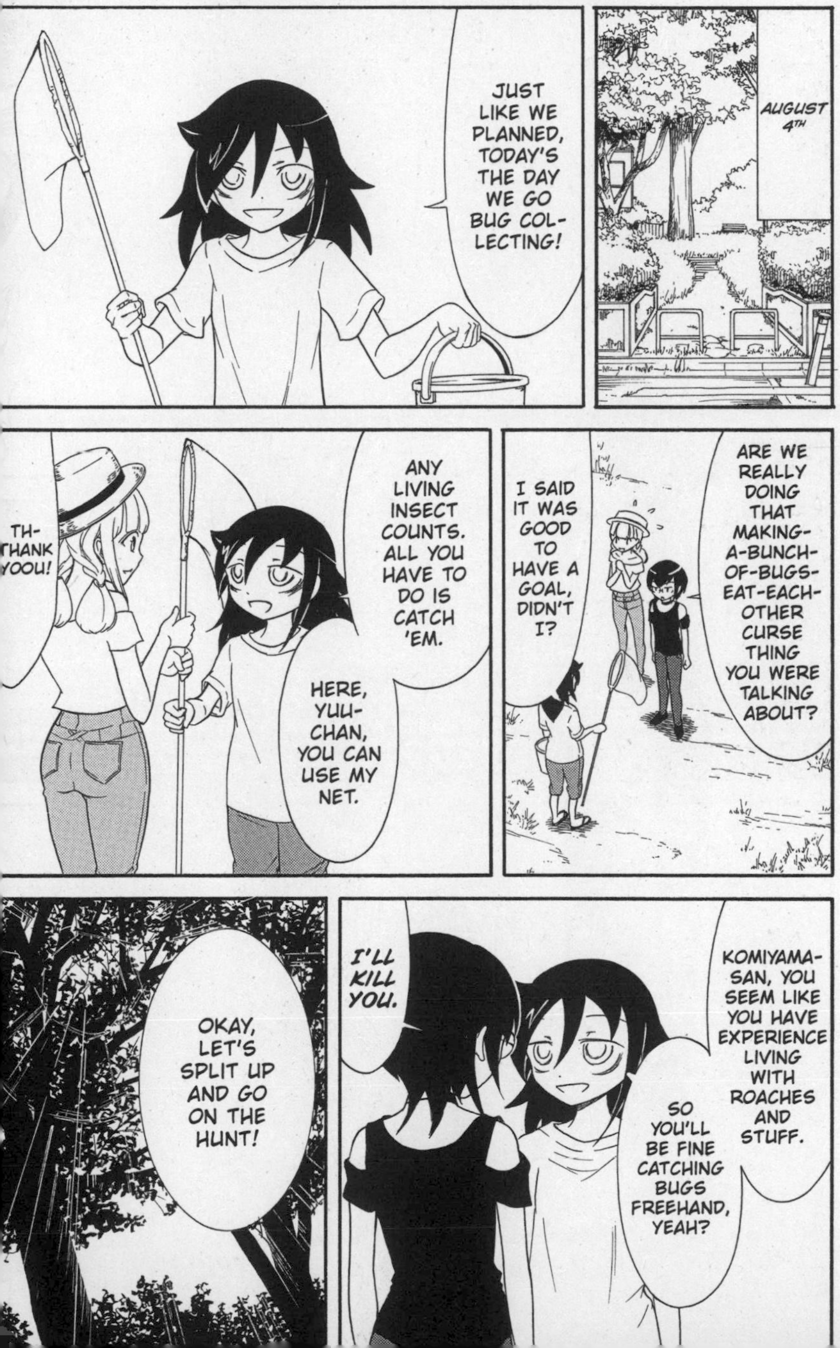
AUGUST 4TH
JUST LIKE WE PLANNED, TODAY'S THE DAY WE GO BUG COL-LECTING!
ARE WE REALLY DOING THAT MAKING-A-BUNCH-OF-BUGS-EAT-EACH-OTHER CURSE THING YOU WERE TALKING ABOUT?
I SAID IT WAS GOOD TO HAVE A GOAL, DIDN'T I?
ANY LIVING INSECT COUNTS. ALL YOU HAVE TO DO IS CATCH 'EM.
HERE, YUU-CHAN, YOU CAN USE MY NET.
TH-THANK YOOU!
KOMIYAMA-SAN, YOU SEEM LIKE YOU HAVE EXPERIENCE LIVING WITH ROACHES AND STUFF.
SO YOU'LL BE FINE CATCHING BUGS FREEHAND, YEAH?
I'LL KILL YOU.
OKAY, LET'S SPLIT UP AND GO ON THE HUNT!

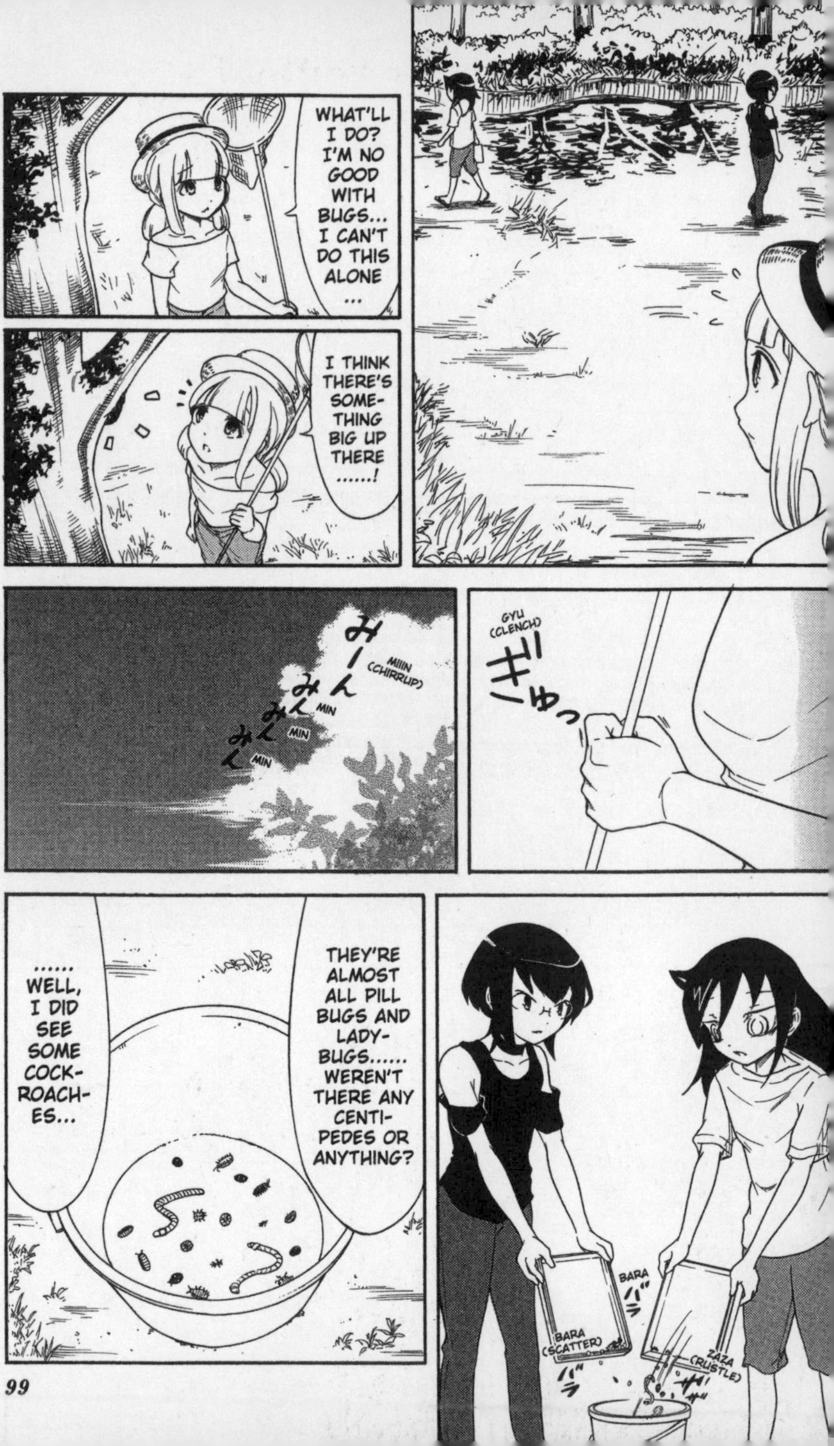
WHAT'LL I DO? I'M NO GOOD WITH BUGS... I CAN'T DO THIS ALONE ...
I THINK THERE'S SOME-THING BIG UP THERE ......!
GYU (CLENCH)
ぎゅっ
みーん
MIIN (CHIRRUP)
みん
MIN
みん
MIN
みん
MIN
バ
BARA
バ
BARA (SCATTER)
ザザ
ZAZA (RUSTLE)
THEY'RE ALMOST ALL PILL BUGS AND LADY-BUGS...... WEREN'T THERE ANY CENTI-PEDES OR ANYTHING?
...... WELL, I DID SEE SOME COCK-ROACH-ES...

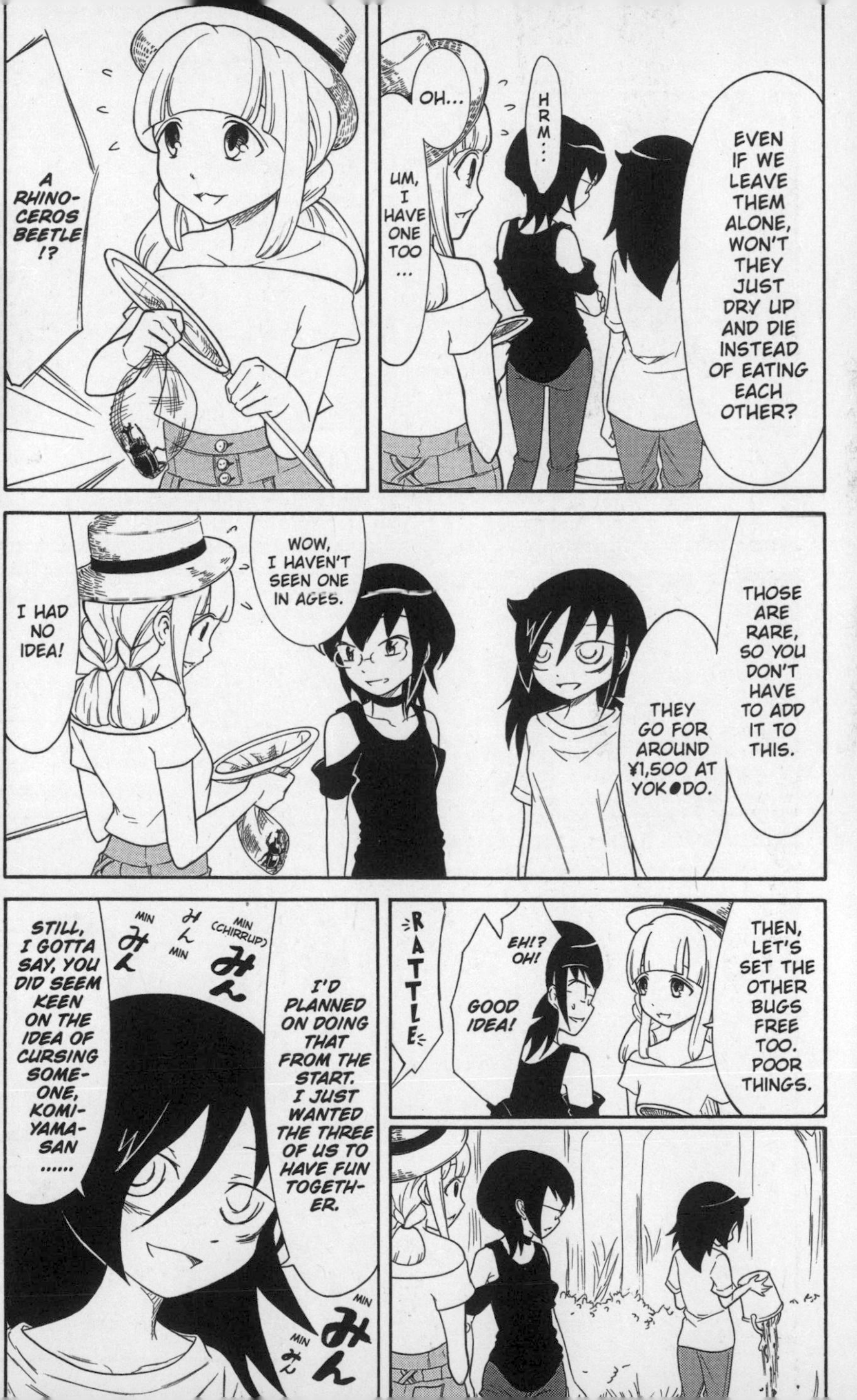
EVEN IF WE LEAVE THEM ALONE, WON'T THEY JUST DRY UP AND DIE INSTEAD OF EATING EACH OTHER?
HRM...
OH...
UM, I HAVE ONE TOO...
A RHINOCEROS BEETLE!?
THOSE ARE RARE, SO YOU DON'T HAVE TO ADD IT TO THIS.
THEY GO FOR AROUND ¥1,500 AT YOKO●DO.
WOW, I HAVEN'T SEEN ONE IN AGES.
I HAD NO IDEA!
THEN, LET'S SET THE OTHER BUGS FREE TOO. POOR THINGS.
RATTLE
EH!? OH!
GOOD IDEA!
みん MIN (CHIRRUP)
みん MIN
みん MIN
I'D PLANNED ON DOING THAT FROM THE START. I JUST WANTED THE THREE OF US TO HAVE FUN TOGETHER.
STILL, I GOTTA SAY, YOU DID SEEM KEEN ON THE IDEA OF CURSING SOMEONE, KOMIYAMA-SAN......
みん MIN
みん MIN

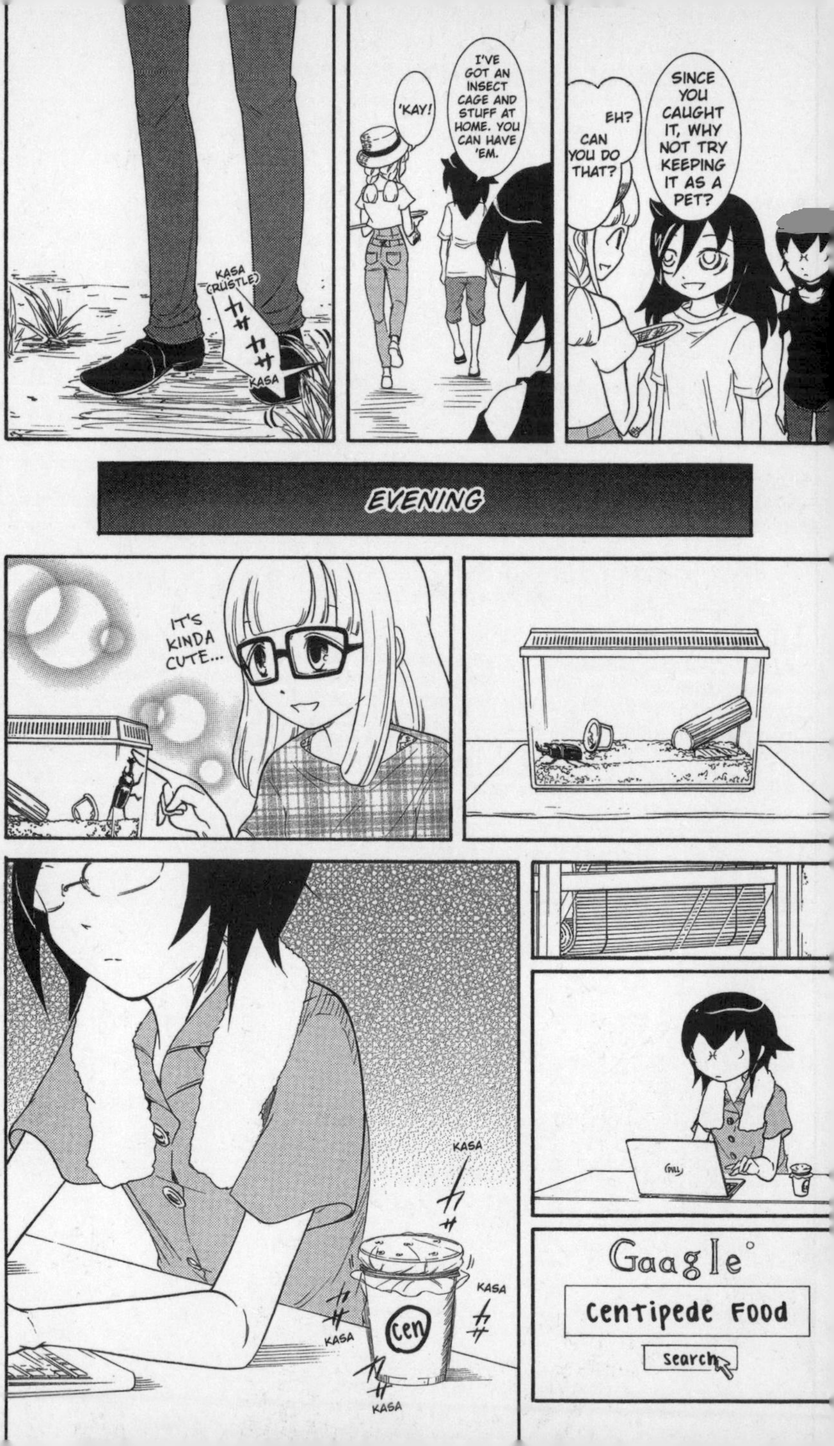
SINCE YOU CAUGHT IT, WHY NOT TRY KEEPING IT AS A PET?
EH? CAN YOU DO THAT?
I'VE GOT AN INSECT CAGE AND STUFF AT HOME. YOU CAN HAVE 'EM.
'KAY!
KASA (RUSTLE)
KASA
EVENING
IT'S KINDA CUTE...
Gaagle
Centipede Food
Search
KASA
KASA
cen
KASA
KASA

AUGUST 10TH • SWIMMING IN THE OCEAN

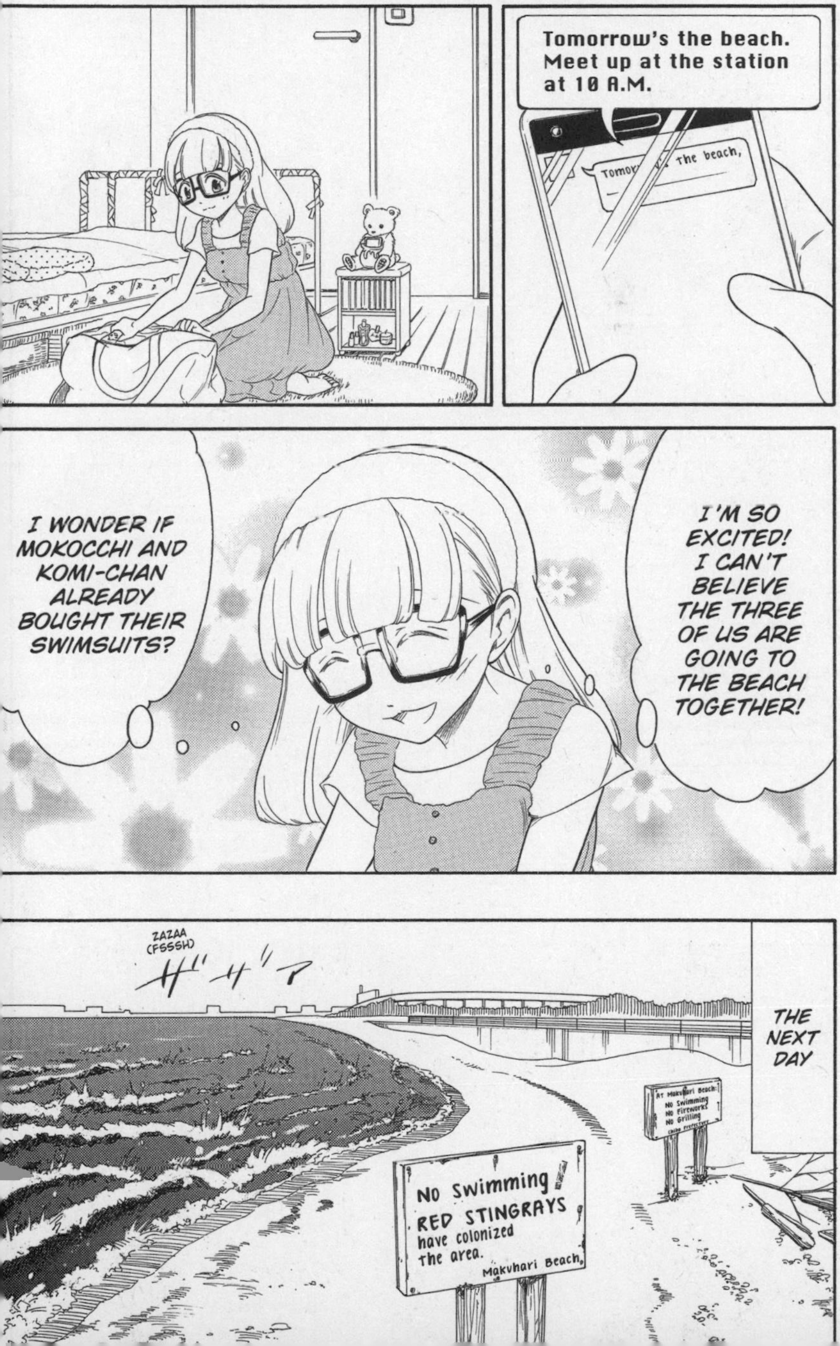
Tomorrow's the beach. Meet up at the station at 10 A.M.
I'M SO EXCITED! I CAN'T BELIEVE THE THREE OF US ARE GOING TO THE BEACH TOGETHER!
I WONDER IF MOKOCCHI AND KOMI-CHAN ALREADY BOUGHT THEIR SWIMSUITS?
THE NEXT DAY
ZAZAA (FSSSH)
ザザァ
At Makuhari Beach: No Swimming No Fireworks No Grilling
No Swimming! RED STINGRAYS have colonized the area. Makuhari Beach

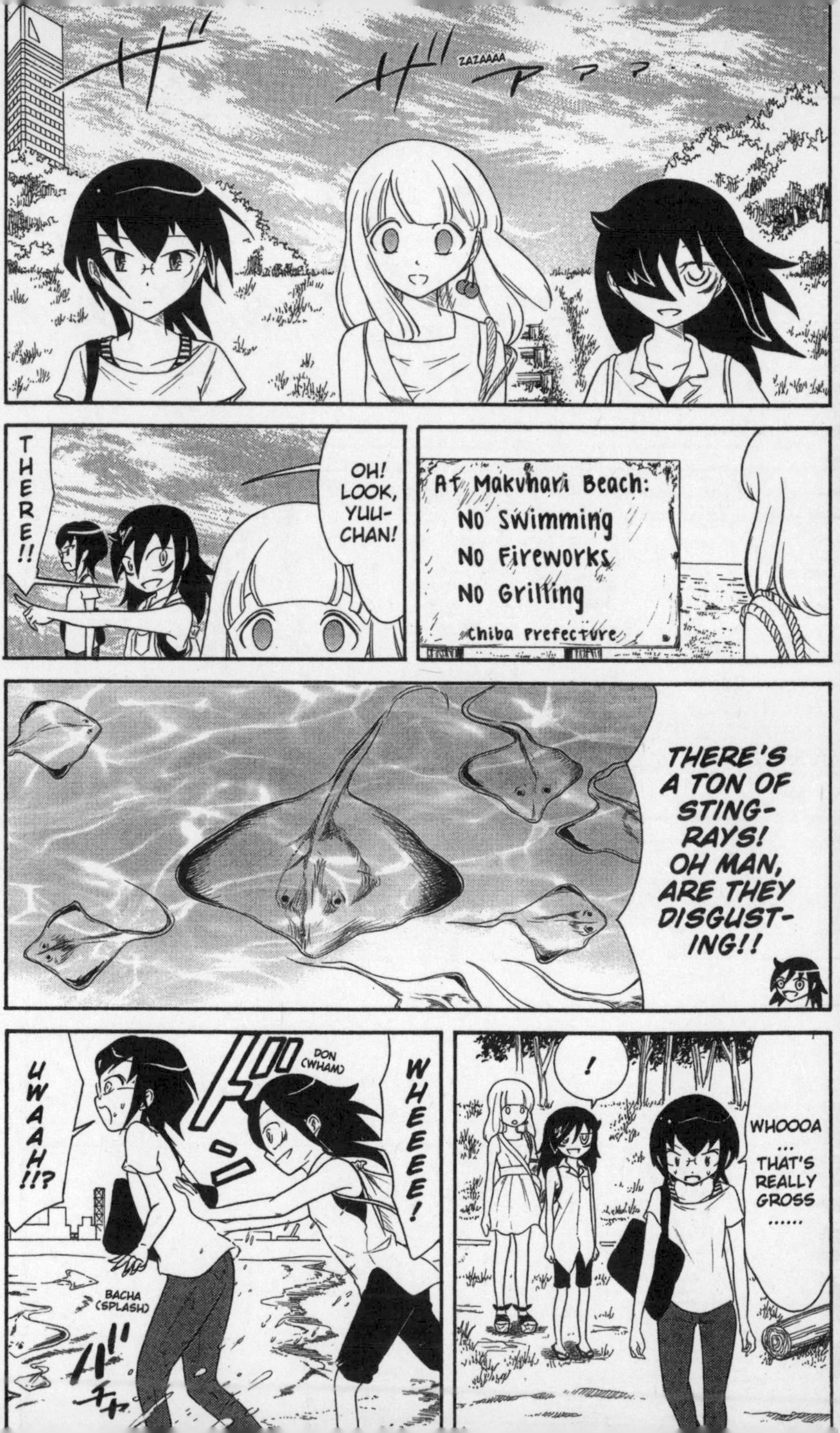
ZAZAAAA
At Makuhari Beach:
No Swimming
No Fireworks
No Grilling
Chiba Prefecture
OH! LOOK, YUU-CHAN!
THERE!!
THERE'S A TON OF STING-RAYS! OH MAN, ARE THEY DISGUST-ING!!
!
WHOOOA ... THAT'S REALLY GROSS ......
WHEEEEE!
DON (WHAM)
UWAAAH!!?
BACHA (SPLASH)

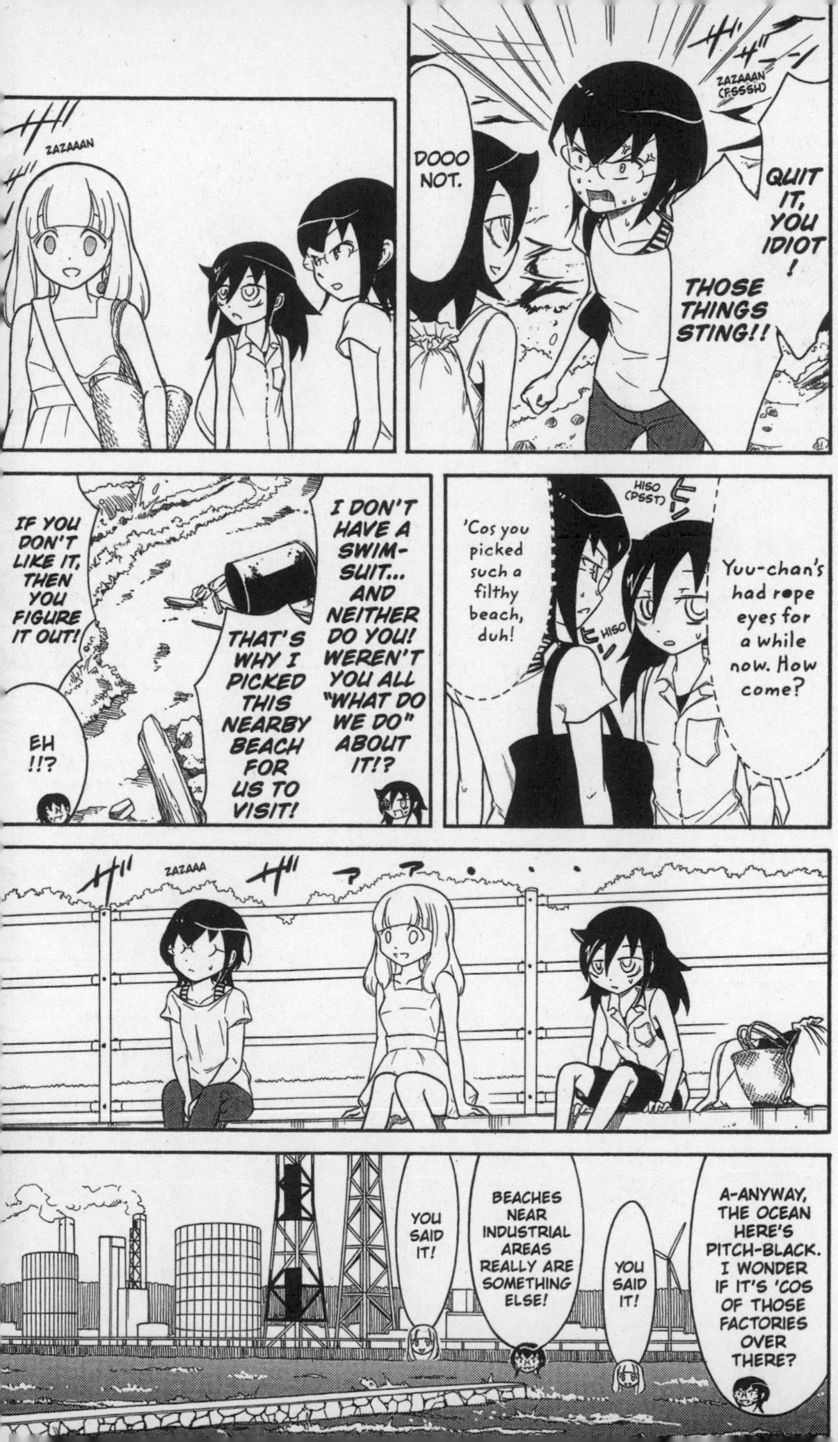
ZAZAAAN (FSSSH)
QUIT IT, YOU IDIOT!
THOSE THINGS STING!!
DOOO NOT.
ZAZAAAN
HISO (PSST)
Yuu-chan's had rope eyes for a while now. How come?
'Cos you picked such a filthy beach, duh!
HISO
I DON'T HAVE A SWIMSUIT... AND NEITHER DO YOU! WEREN'T YOU ALL "WHAT DO WE DO" ABOUT IT!?
THAT'S WHY I PICKED THIS NEARBY BEACH FOR US TO VISIT!
IF YOU DON'T LIKE IT, THEN YOU FIGURE IT OUT!
EH!!?
ZAZAAA
A-ANYWAY, THE OCEAN HERE'S PITCH-BLACK. I WONDER IF IT'S 'COS OF THOSE FACTORIES OVER THERE?
YOU SAID IT!
BEACHES NEAR INDUSTRIAL AREAS REALLY ARE SOMETHING ELSE!
YOU SAID IT!

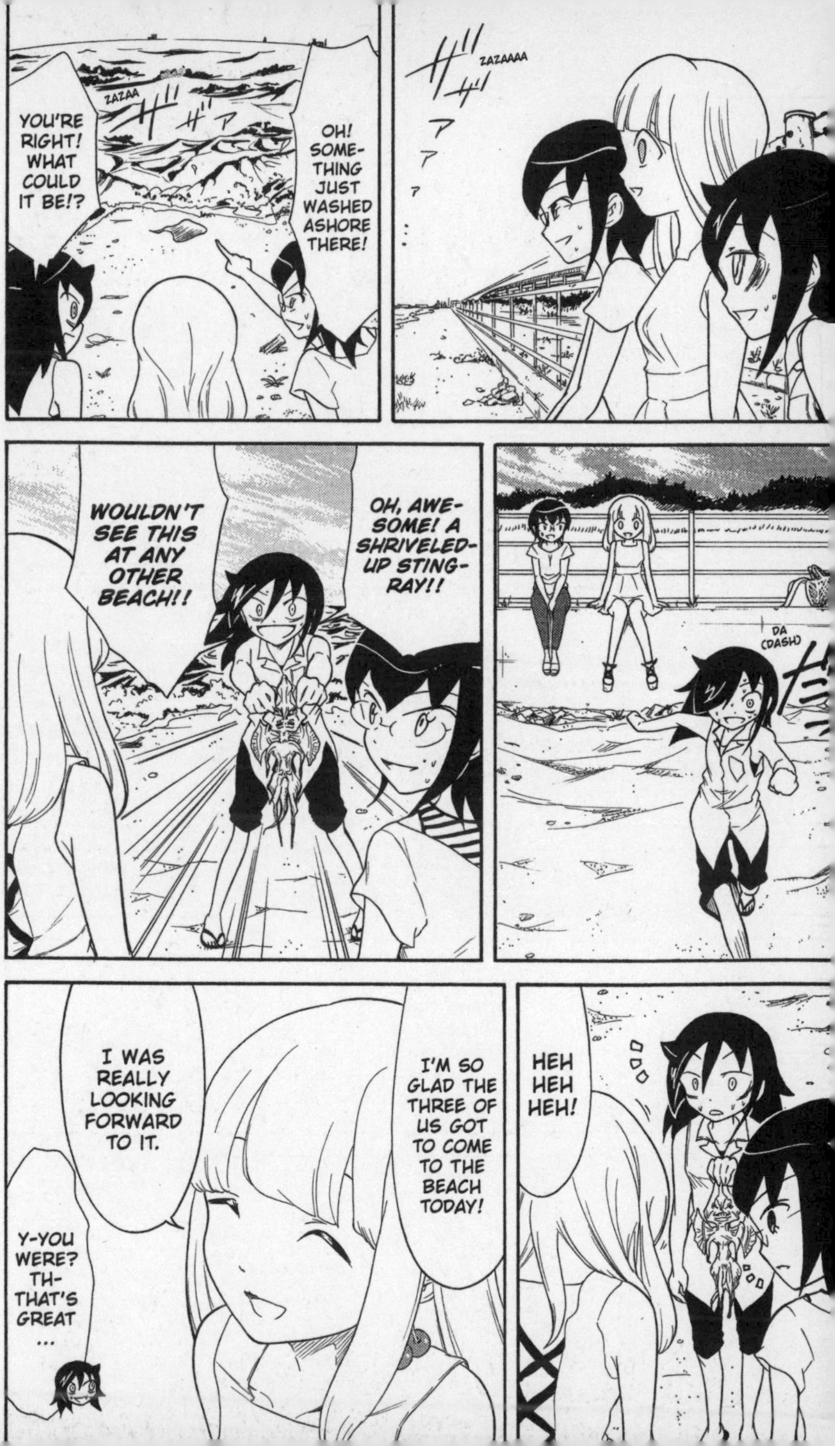
ZAZAAAA
OH! SOME-THING JUST WASHED ASHORE THERE!
YOU'RE RIGHT! WHAT COULD IT BE!?
ZAZAA
DA (DASH)
OH, AWE-SOME! A SHRIVELED-UP STING-RAY!!
WOULDN'T SEE THIS AT ANY OTHER BEACH!!
HEH HEH HEH!
I'M SO GLAD THE THREE OF US GOT TO COME TO THE BEACH TODAY!
I WAS REALLY LOOKING FORWARD TO IT.
Y-YOU WERE? TH-THAT'S GREAT...

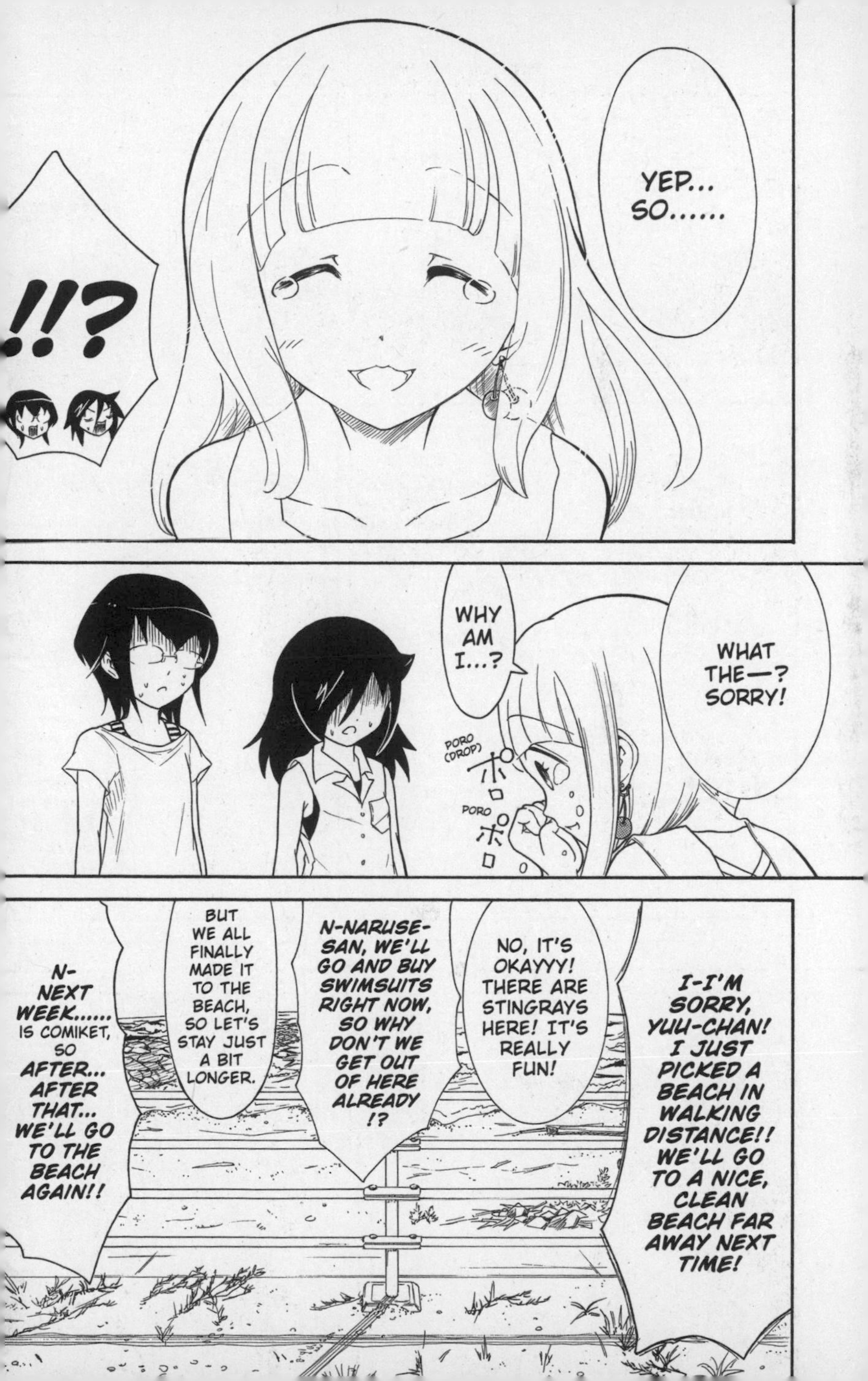
YEP... SO......
!!?
WHAT THE—? SORRY!
WHY AM I...?
PORO (DROP)
PORO
I-I'M SORRY, YUU-CHAN! I JUST PICKED A BEACH IN WALKING DISTANCE!! WE'LL GO TO A NICE, CLEAN BEACH FAR AWAY NEXT TIME!
NO, IT'S OKAYYY! THERE ARE STINGRAYS HERE! IT'S REALLY FUN!
N-NARUSE-SAN, WE'LL GO AND BUY SWIMSUITS RIGHT NOW, SO WHY DON'T WE GET OUT OF HERE ALREADY!?
BUT WE ALL FINALLY MADE IT TO THE BEACH, SO LET'S STAY JUST A BIT LONGER.
N-NEXT WEEK...... IS COMIKET, SO AFTER... AFTER THAT... WE'LL GO TO THE BEACH AGAIN!!

AUGUST 17TH • COMIKET

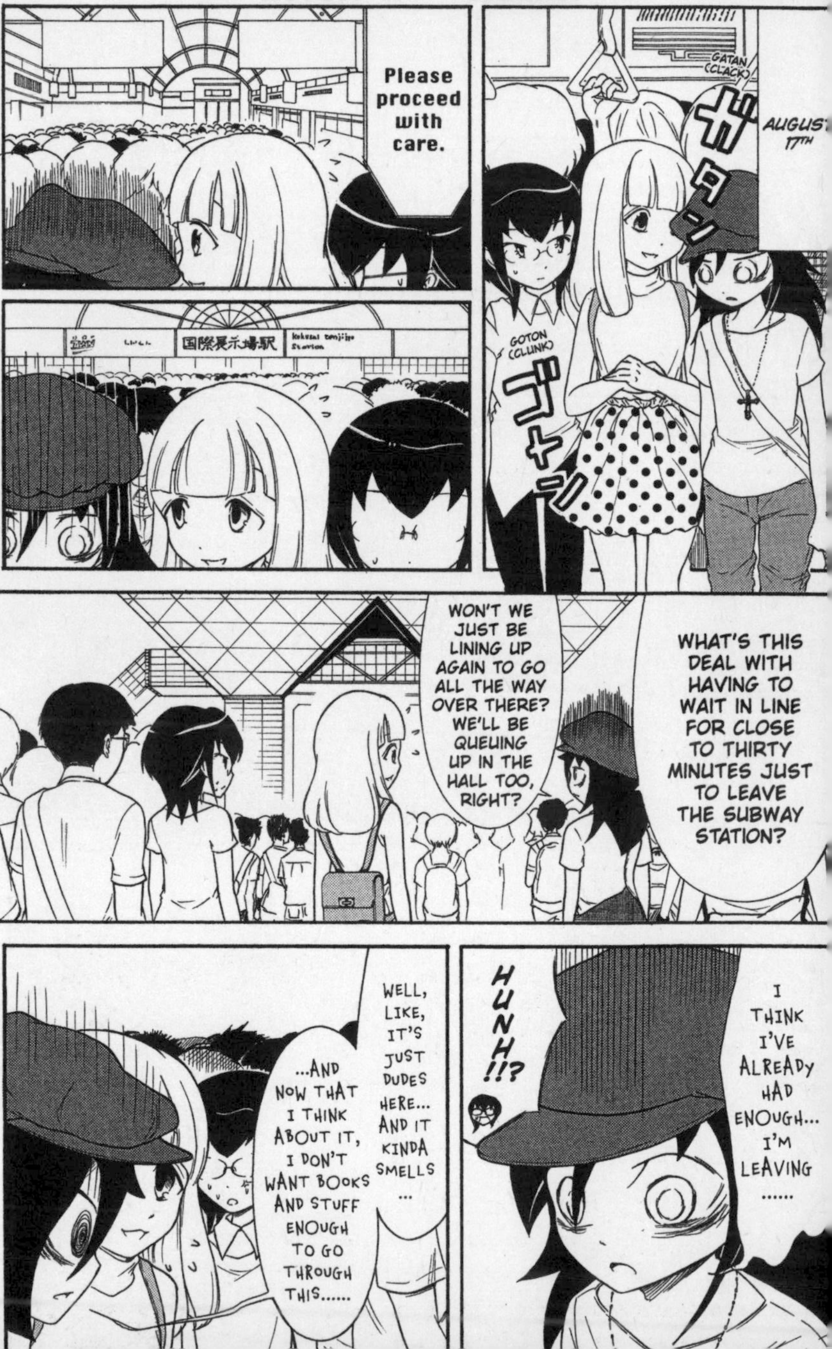

GATAN (CLACK)
ガタン
AUGUST 17TH
GOTON (CLUNK)
ゴトン
Please proceed with care.
国際展示場駅
WHAT'S THIS DEAL WITH HAVING TO WAIT IN LINE FOR CLOSE TO THIRTY MINUTES JUST TO LEAVE THE SUBWAY STATION?
WON'T WE JUST BE LINING UP AGAIN TO GO ALL THE WAY OVER THERE? WE'LL BE QUEUING UP IN THE HALL TOO, RIGHT?
I THINK I'VE ALREADY HAD ENOUGH... I'M LEAVING......
HUNH!!?
WELL, LIKE, IT'S JUST DUDES HERE... AND IT KINDA SMELLS...
...AND NOW THAT I THINK ABOUT IT, I DON'T WANT BOOKS AND STUFF ENOUGH TO GO THROUGH THIS......

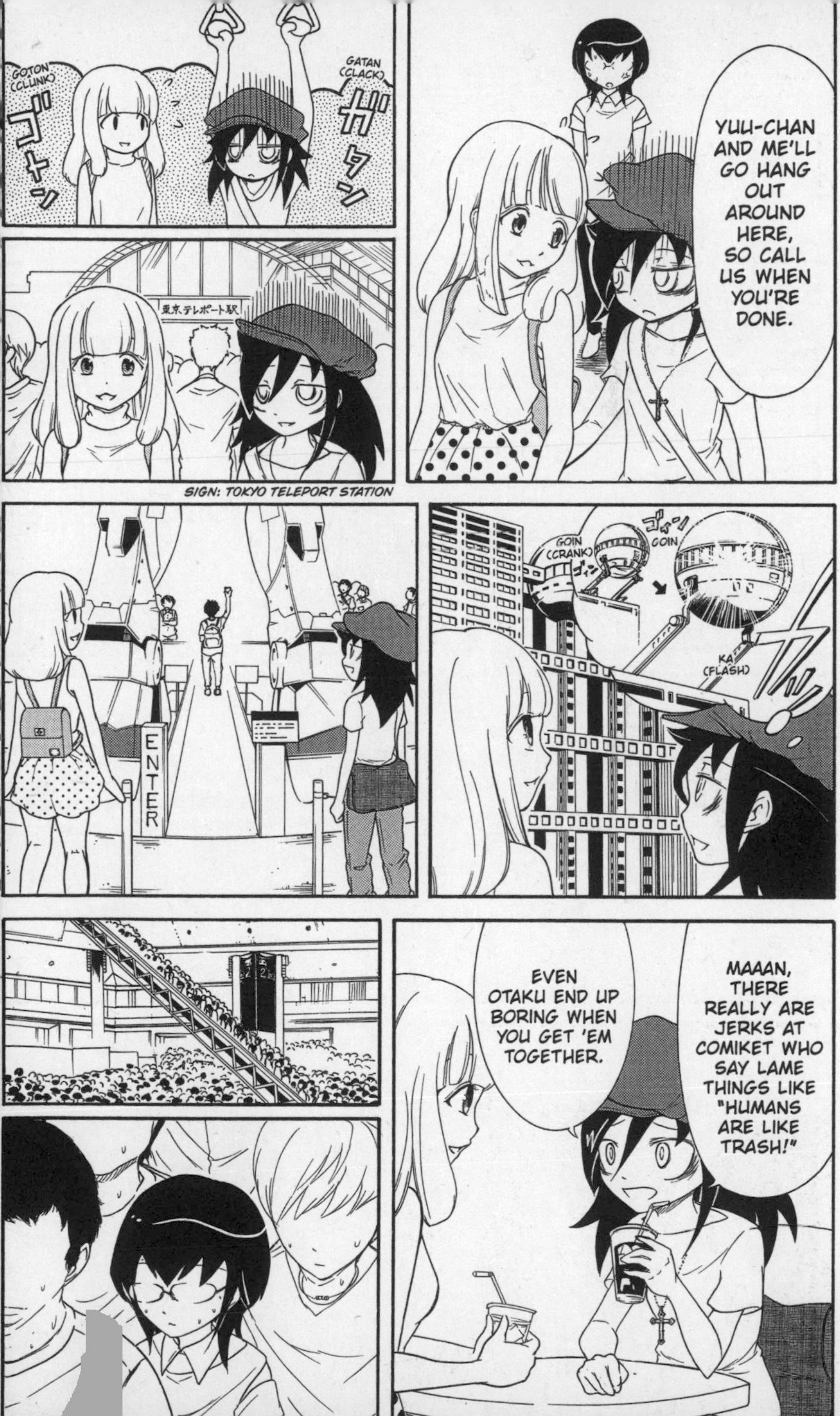
YUU-CHAN AND ME'LL GO HANG OUT AROUND HERE, SO CALL US WHEN YOU'RE DONE.
GATAN (CLACK)
GOTON (CLUNK)
東京テレポート駅
SIGN: TOKYO TELEPORT STATION
GOIN
GOIN (CRANK)
KA (FLASH)
ENTER
MAAAN, THERE REALLY ARE JERKS AT COMIKET WHO SAY LAME THINGS LIKE "HUMANS ARE LIKE TRASH!"
EVEN OTAKU END UP BORING WHEN YOU GET 'EM TOGETHER.

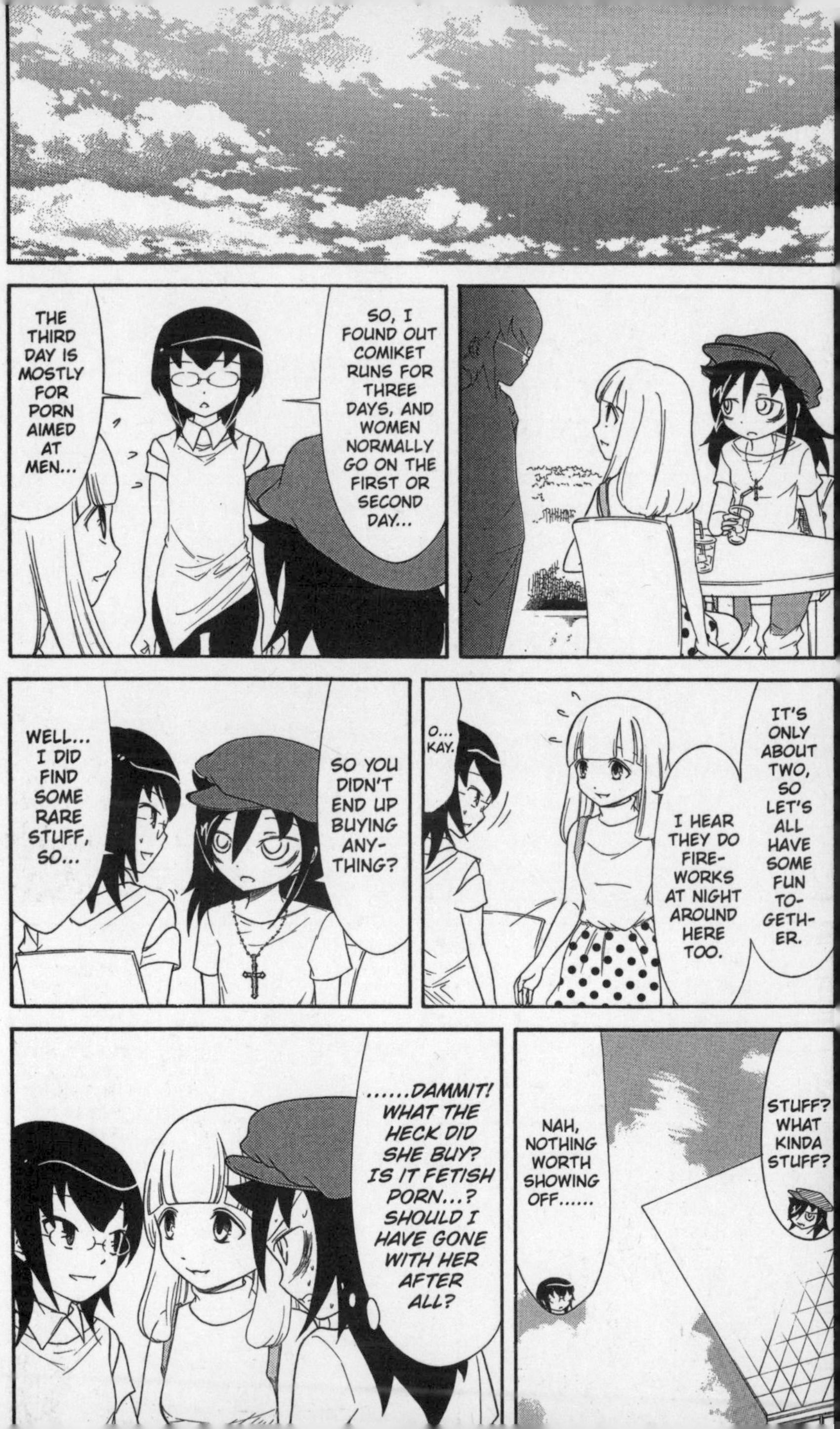
SO, I FOUND OUT COMIKET RUNS FOR THREE DAYS, AND WOMEN NORMALLY GO ON THE FIRST OR SECOND DAY...
THE THIRD DAY IS MOSTLY FOR PORN AIMED AT MEN...
IT'S ONLY ABOUT TWO, SO LET'S ALL HAVE SOME FUN TO-GETH-ER.
I HEAR THEY DO FIRE-WORKS AT NIGHT AROUND HERE TOO.
O... KAY.
SO YOU DIDN'T END UP BUYING ANY-THING?
WELL... I DID FIND SOME RARE STUFF, SO...
STUFF? WHAT KINDA STUFF?
NAH, NOTHING WORTH SHOWING OFF......
......DAMMIT! WHAT THE HECK DID SHE BUY? IS IT FETISH PORN...? SHOULD I HAVE GONE WITH HER AFTER ALL?

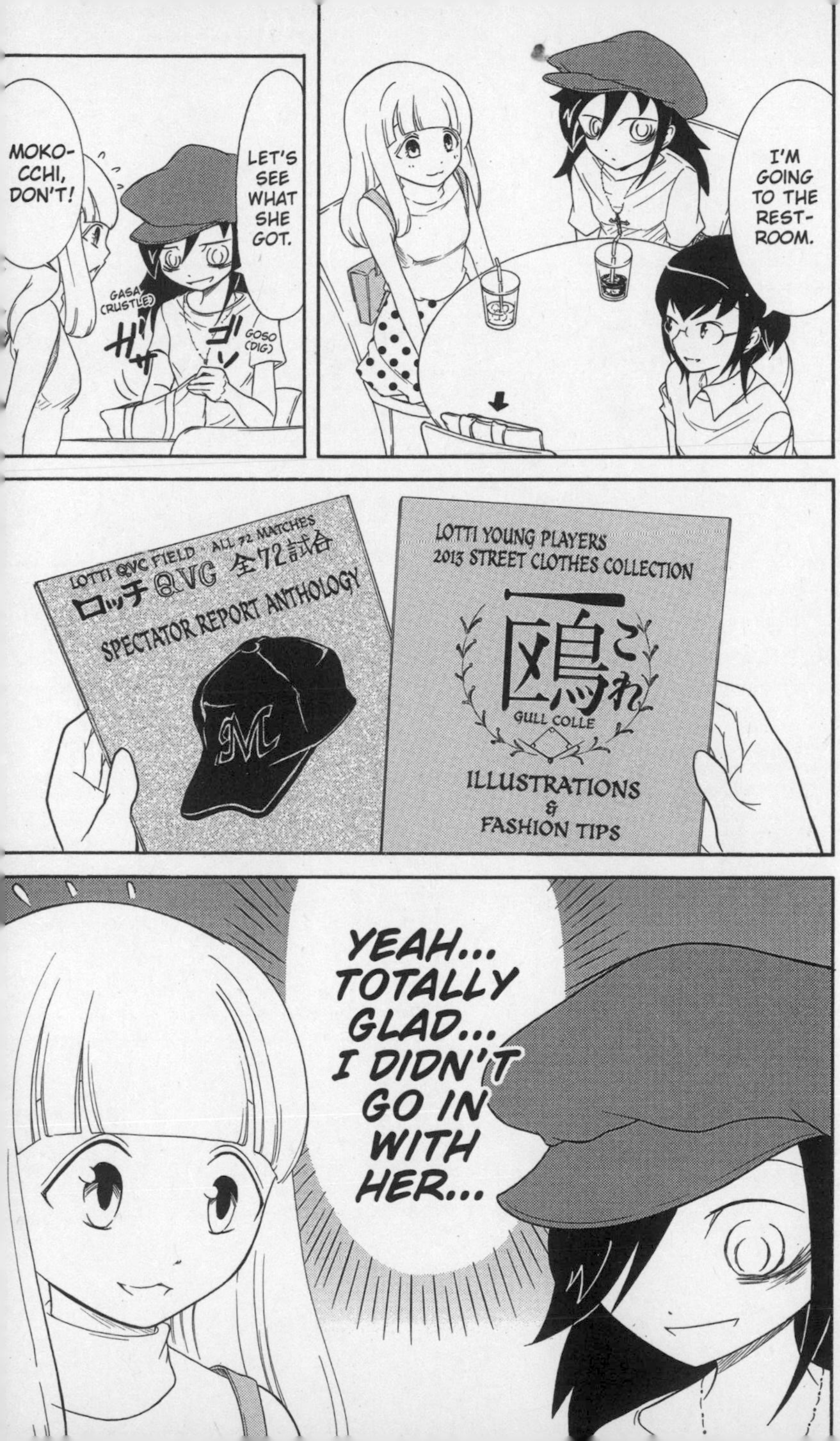
I'M GOING TO THE REST-ROOM.
LET'S SEE WHAT SHE GOT.
MOKO-CCHI, DON'T!
GASA (RUSTLE)
ガサ
ゴソ
GOSO (DIG)
LOTTI YOUNG PLAYERS
2013 STREET CLOTHES COLLECTION
鴎これ
GULL COLLE
ILLUSTRATIONS & FASHION TIPS
LOTTI QVC FIELD · ALL 72 MATCHES
ロッチ QVC 全72試合
SPECTATOR REPORT ANTHOLOGY
YEAH... TOTALLY GLAD... I DIDN'T GO IN WITH HER...

No Matter How I Look at It, It's You Guys' Fault I'm Not Popular!

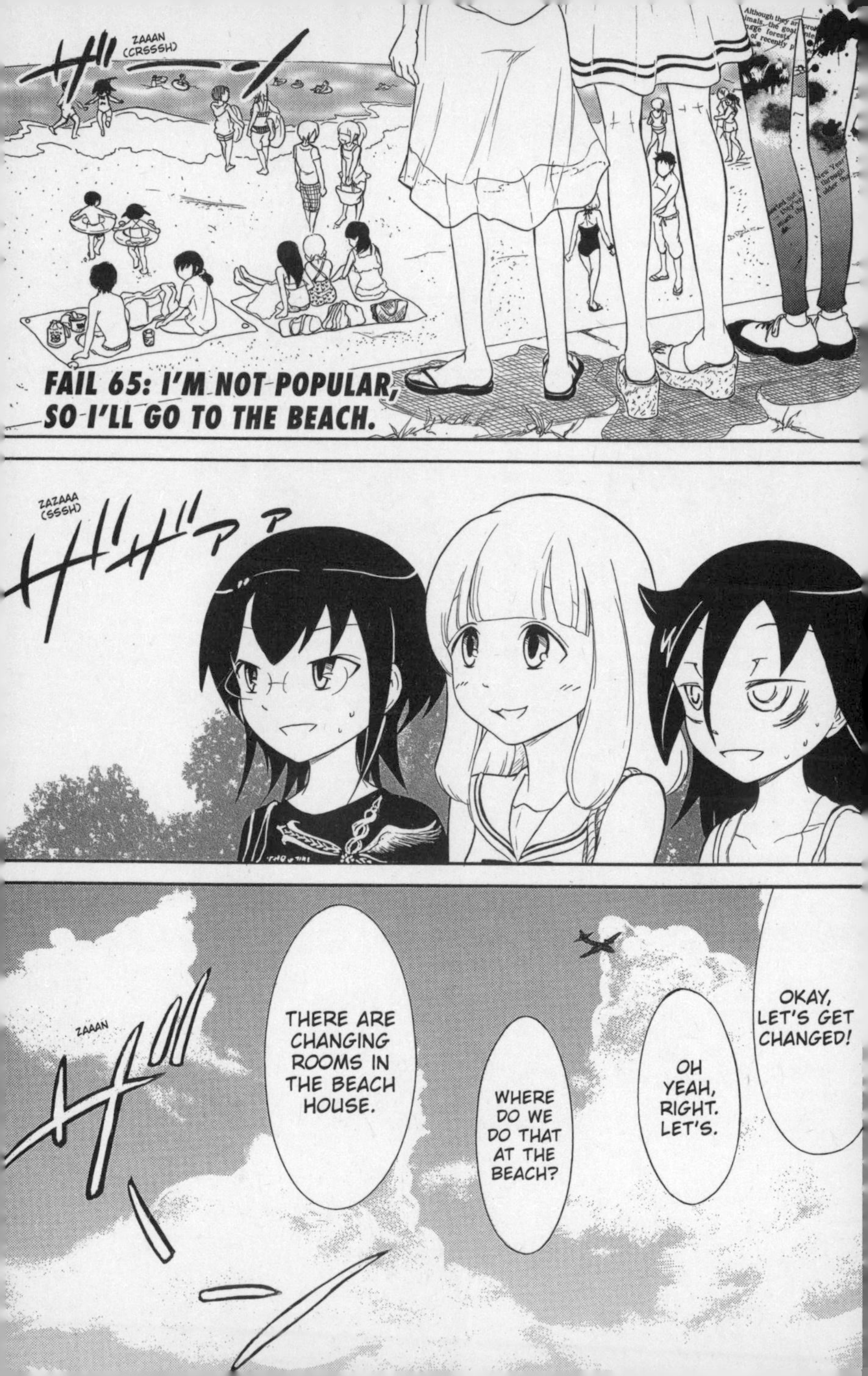
ZAAAN (CRSSSH)
FAIL 65: I'M NOT POPULAR, SO I'LL GO TO THE BEACH.
ZAZAAA (SSSH)
OKAY, LET'S GET CHANGED!
OH YEAH, RIGHT. LET'S.
WHERE DO WE DO THAT AT THE BEACH?
THERE ARE CHANGING ROOMS IN THE BEACH HOUSE.
ZAAAN

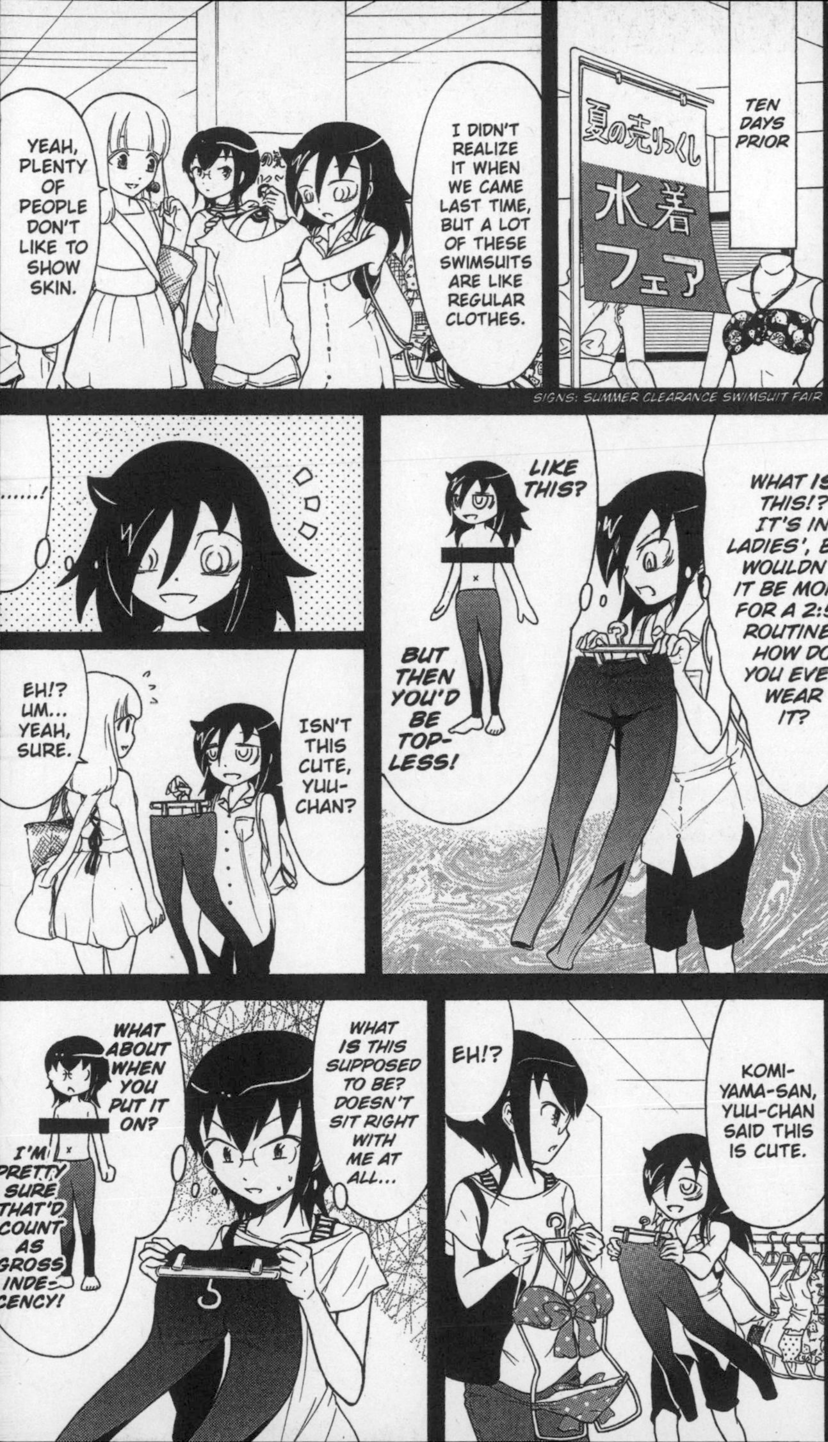
TEN DAYS PRIOR
夏の売りつくし
水着フェア
I DIDN'T REALIZE IT WHEN WE CAME LAST TIME, BUT A LOT OF THESE SWIMSUITS ARE LIKE REGULAR CLOTHES.
YEAH, PLENTY OF PEOPLE DON'T LIKE TO SHOW SKIN.
SIGNS: SUMMER CLEARANCE SWIMSUIT FAIR
WHAT IS THIS!? IT'S IN LADIES', BUT WOULDN'T IT BE MORE FOR A 2:50 ROUTINE? HOW DO YOU EVEN WEAR IT?
LIKE THIS?
BUT THEN YOU'D BE TOP-LESS!
......!
ISN'T THIS CUTE, YUU-CHAN?
EH!? UM... YEAH, SURE.
KOMI-YAMA-SAN, YUU-CHAN SAID THIS IS CUTE.
EH!?
WHAT IS THIS SUPPOSED TO BE? DOESN'T SIT RIGHT WITH ME AT ALL...
WHAT ABOUT WHEN YOU PUT IT ON?
I'M PRETTY SURE THAT'D COUNT AS GROSS INDE-CENCY!

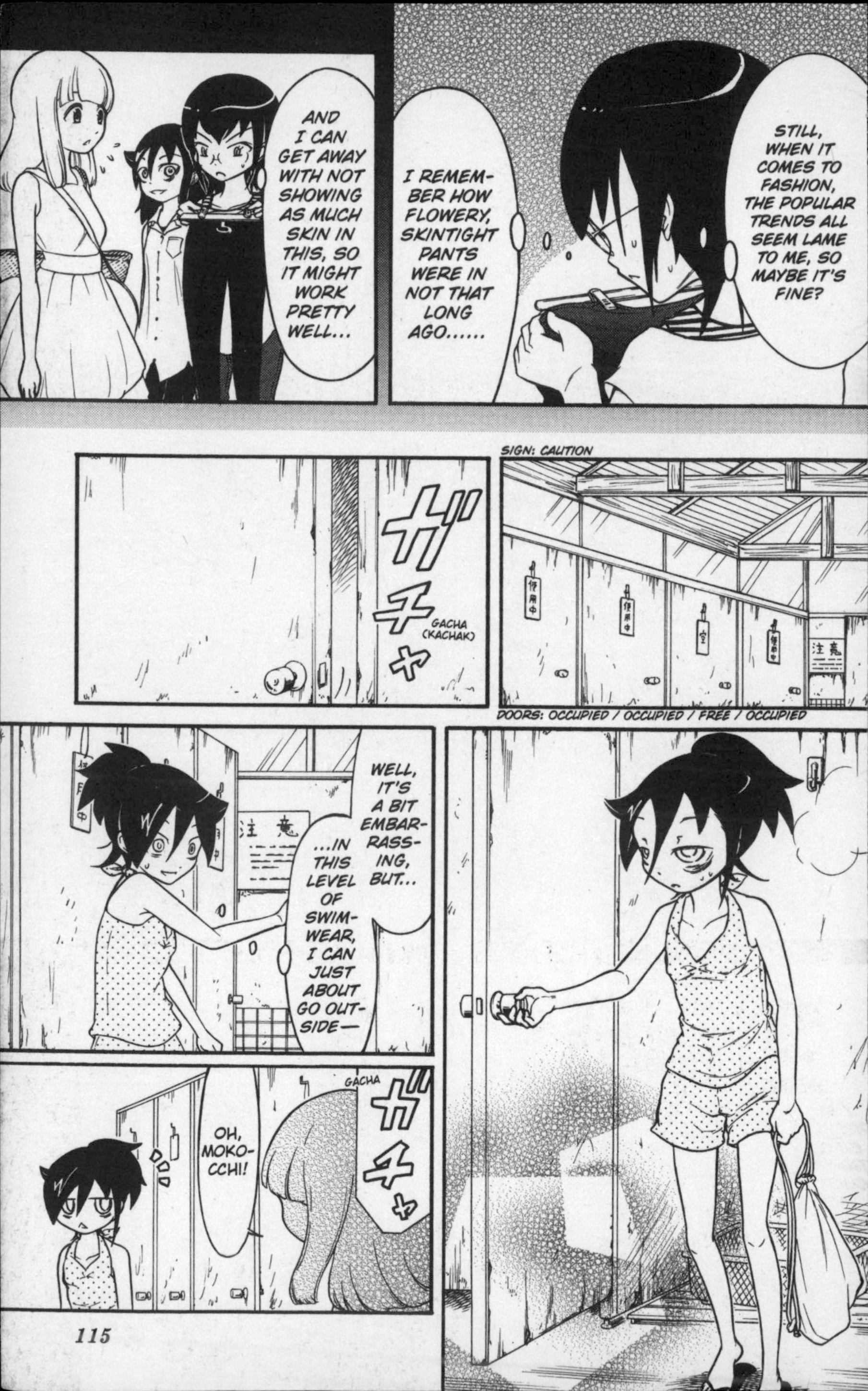
STILL, WHEN IT COMES TO FASHION, THE POPULAR TRENDS ALL SEEM LAME TO ME, SO MAYBE IT'S FINE?
I REMEMBER HOW FLOWERY, SKINTIGHT PANTS WERE IN NOT THAT LONG AGO......
AND I CAN GET AWAY WITH NOT SHOWING AS MUCH SKIN IN THIS, SO IT MIGHT WORK PRETTY WELL...
SIGN: CAUTION
DOORS: OCCUPIED / OCCUPIED / FREE / OCCUPIED
GACHA (KACHAK)
WELL, IT'S A BIT EMBARRASSING, BUT...
...IN THIS LEVEL OF SWIMWEAR, I CAN JUST ABOUT GO OUTSIDE—
GACHA
OH, MOKOCCHI!

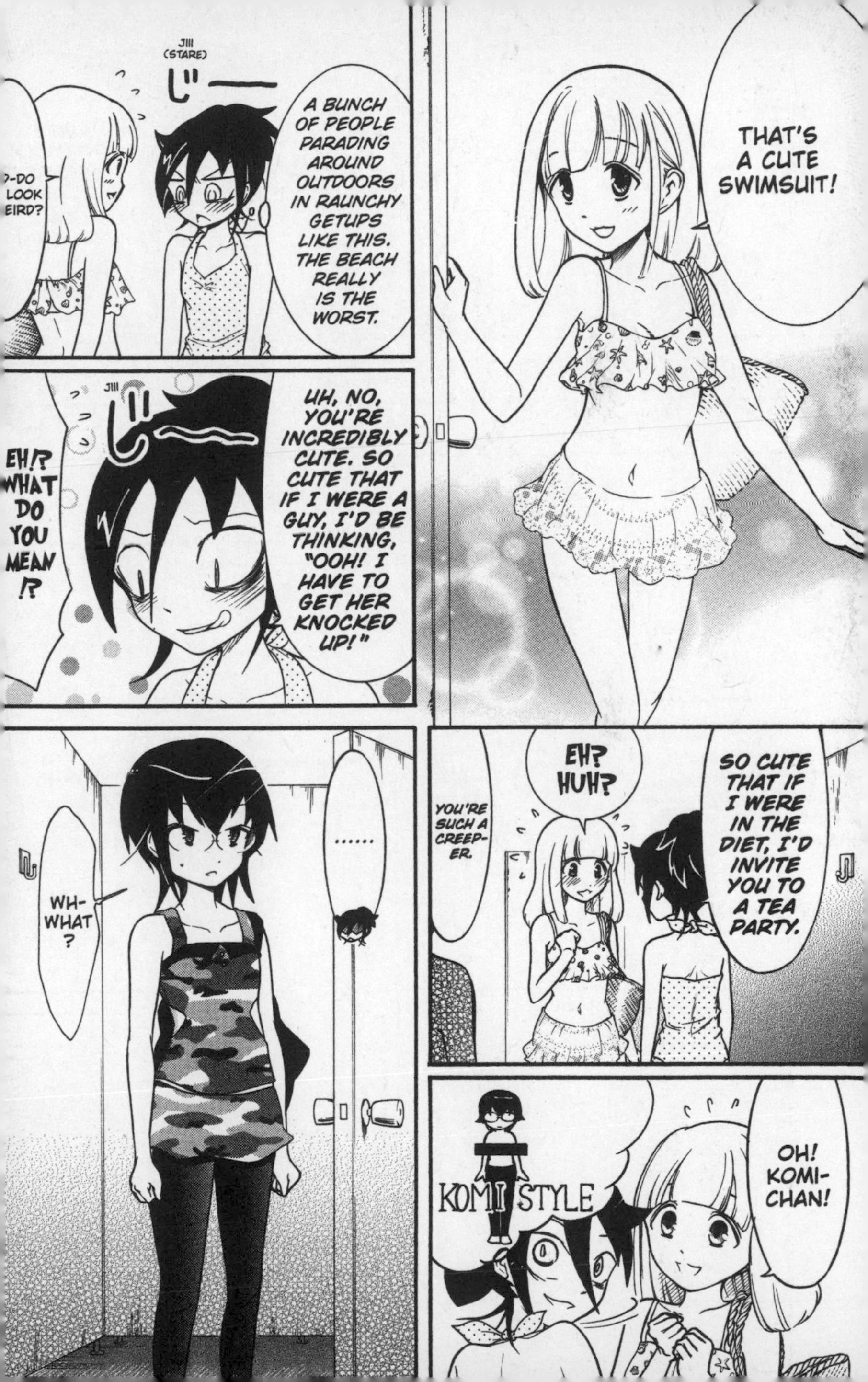
THAT'S A CUTE SWIMSUIT!
JIII (STARE)
じー
A BUNCH OF PEOPLE PARADING AROUND OUTDOORS IN RAUNCHY GETUPS LIKE THIS. THE BEACH REALLY IS THE WORST.
-DO LOOK EIRD?
JIII
じ
UH, NO, YOU'RE INCREDIBLY CUTE. SO CUTE THAT IF I WERE A GUY, I'D BE THINKING, "OOH! I HAVE TO GET HER KNOCKED UP!"
EH!? WHAT DO YOU MEAN !?
SO CUTE THAT IF I WERE IN THE DIET, I'D INVITE YOU TO A TEA PARTY.
EH? HUH?
YOU'RE SUCH A CREEPER.
OH! KOMI-CHAN!
KOMI STYLE
......
WH-WHAT ?

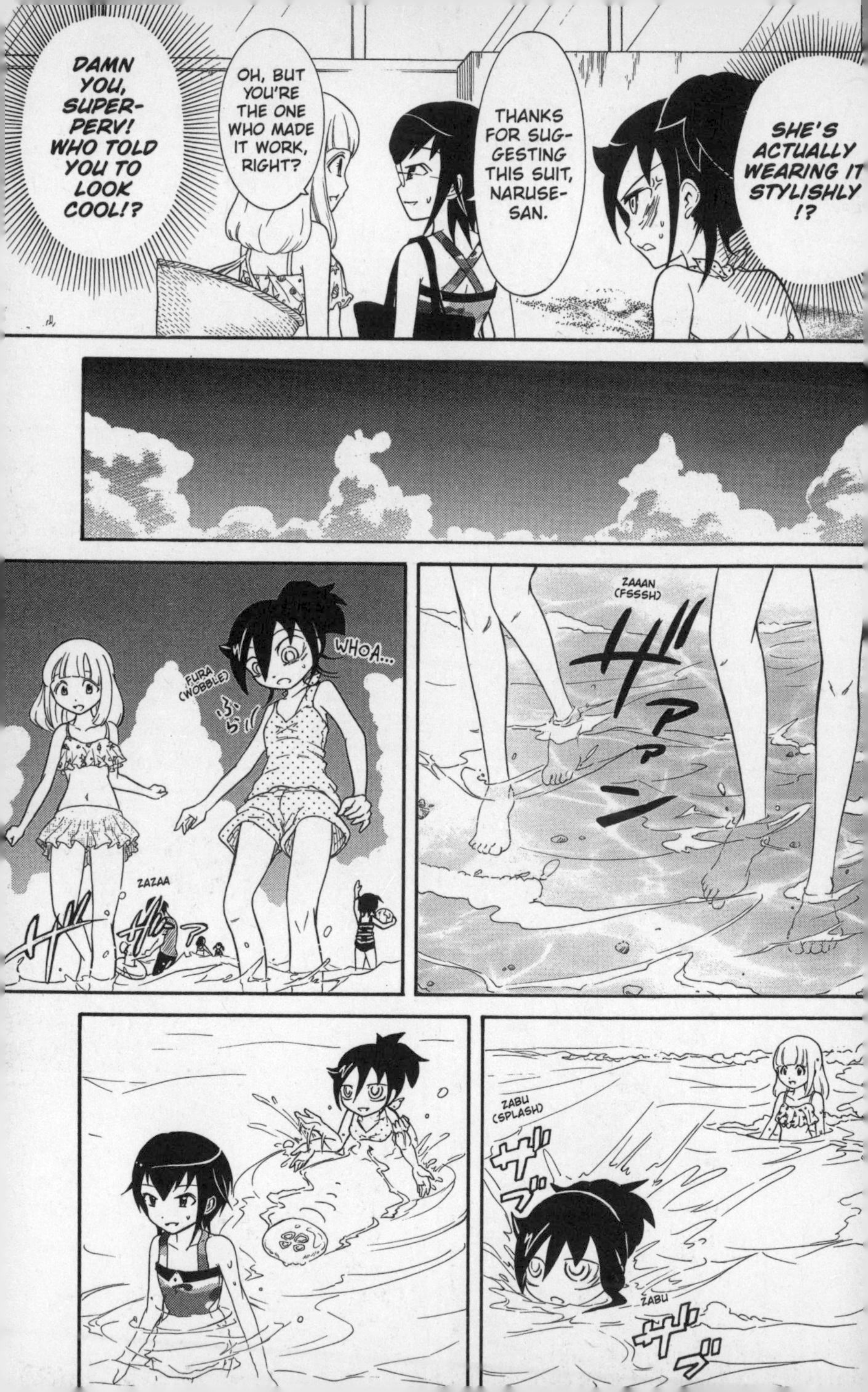

SHE'S ACTUALLY WEARING IT STYLISHLY!?
THANKS FOR SUG-GESTING THIS SUIT, NARUSE-SAN.
OH, BUT YOU'RE THE ONE WHO MADE IT WORK, RIGHT?
DAMN YOU, SUPER-PERV! WHO TOLD YOU TO LOOK COOL!?
ZAAAN (FSSSH)
WHOA...
FURA (WOBBLE)
ZAZAA
ZABU (SPLASH)
ZABU

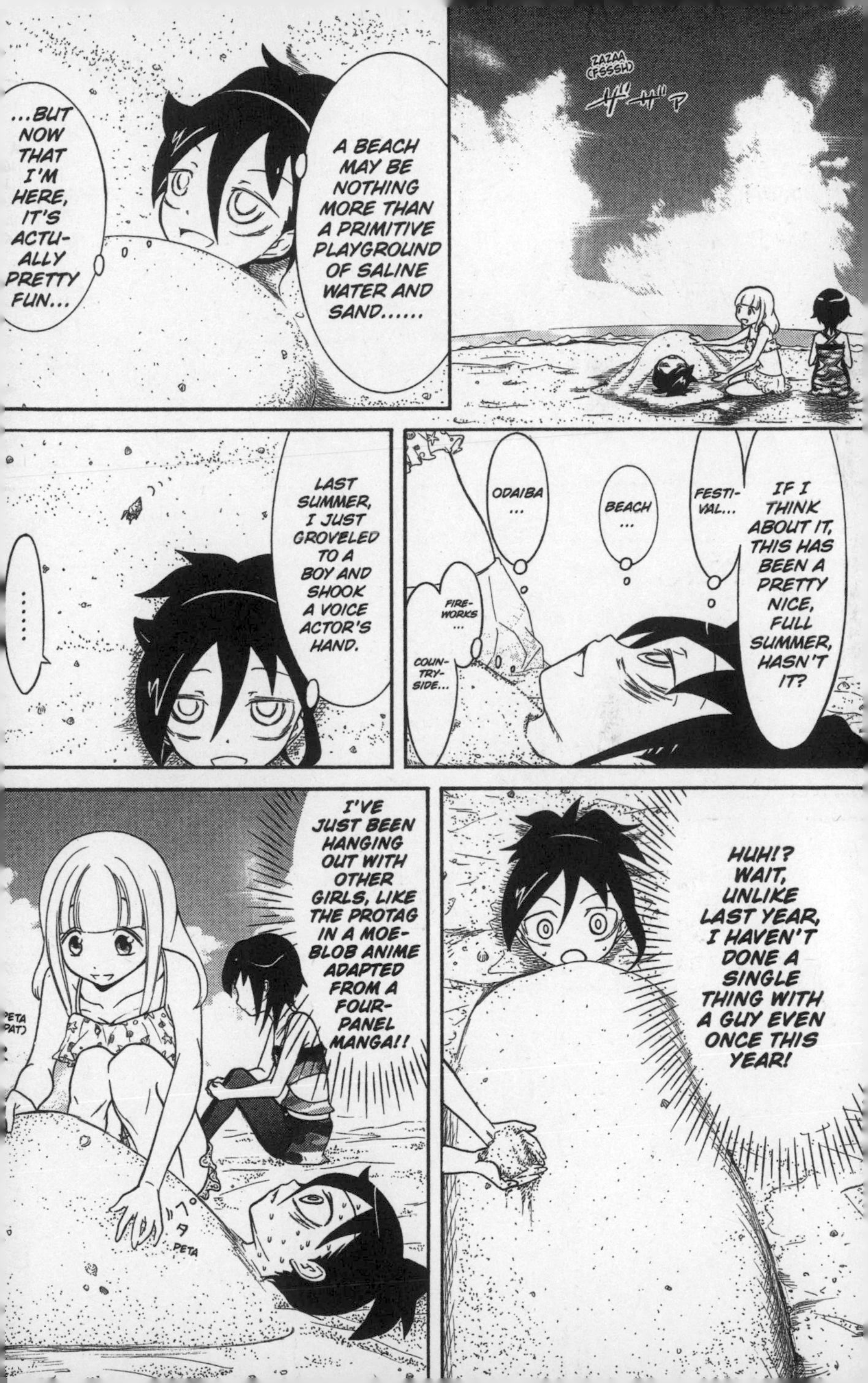
ZAZAA (FSSSH)
A BEACH MAY BE NOTHING MORE THAN A PRIMITIVE PLAYGROUND OF SALINE WATER AND SAND......
...BUT NOW THAT I'M HERE, IT'S ACTUALLY PRETTY FUN...
IF I THINK ABOUT IT, THIS HAS BEEN A PRETTY NICE, FULL SUMMER, HASN'T IT?
FESTIVAL...
BEACH...
ODAIBA...
FIREWORKS...
COUNTRYSIDE...
LAST SUMMER, I JUST GROVELED TO A BOY AND SHOOK A VOICE ACTOR'S HAND.
......
HUH!? WAIT, UNLIKE LAST YEAR, I HAVEN'T DONE A SINGLE THING WITH A GUY EVEN ONCE THIS YEAR!
I'VE JUST BEEN HANGING OUT WITH OTHER GIRLS, LIKE THE PROTAG IN A MOE-BLOB ANIME ADAPTED FROM A FOUR-PANEL MANGA!!
PETA (PAT)
PETA

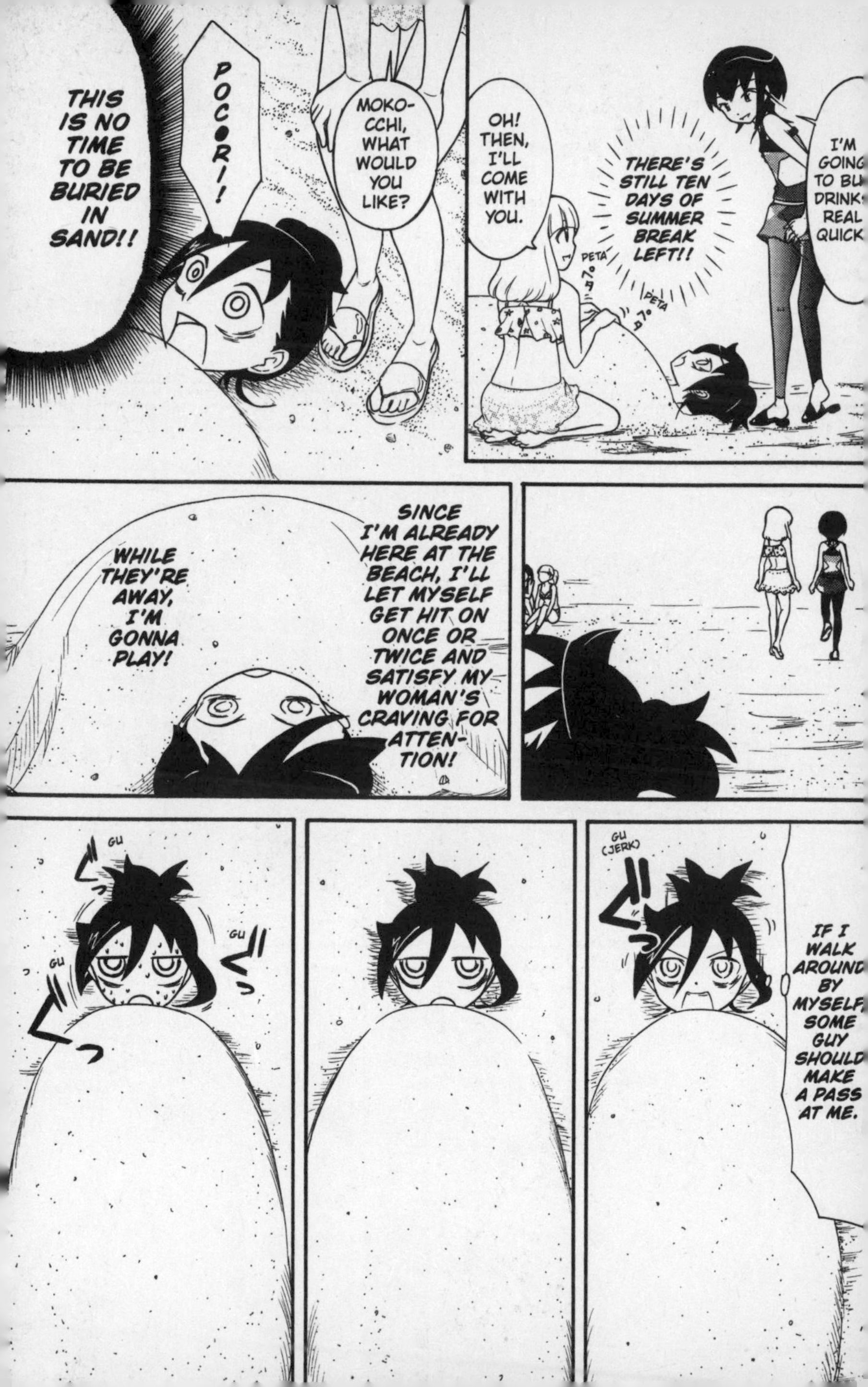
I'M GOING TO BU DRINK REAL QUICK
THERE'S STILL TEN DAYS OF SUMMER BREAK LEFT!!
OH! THEN, I'LL COME WITH YOU.
PETA
PETA
MOKO-CCHI, WHAT WOULD YOU LIKE?
POCORI!
THIS IS NO TIME TO BE BURIED IN SAND!!
SINCE I'M ALREADY HERE AT THE BEACH, I'LL LET MYSELF GET HIT ON ONCE OR TWICE AND SATISFY MY WOMAN'S CRAVING FOR ATTEN-TION!
WHILE THEY'RE AWAY, I'M GONNA PLAY!
IF I WALK AROUND BY MYSELF, SOME GUY SHOULD MAKE A PASS AT ME.
GU (JERK)
GU
GU
GU

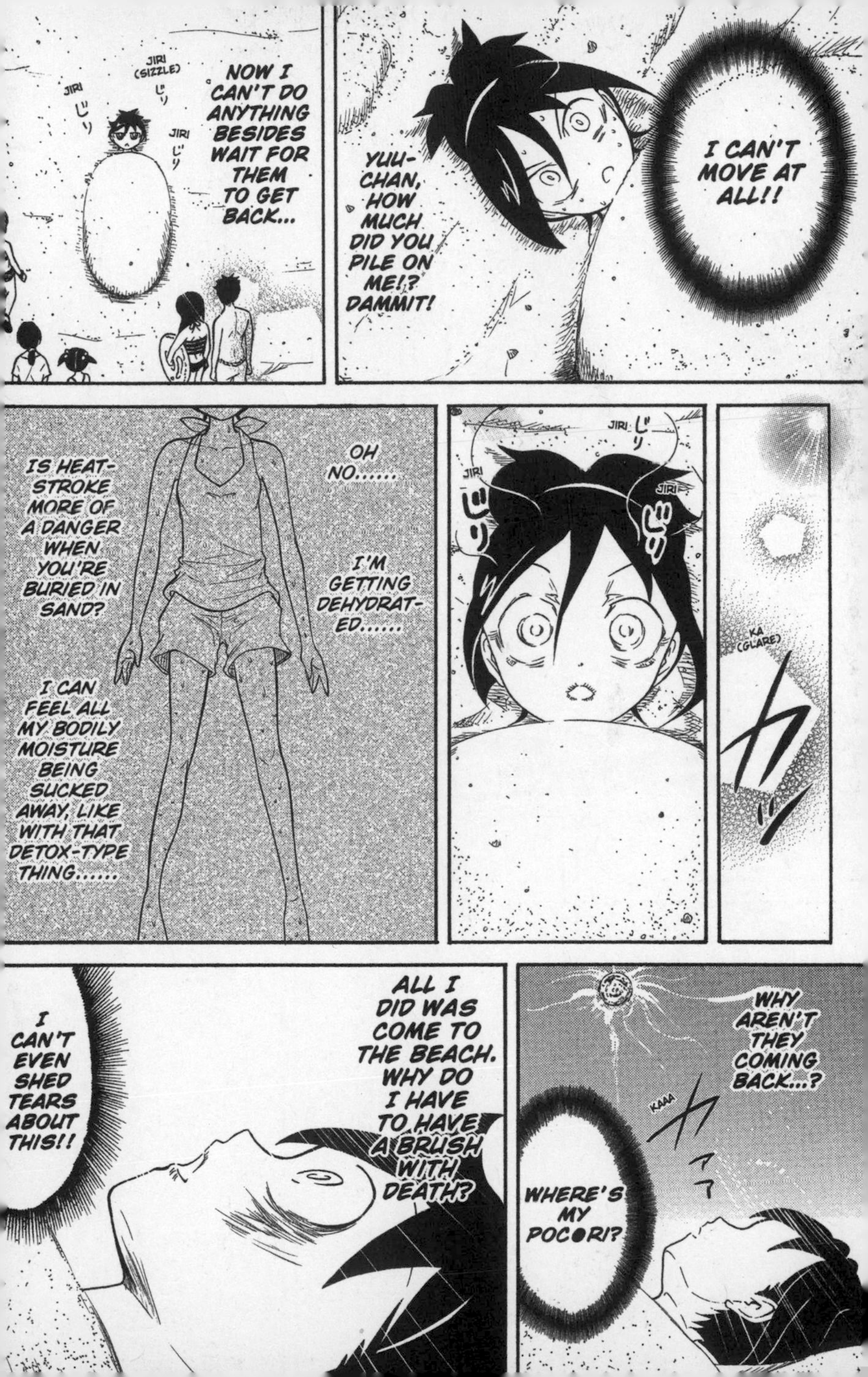
I CAN'T MOVE AT ALL!!
YUU-CHAN, HOW MUCH DID YOU PILE ON ME!? DAMMIT!
NOW I CAN'T DO ANYTHING BESIDES WAIT FOR THEM TO GET BACK...
JIRI (SIZZLE)
じり
JIRI
じり
JIRI
じり
KA (GLARE)
カッ
JIRI
じり
JIRI
じり
JIRI
じり
OH NO......
I'M GETTING DEHYDRAT-ED......
IS HEAT-STROKE MORE OF A DANGER WHEN YOU'RE BURIED IN SAND?
I CAN FEEL ALL MY BODILY MOISTURE BEING SUCKED AWAY, LIKE WITH THAT DETOX-TYPE THING......
WHY AREN'T THEY COMING BACK...?
KAAA
カァァ
WHERE'S MY POCORI?
ALL I DID WAS COME TO THE BEACH. WHY DO I HAVE TO HAVE A BRUSH WITH DEATH?
I CAN'T EVEN SHED TEARS ABOUT THIS!!

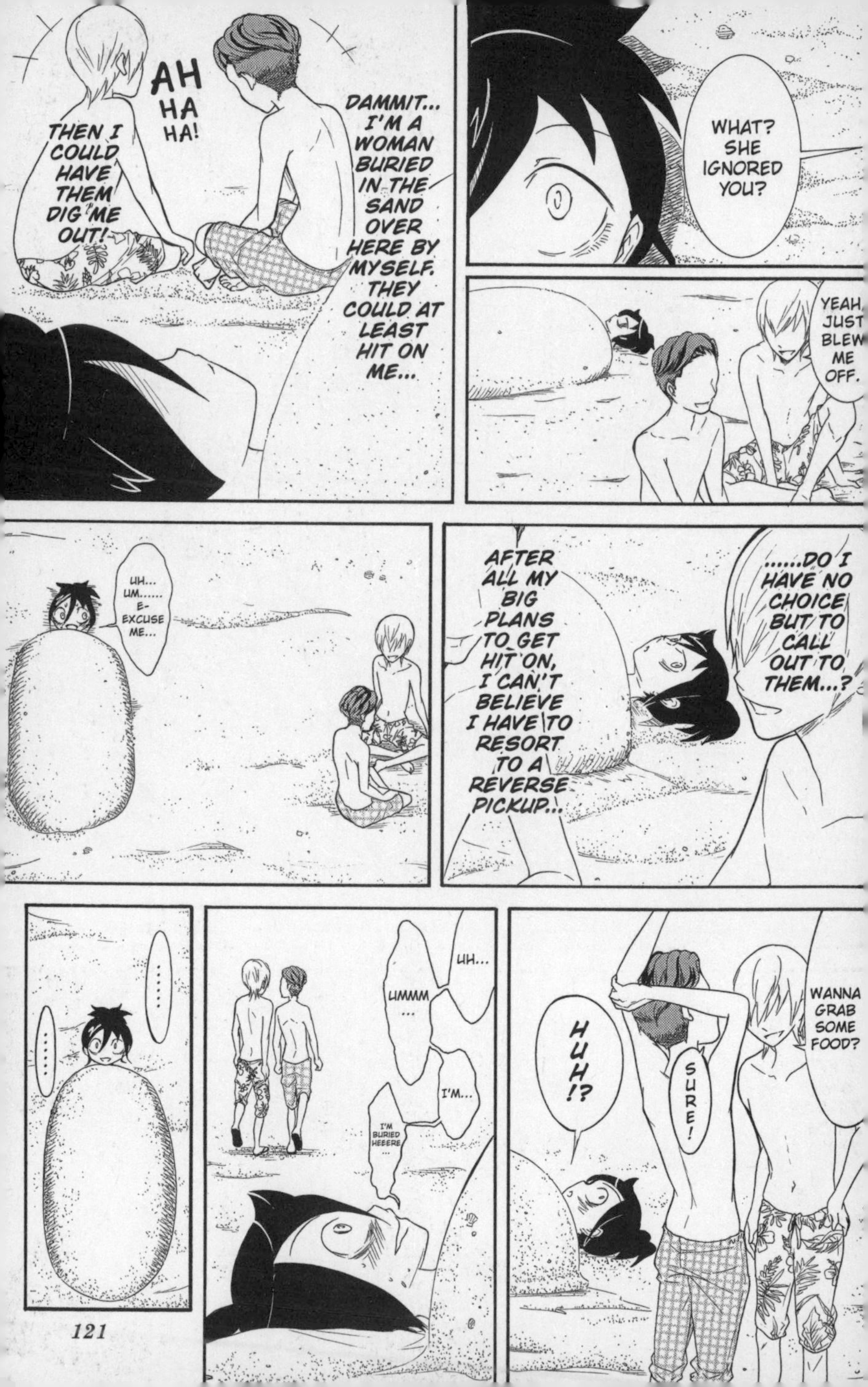

WHAT? SHE IGNORED YOU?
YEAH, JUST BLEW ME OFF.
DAMMIT... I'M A WOMAN BURIED IN THE SAND OVER HERE BY MYSELF. THEY COULD AT LEAST HIT ON ME...
AH HA HA!
THEN I COULD HAVE THEM DIG ME OUT!
......DO I HAVE NO CHOICE BUT TO CALL OUT TO THEM...?
AFTER ALL MY BIG PLANS TO GET HIT ON, I CAN'T BELIEVE I HAVE TO RESORT TO A REVERSE PICKUP...
UH... UM...... E-EXCUSE ME...
WANNA GRAB SOME FOOD?
SURE!
HUH!?
UH...
UMMM...
I'M...
I'M BURIED HEEERE...
......
......

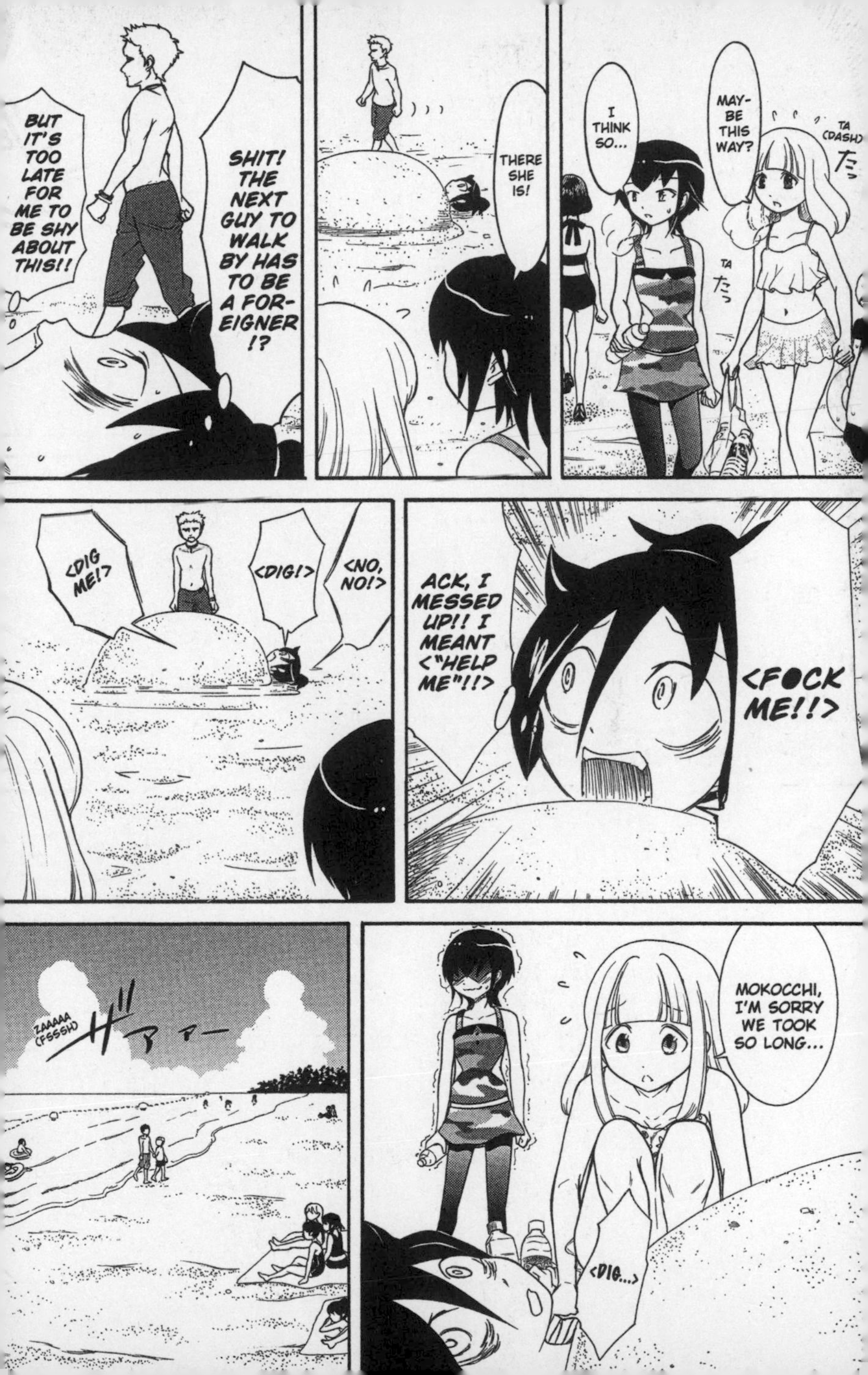
MAY-BE THIS WAY?
TA (DASH)
I THINK SO...
TA
THERE SHE IS!
SHIT! THE NEXT GUY TO WALK BY HAS TO BE A FOR-EIGNER!?
BUT IT'S TOO LATE FOR ME TO BE SHY ABOUT THIS!!
<FOCK ME!!>
ACK, I MESSED UP!! I MEANT <"HELP ME"!!>
<NO, NO!>
<DIG!>
<DIG ME!>
MOKOCCHI, I'M SORRY WE TOOK SO LONG...
<DIG...>
ZAAAAA (FSSSH)

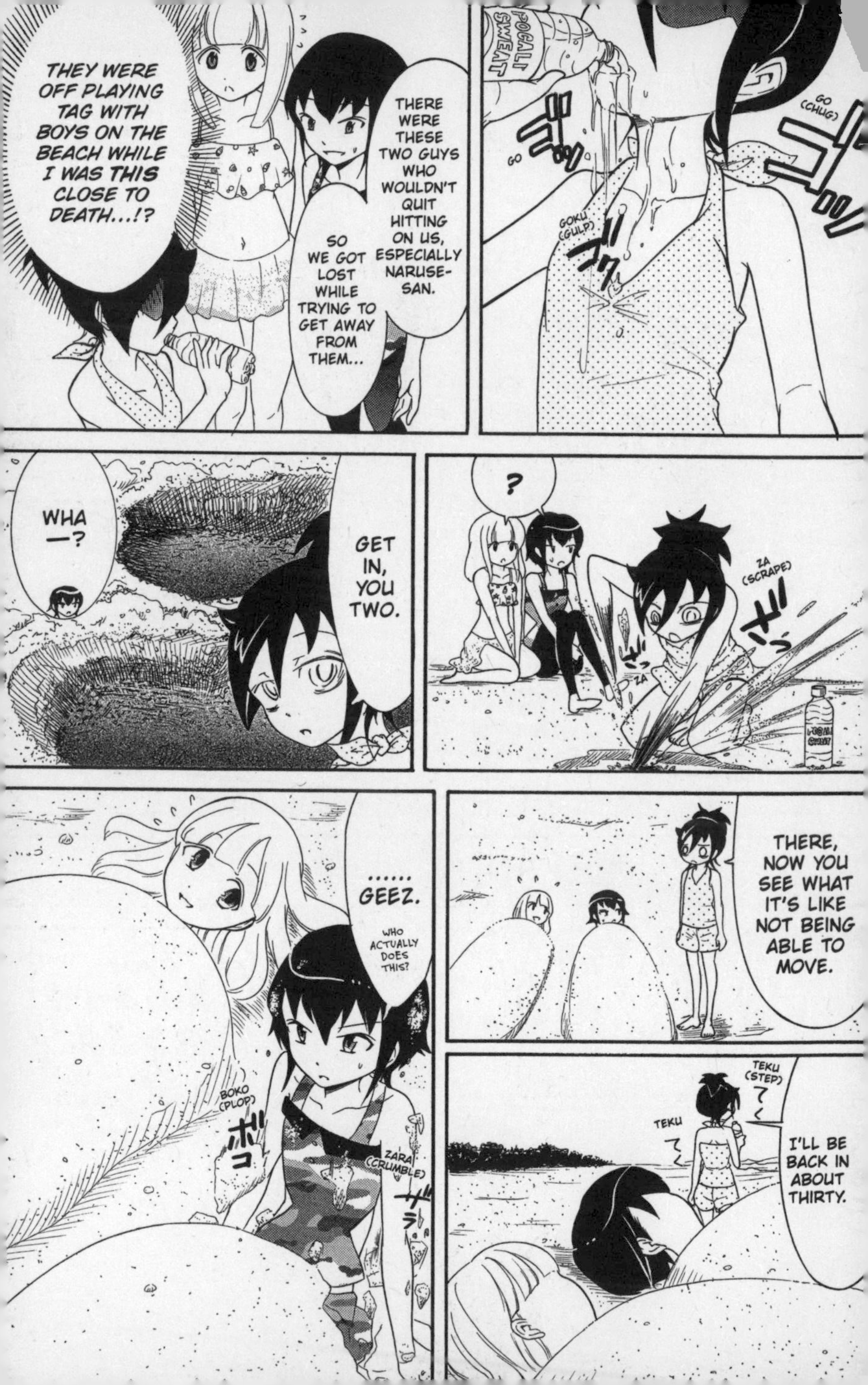
POGALI SWEAT
GO (CHUG)
GO
GOKU (GULP)
THERE WERE THESE TWO GUYS WHO WOULDN'T QUIT HITTING ON US, ESPECIALLY NARUSE-SAN.
SO WE GOT LOST WHILE TRYING TO GET AWAY FROM THEM...
THEY WERE OFF PLAYING TAG WITH BOYS ON THE BEACH WHILE I WAS THIS CLOSE TO DEATH...!?
?
ZA (SCRAPE)
ZA
GET IN, YOU TWO.
WHA—?
THERE, NOW YOU SEE WHAT IT'S LIKE NOT BEING ABLE TO MOVE.
TEKU (STEP)
TEKU
I'LL BE BACK IN ABOUT THIRTY.
......GEEZ.
WHO ACTUALLY DOES THIS?
BOKO (PLOP)
ZARA (CRUMBLE)

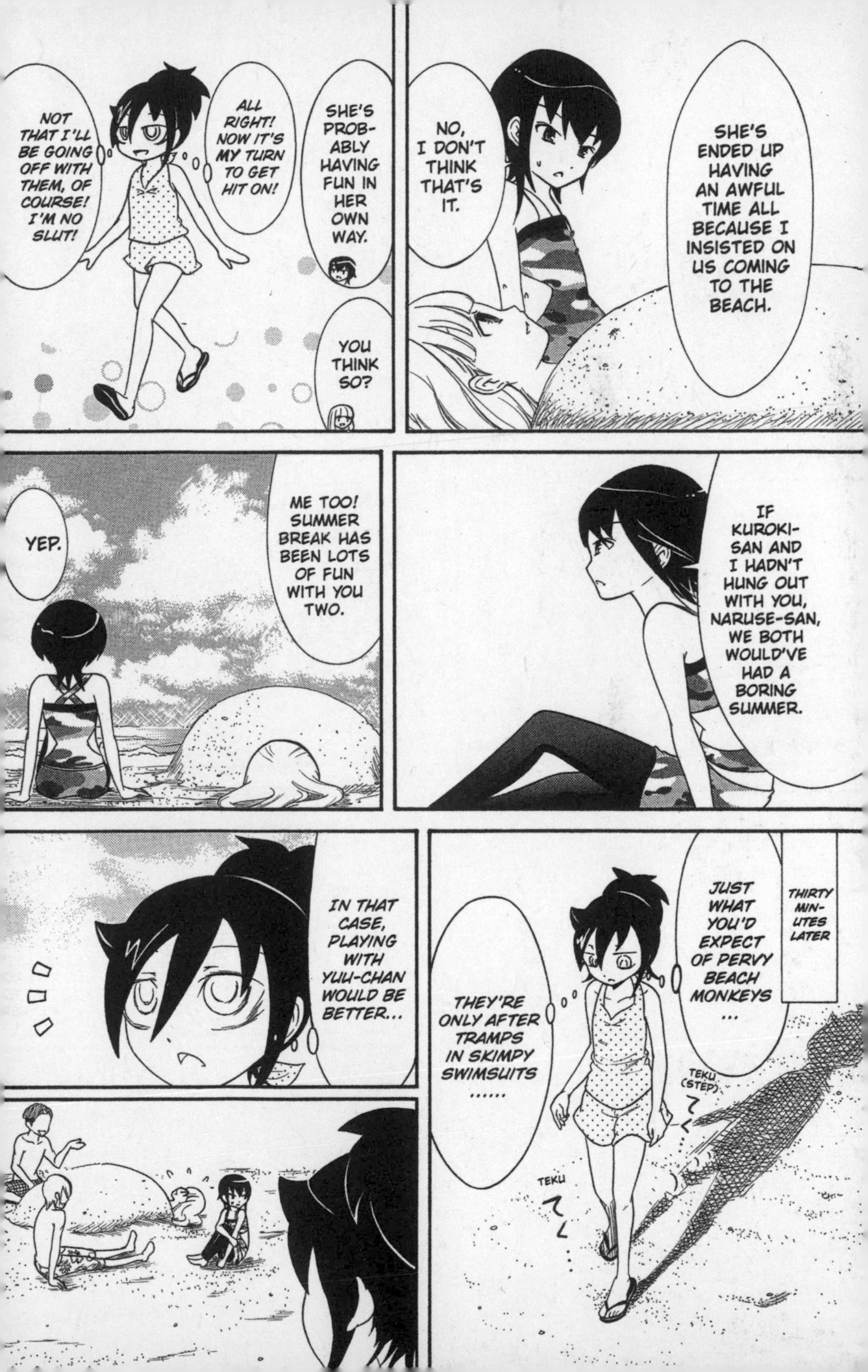
SHE'S ENDED UP HAVING AN AWFUL TIME ALL BECAUSE I INSISTED ON US COMING TO THE BEACH.
NO, I DON'T THINK THAT'S IT.
SHE'S PROBABLY HAVING FUN IN HER OWN WAY.
YOU THINK SO?
ALL RIGHT! NOW IT'S MY TURN TO GET HIT ON!
NOT THAT I'LL BE GOING OFF WITH THEM, OF COURSE! I'M NO SLUT!
IF KUROKI-SAN AND I HADN'T HUNG OUT WITH YOU, NARUSE-SAN, WE BOTH WOULD'VE HAD A BORING SUMMER.
ME TOO! SUMMER BREAK HAS BEEN LOTS OF FUN WITH YOU TWO.
YEP.
THIRTY MINUTES LATER
JUST WHAT YOU'D EXPECT OF PERVY BEACH MONKEYS ...
THEY'RE ONLY AFTER TRAMPS IN SKIMPY SWIMSUITS ......
TEKU (STEP)
TEKU
IN THAT CASE, PLAYING WITH YUU-CHAN WOULD BE BETTER...

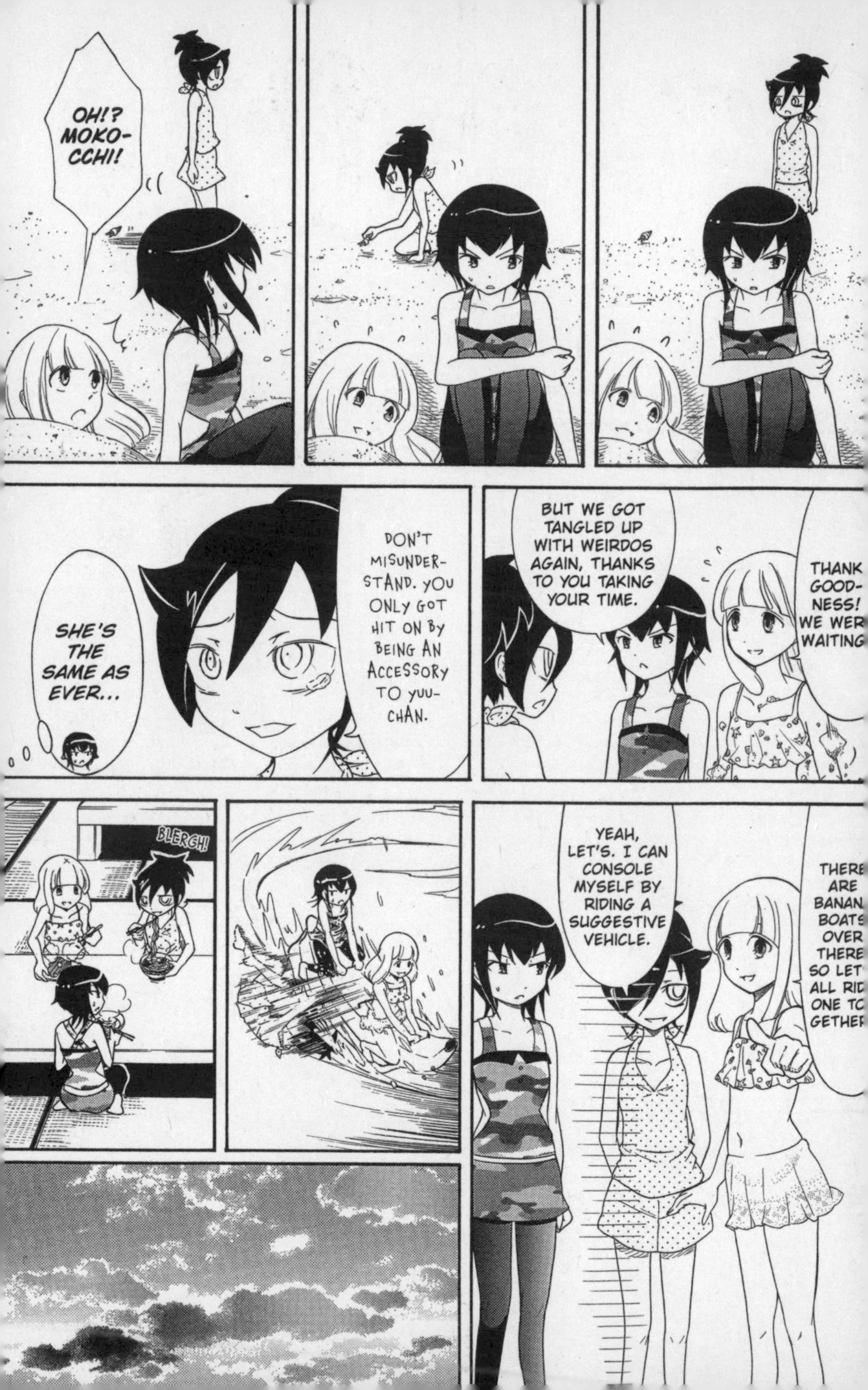
OH!? MOKO-CCHI!
THANK GOOD-NESS! WE WER WAITING
BUT WE GOT TANGLED UP WITH WEIRDOS AGAIN, THANKS TO YOU TAKING YOUR TIME.
DON'T MISUNDER-STAND. YOU ONLY GOT HIT ON BY BEING AN ACCESSORY TO YUU-CHAN.
SHE'S THE SAME AS EVER...
THERE ARE BANAN BOATS OVER THERE SO LET ALL RID ONE TO GETHER
YEAH, LET'S. I CAN CONSOLE MYSELF BY RIDING A SUGGESTIVE VEHICLE.
BLERGH!

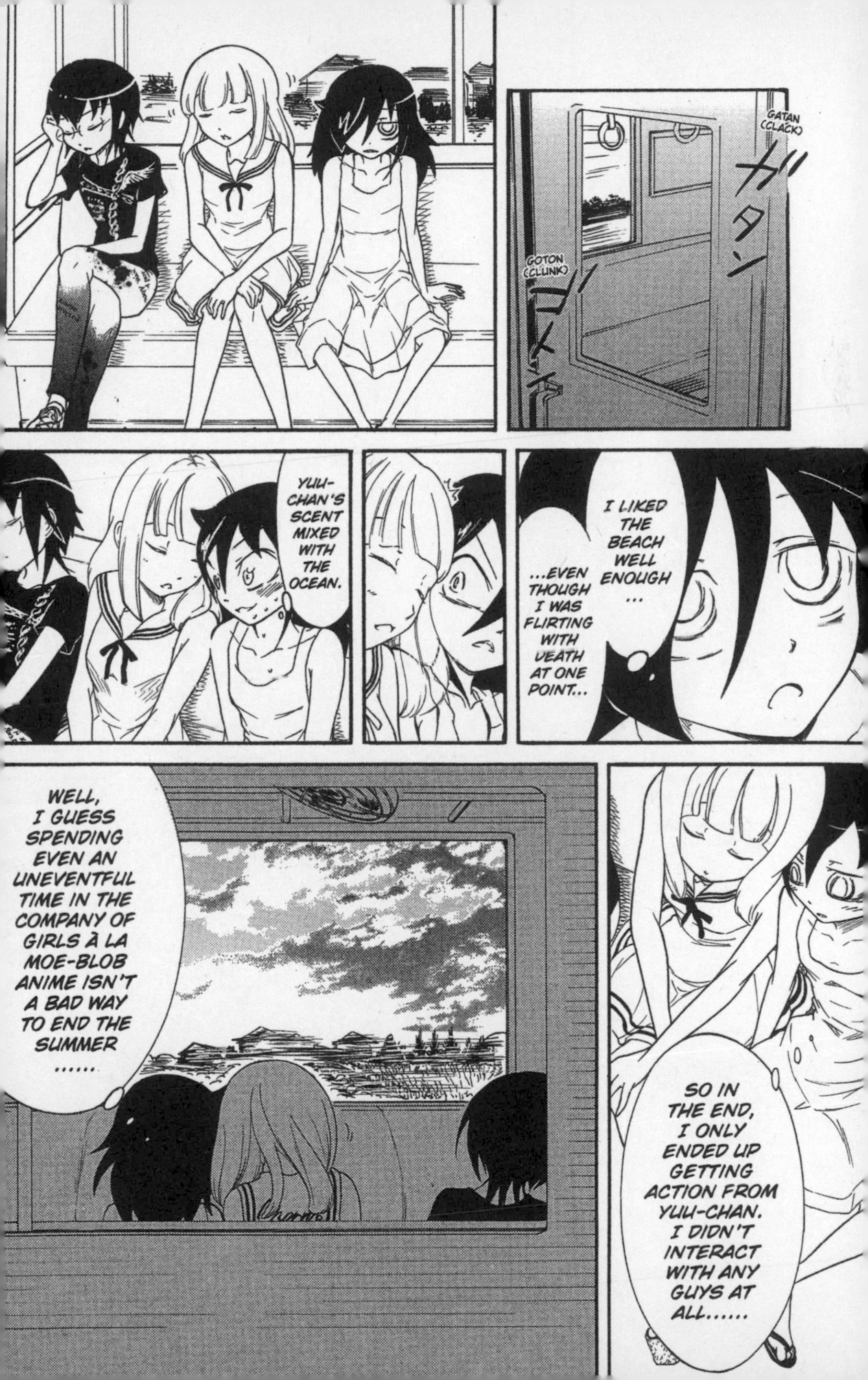
GATAN (CLACK)
ガタン
GOTON (CLUNK)
ゴトン
I LIKED THE BEACH WELL ENOUGH ...
...EVEN THOUGH I WAS FLIRTING WITH DEATH AT ONE POINT...
YUU-CHAN'S SCENT MIXED WITH THE OCEAN.
SO IN THE END, I ONLY ENDED UP GETTING ACTION FROM YUU-CHAN. I DIDN'T INTERACT WITH ANY GUYS AT ALL......
WELL, I GUESS SPENDING EVEN AN UNEVENTFUL TIME IN THE COMPANY OF GIRLS À LA MOE-BLOB ANIME ISN'T A BAD WAY TO END THE SUMMER ......

No Matter How I Look at It, It's You Guys' Fault I'm Not Popular!

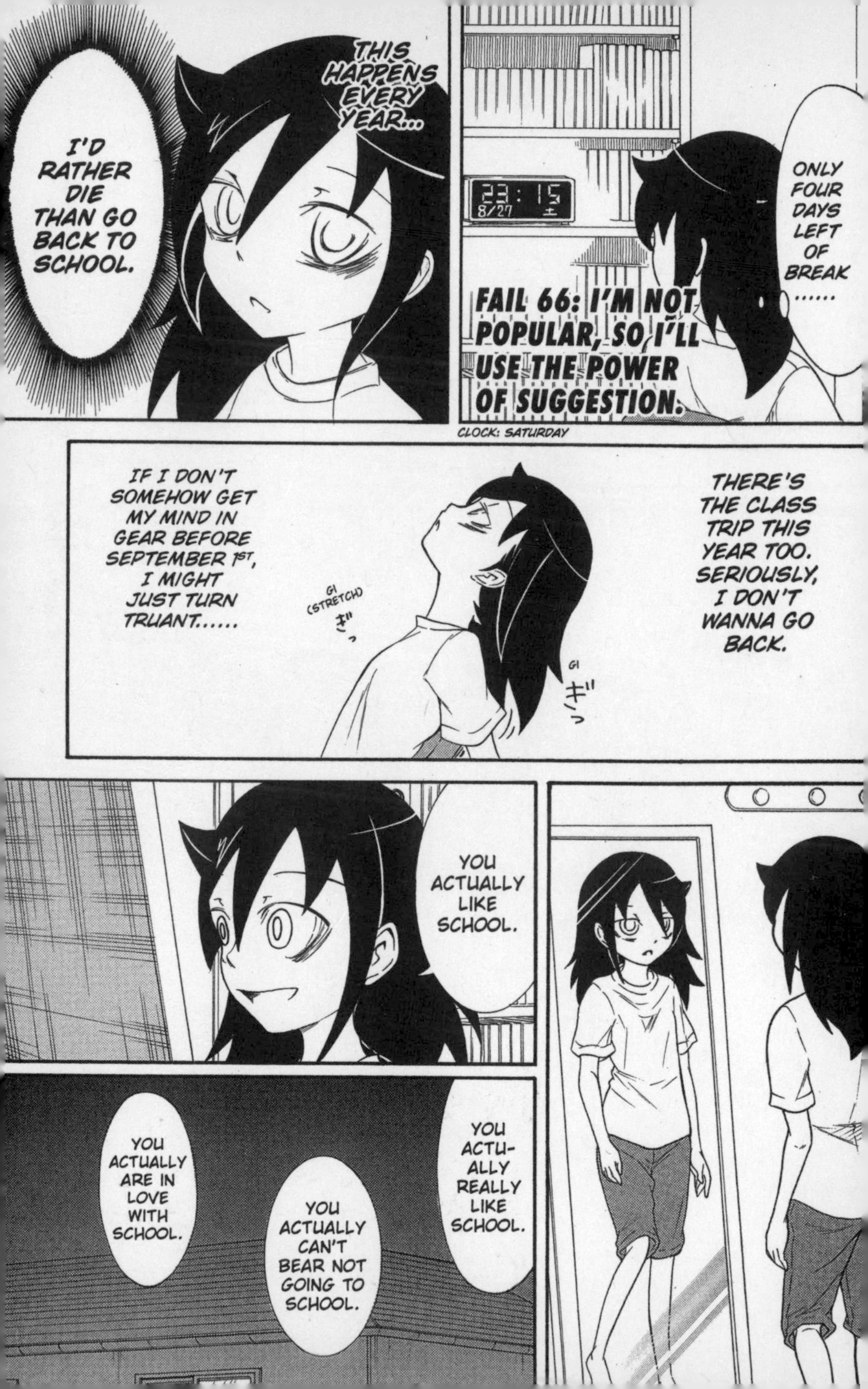
23:15
8/27 土
ONLY FOUR DAYS LEFT OF BREAK......
FAIL 66: I'M NOT POPULAR, SO I'LL USE THE POWER OF SUGGESTION.
CLOCK: SATURDAY
THIS HAPPENS EVERY YEAR...
I'D RATHER DIE THAN GO BACK TO SCHOOL.
THERE'S THE CLASS TRIP THIS YEAR TOO. SERIOUSLY, I DON'T WANNA GO BACK.
GI
ギッ
GI (STRETCH)
ぎっ
IF I DON'T SOMEHOW GET MY MIND IN GEAR BEFORE SEPTEMBER 1ST, I MIGHT JUST TURN TRUANT......
YOU ACTUALLY LIKE SCHOOL.
YOU ACTUALLY REALLY LIKE SCHOOL.
YOU ACTUALLY CAN'T BEAR NOT GOING TO SCHOOL.
YOU ACTUALLY ARE IN LOVE WITH SCHOOL.

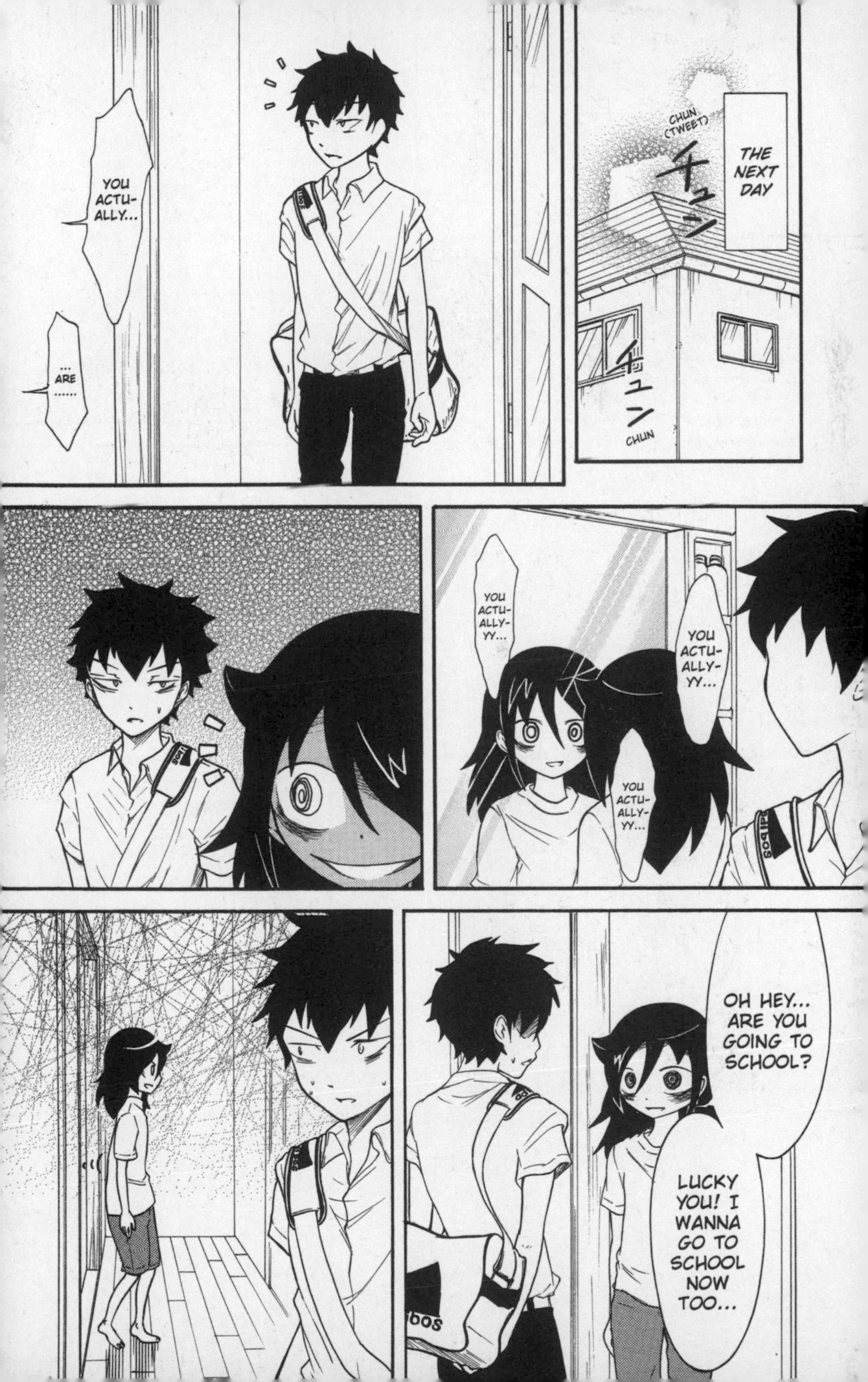
THE NEXT DAY
CHUN (TWEET)
CHUN
YOU ACTU-ALLY...
... ARE ......
YOU ACTU-ALLY-YY...
YOU ACTU-ALLY-YY...
YOU ACTU-ALLY-YY...
OH HEY... ARE YOU GOING TO SCHOOL?
LUCKY YOU! I WANNA GO TO SCHOOL NOW TOO...

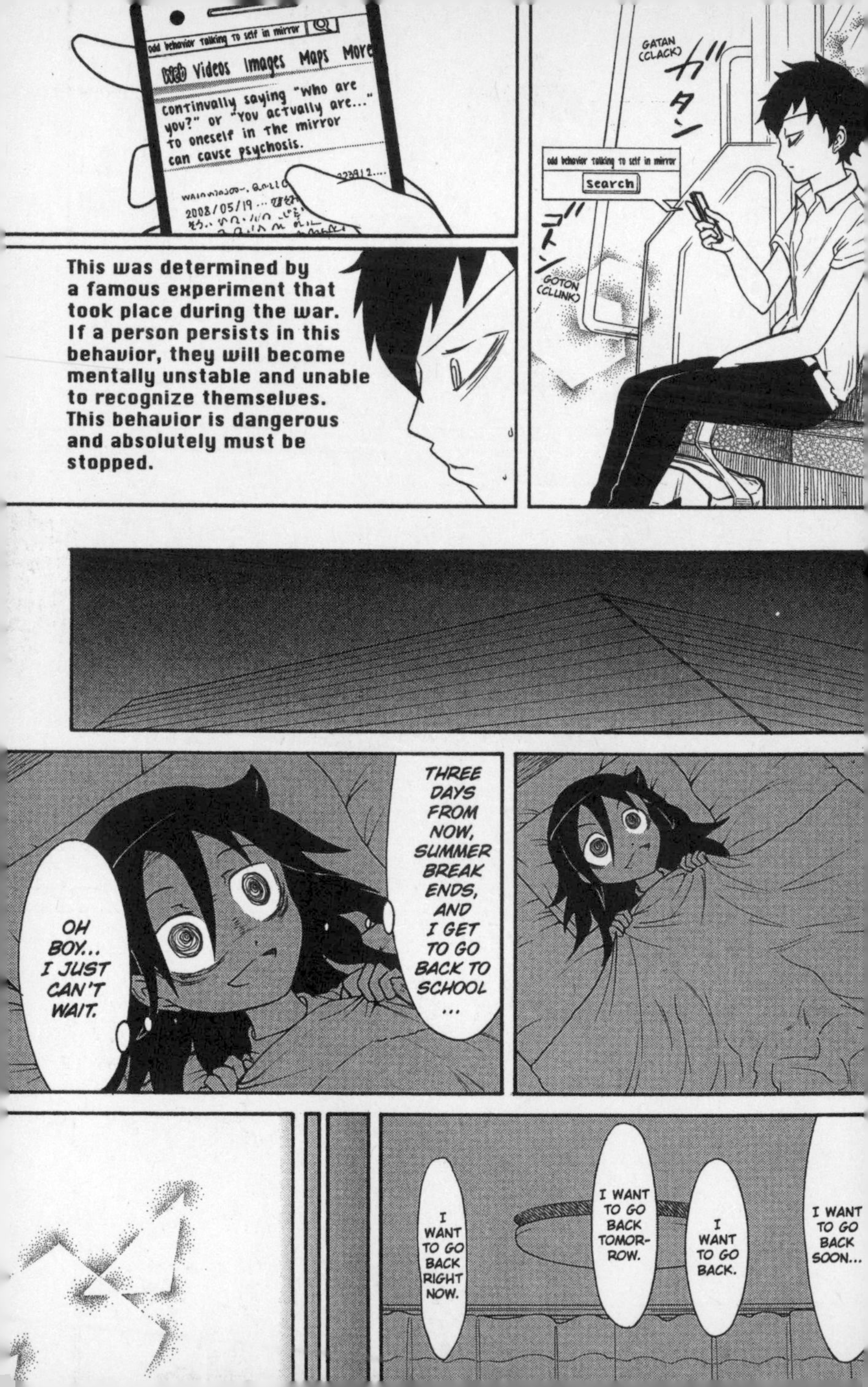

GATAN (CLACK)
ガタン
odd behavior talking to self in mirror
Search
ゴトン
GOTON (CLUNK)
odd behavior talking to self in mirror
Web Videos Images Maps More
continually saying "who are you?" or "you actually are..." to oneself in the mirror can cause psychosis.
This was determined by a famous experiment that took place during the war. If a person persists in this behavior, they will become mentally unstable and unable to recognize themselves. This behavior is dangerous and absolutely must be stopped.
THREE DAYS FROM NOW, SUMMER BREAK ENDS, AND I GET TO GO BACK TO SCHOOL...
OH BOY... I JUST CAN'T WAIT.
I WANT TO GO BACK SOON...
I WANT TO GO BACK.
I WANT TO GO BACK TOMORROW.
I WANT TO GO BACK RIGHT NOW.

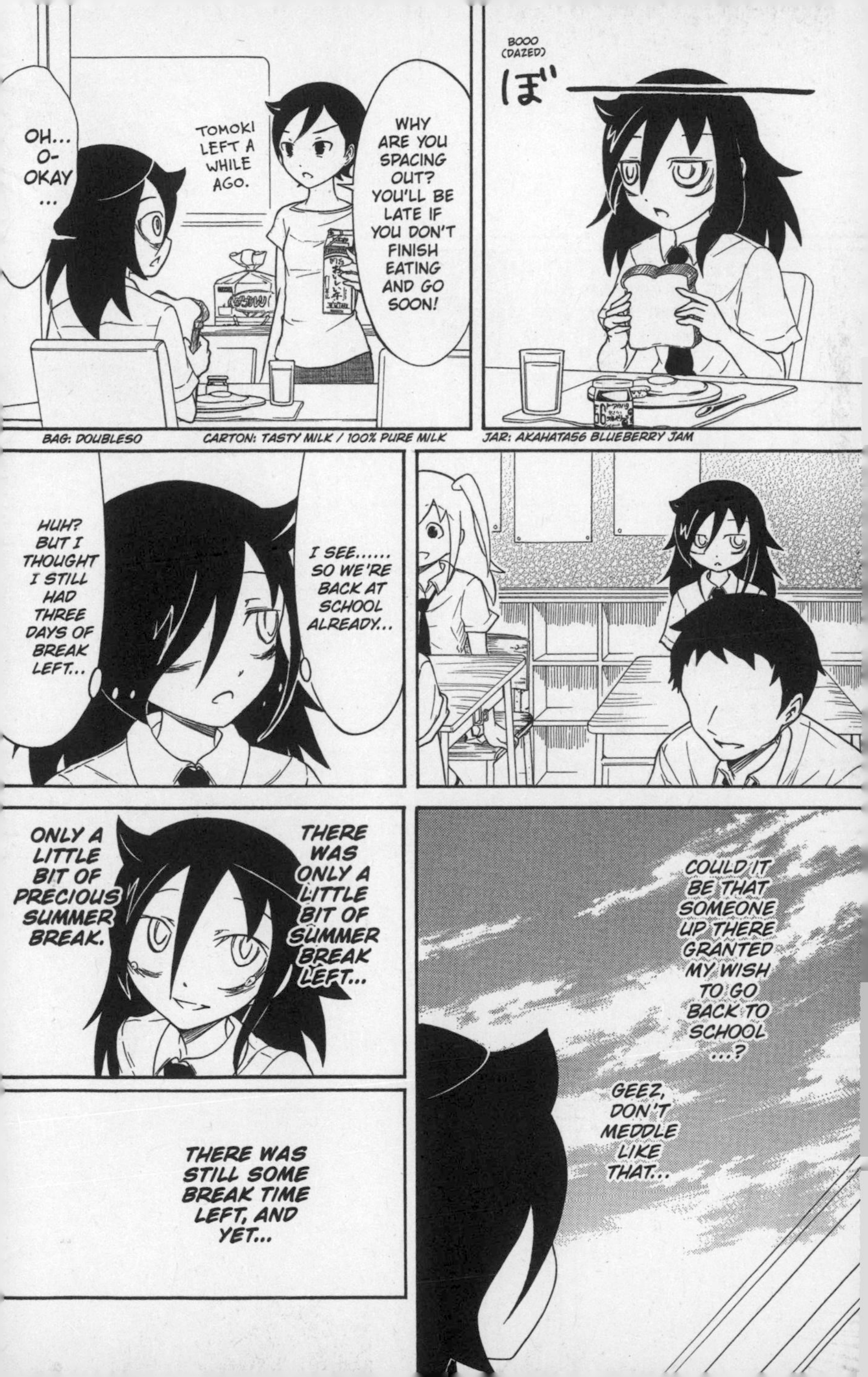
BOOO (DAZED)
ぼ
WHY ARE YOU SPACING OUT? YOU'LL BE LATE IF YOU DON'T FINISH EATING AND GO SOON!
TOMOKI LEFT A WHILE AGO.
OH... O-OKAY...
JAR: AKAHATA56 BLUEBERRY JAM
CARTON: TASTY MILK / 100% PURE MILK
BAG: DOUBLESO
I SEE...... SO WE'RE BACK AT SCHOOL ALREADY...
HUH? BUT I THOUGHT I STILL HAD THREE DAYS OF BREAK LEFT...
COULD IT BE THAT SOMEONE UP THERE GRANTED MY WISH TO GO BACK TO SCHOOL ...?
GEEZ, DON'T MEDDLE LIKE THAT...
THERE WAS ONLY A LITTLE BIT OF SUMMER BREAK LEFT...
ONLY A LITTLE BIT OF PRECIOUS SUMMER BREAK.
THERE WAS STILL SOME BREAK TIME LEFT, AND YET...

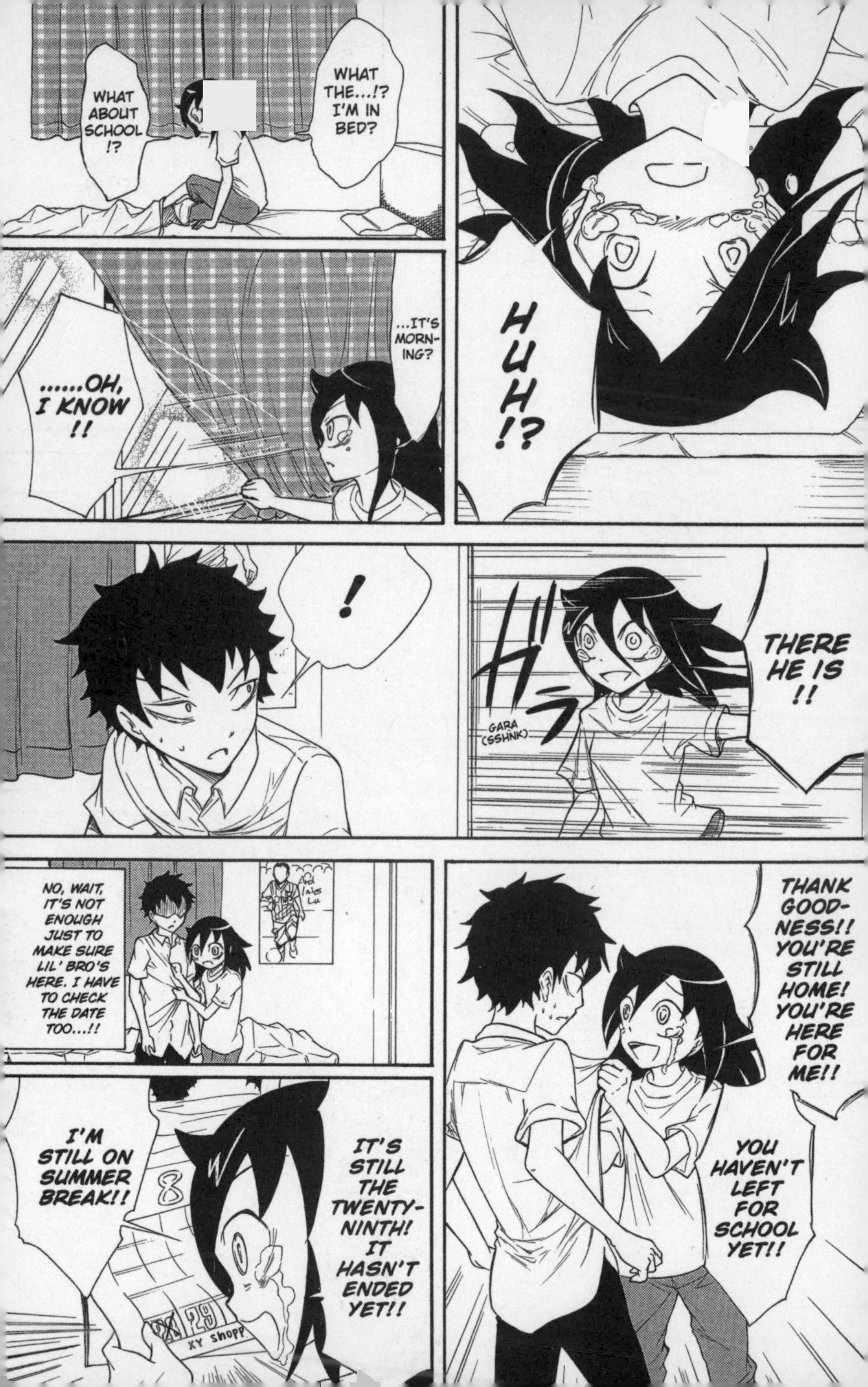
HUH!?
WHAT THE...!? I'M IN BED?
WHAT ABOUT SCHOOL!?
...IT'S MORNING?
......OH, I KNOW!!
ガラ
GARA (SSHNK)
THERE HE IS!!
!
THANK GOODNESS!! YOU'RE STILL HOME! YOU'RE HERE FOR ME!!
YOU HAVEN'T LEFT FOR SCHOOL YET!!
NO, WAIT, IT'S NOT ENOUGH JUST TO MAKE SURE LIL' BRO'S HERE. I HAVE TO CHECK THE DATE TOO...!!
IT'S STILL THE TWENTY-NINTH! IT HASN'T ENDED YET!!
I'M STILL ON SUMMER BREAK!!
8
29
XY Shopp

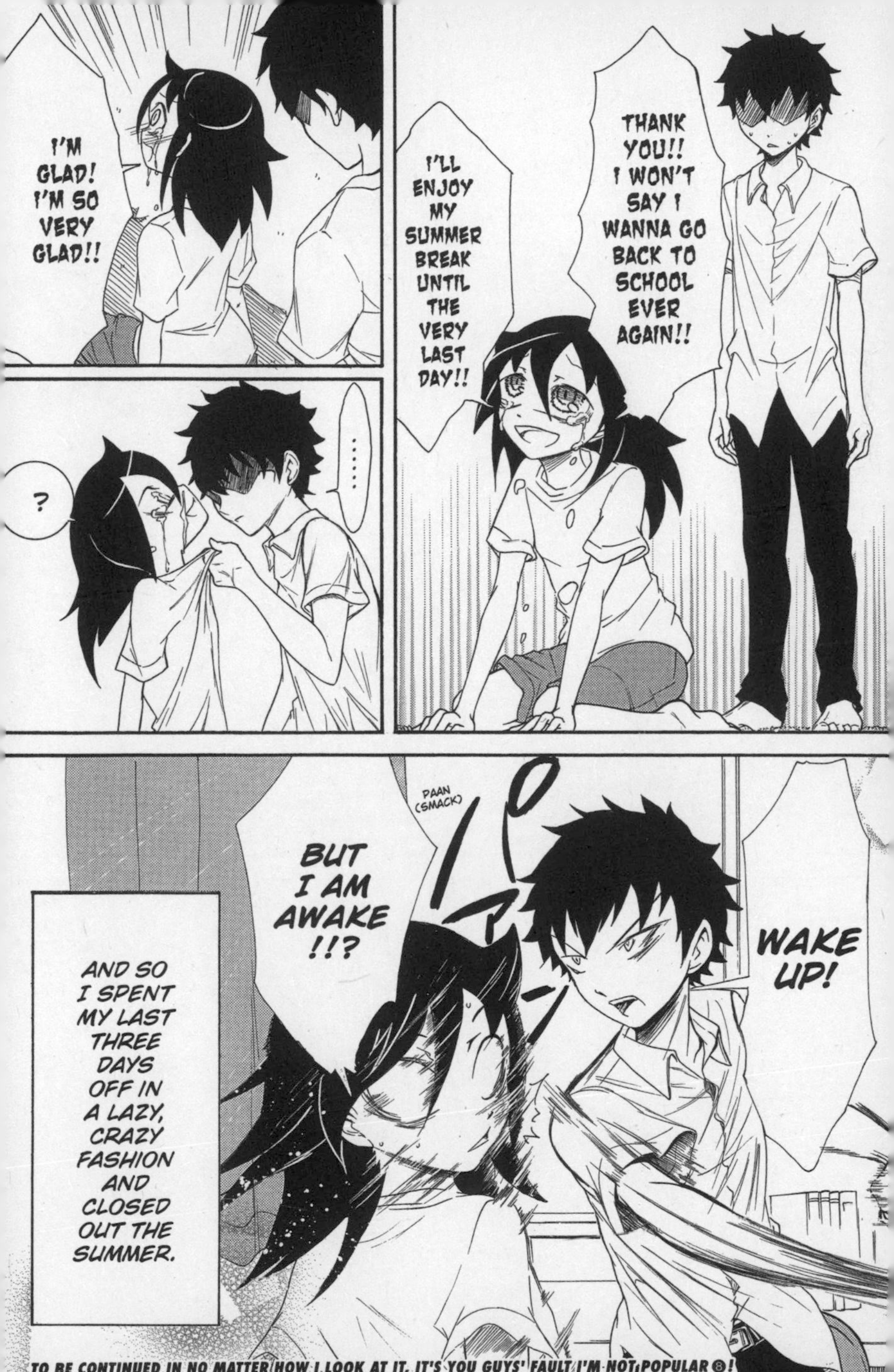
THANK YOU!! I WON'T SAY I WANNA GO BACK TO SCHOOL EVER AGAIN!!
I'LL ENJOY MY SUMMER BREAK UNTIL THE VERY LAST DAY!!
I'M GLAD! I'M SO VERY GLAD!!
......
?
WAKE UP!
PAAN (SMACK)
BUT I AM AWAKE!!?
AND SO I SPENT MY LAST THREE DAYS OFF IN A LAZY, CRAZY FASHION AND CLOSED OUT THE SUMMER.

TO BE CONTINUED IN NO MATTER HOW I LOOK AT IT, IT'S YOU GUYS' FAULT I'M NOT POPULAR ⑧!

BONUS

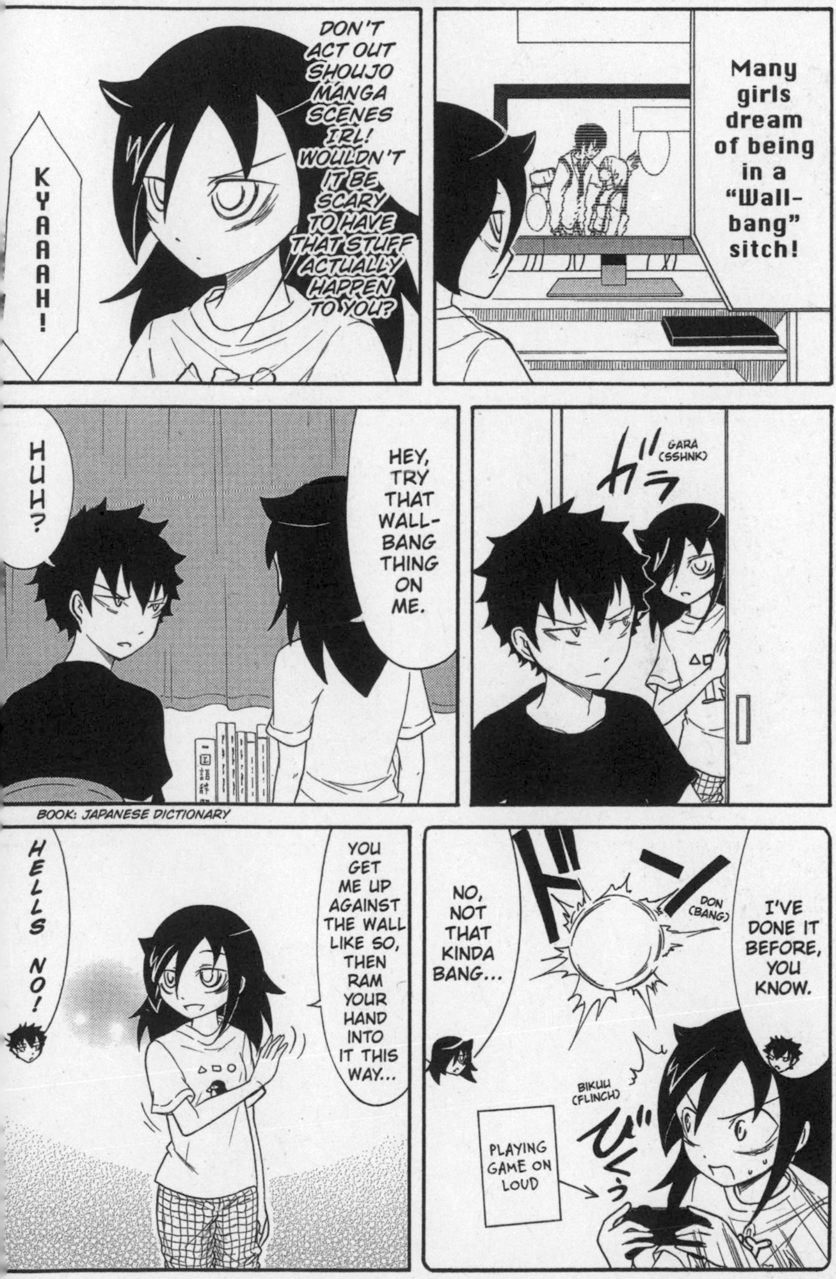
Many girls dream of being in a "Wall-bang" sitch!
DON'T ACT OUT SHOUJO MANGA SCENES IRL! WOULDN'T IT BE SCARY TO HAVE THAT STUFF ACTUALLY HAPPEN TO YOU?
KYAAAAH!
GARA (SSHNK)
HEY, TRY THAT WALL-BANG THING ON ME.
HUH?
BOOK: JAPANESE DICTIONARY
I'VE DONE IT BEFORE, YOU KNOW.
DON (BANG)
NO, NOT THAT KINDA BANG...
BIKUU (FLINCH)
PLAYING GAME ON LOUD
YOU GET ME UP AGAINST THE WALL LIKE SO, THEN RAM YOUR HAND INTO IT THIS WAY...
HELLS NO!

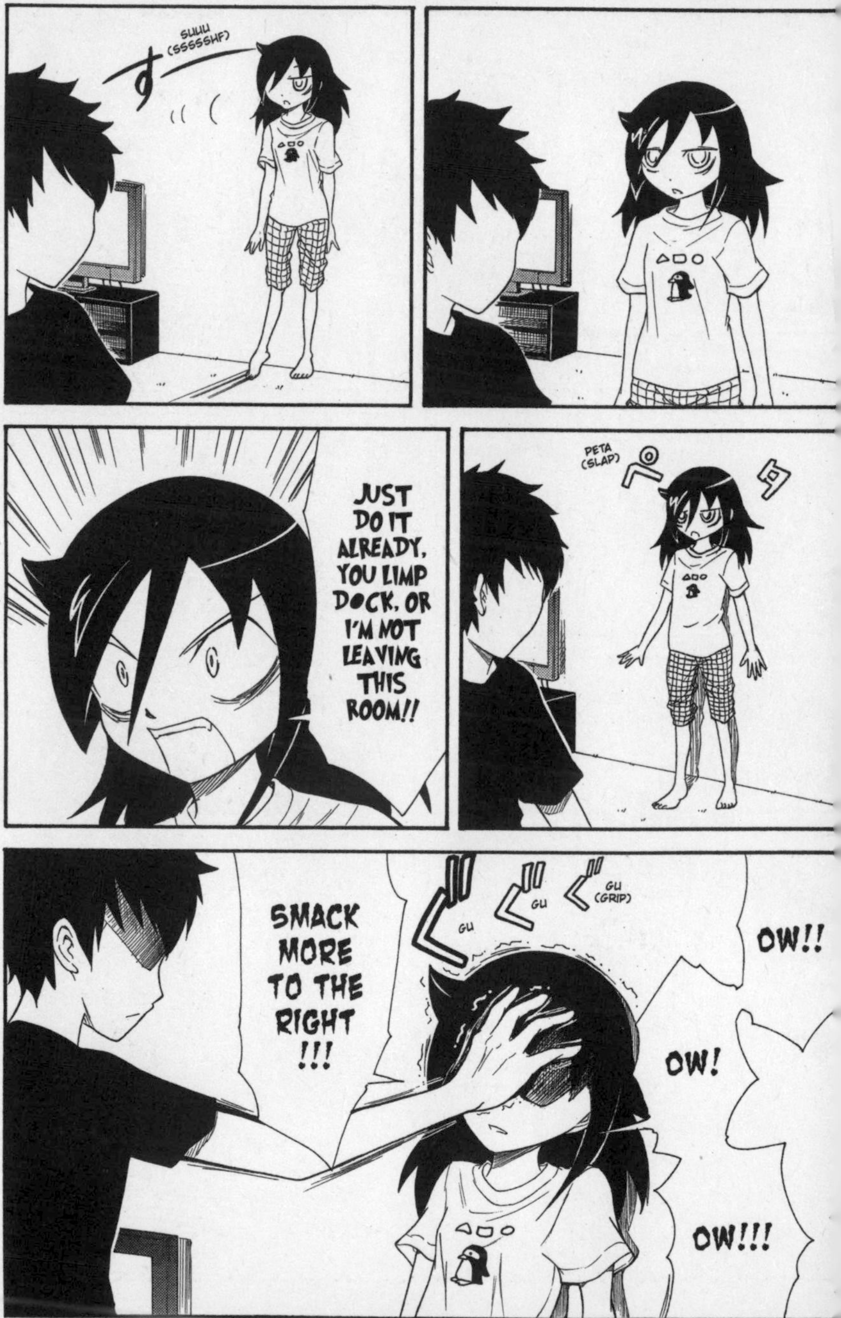
SUUU (SSSSSHF)
す
PETA (SLAP)
ペタ
JUST DO IT ALREADY, YOU LIMP DOCK, OR I'M NOT LEAVING THIS ROOM!!
GU (GRIP)
GU
GU
SMACK MORE TO THE RIGHT!!!
OW!!
OW!
OW!!!

WITH THE HELP OF ASSISTANT YUUJI ASAKURA-SAN

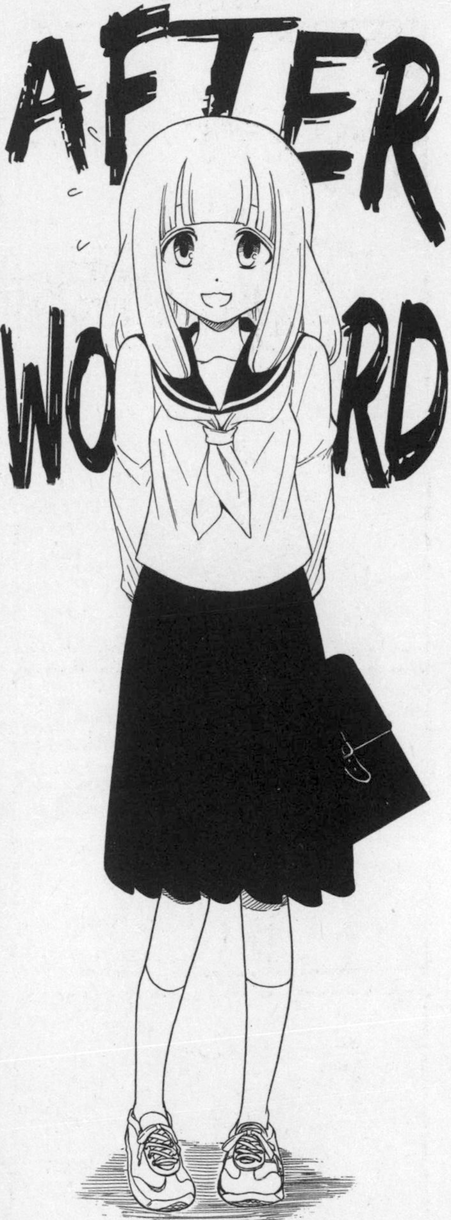
AFTER
WO
RD

AT WORK ONE DAY (1)

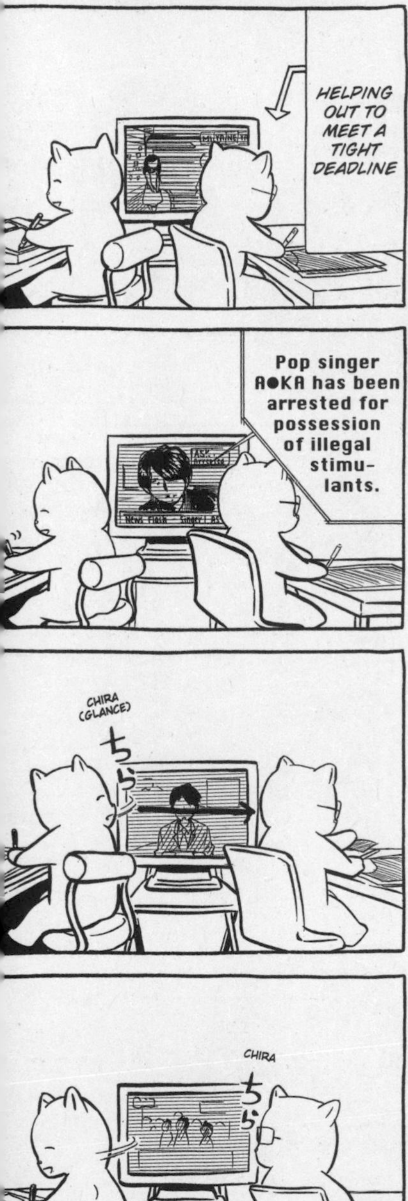
HELPING OUT TO MEET A TIGHT DEADLINE
Pop singer A●KA has been arrested for possession of illegal stimulants.
ちら
CHIRA (GLANCE)
ちら
CHIRA

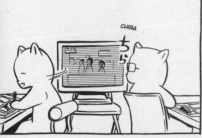

AT WORK ONE DAY (2)

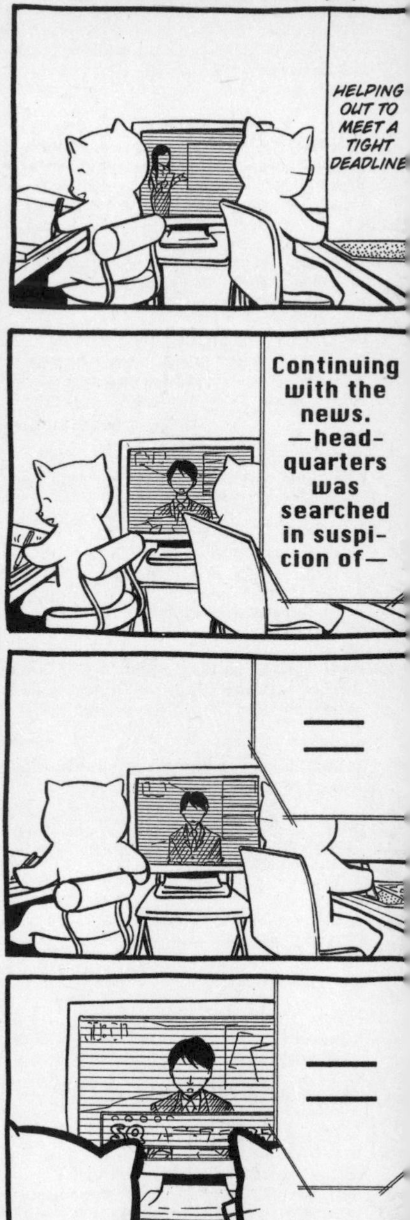
HELPING OUT TO MEET A TIGHT DEADLINE
Continuing with the news. —headquarters was searched in suspicion of—

REVISION

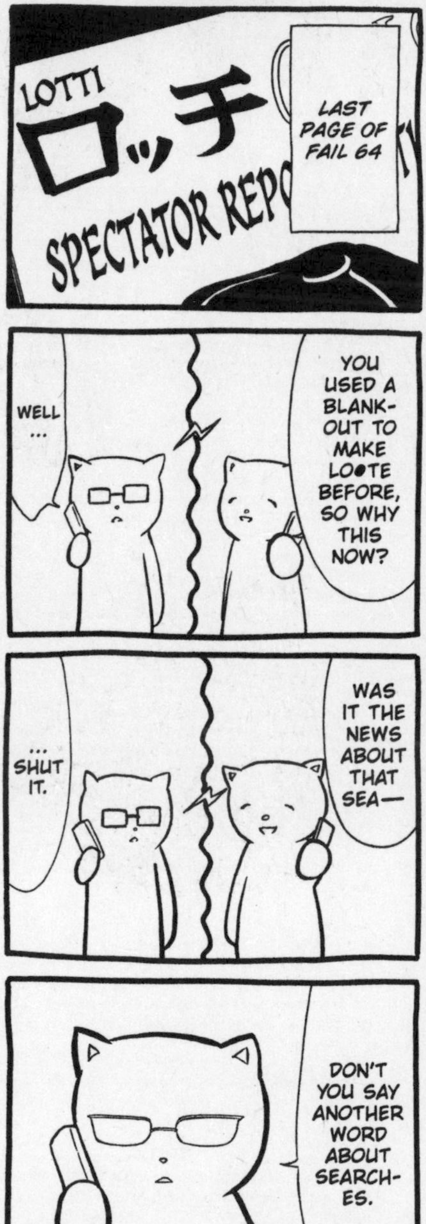
LAST PAGE OF FAIL 64
LOTTI
ロッチ
SPECTATOR REPO
YOU USED A BLANK-OUT TO MAKE LO●TE BEFORE, SO WHY THIS NOW?
WELL ...
WAS IT THE NEWS ABOUT THAT SEA—
... SHUT IT.
DON'T YOU SAY ANOTHER WORD ABOUT SEARCH-ES.

PAGE 4
The show that makes Tomoko late is Hasbro's *My Little Pony: Friendship Is Magic*, in which Rainbow Dash is a main character. Rainbow Dash's Japanese voice actress is Izumi Kitta, who also voices Tomoko in the *WataMote* anime series.

PAGE 5
Ignite Pass Kai is a reference to one of the protagonist Kuroko's pass techniques from the manga and anime series *Kuroko's Basketball* by Tadatoshi Fujimaki. This upgrade of Kuroko's original Ignite Pass adds spin to the ball, making it travel in a corkscrew-like path.

PAGE 8
My big sister can't... is another reference to the light novel/anime/manga series, *Oreimo: My Little Sister Can't Be This Cute (Ore no Imouto ga Konna ni Kawaii Wake ga Nai)*.

PAGE 15
Japan's high school baseball **nationals** are a huge deal, and the finals held at Koshien Stadium in Osaka are televised and bring in a massive viewership annually.

PAGE 21
Kodoku (literally "worm poison") is an actual Japanese curse technique based on legend and folklore. It often appears in fictional stories in everything from light novels and manga to television shows.

PAGE 23
The **costume** Komi is thinking of belongs to Shimakaze from *Kantai Collection*, or *~KanColle~*, which features personifications of World War II warships as cute girls. The property started out as a card game but has since expanded to anime and other media.

PAGE 24
Comiket is short for Comic Market, a three-day event held twice a year at the Tokyo International Exhibition Center (aka Big Sight) for buying and selling comics, most of them independent or fan-made works.

PAGE 29
The **holiday** Tomoko is referring to is almost certainly Ocean Day (*Umi no Hi*), which annually falls on the third Monday of July.

PAGE 31
Teppanyaki is a Japanese style of food preparation in which dishes are cooked on a hot metal griddle.

PAGE 32
The **first TV screen** on this page shows Ene, the whimsical A.I. girl from the *Mekakucity Actors* anime, which is based on the *Kagerou Project* property created by Jin. This scene is from the first episode of the anime, which aired in spring 2014.

PAGE 32
This **weird cat picture** of a feline with a couple legs and tail is one that was (supposedly) partially caught by a Google Street View camera in May 2013. It went viral with Japanese netizens, featuring the caption, "Just Passing Through..."

PAGE 32
The scene on the **second TV screen** is from the first episode of the anime adaptation of the light novel series *The Irregular at Magic High School (Mahouka Koukou no Rettousei)*, which aired in spring/summer 2014. Here, the main character is responding to his discovery that the girl with glasses in the next panel can read auras.

PAGE 33
The **birdsong** Tomoko is hearing is the call of an Eastern turtledove, also known as an Oriental turtledove.

PAGE 33
At 7/11 convenience stores in Japan, you buy iced **coffee** by purchasing the cup with ice in it, then adding the coffee at a self-service dispenser.

PAGE 34
The **gameplay vid** Tomoko is watching features *Super Mario World*.

PAGE 41
Yuuhi Shimbun ("Evening Sun Newspaper") is a play on *Asahi Shimbun*, an actual Japanese newspaper, the name of which literally means "Morning Sun Newspaper."

PAGE 62
POPTEEN is a parody of *POPTEEN*, a monthly teen girls' fashion magazine published by Kadokawa. The issue here appears to be from June 2014.

PAGE 63
Taiyaki is a Japanese pastry in the shape of a red snapper fish, usually containing a sweet filling, like red bean paste.

PAGE 64
The **candy cutout game** (*katanuki*) is popular at Japanese festivals and utilizes small sheets of sugar candy with shapes pressed into them that must be poked out very carefully since they break easily.

PAGE 65
Kachiwari is a frozen treat similar to shaved ice but is more of a clump of ice in a plastic bag with a straw, often with diluted syrup added for flavor. It's known as a treat sold at Koshien Stadium in Osaka, where the national high school baseball championships are held.

PAGE 68
Pudding is a reference to the comedy horror manga series *Franken Fran* by Katsuhisa Kigitsu, in which a girl's dead dog named Pudding is brought back to life by transplanting its brain into the corpse of a dead middle-aged man.

PAGE 72
Of the **creepy sounds** Tomoko is making here, the first two are net slang used when making fun of people or teasing "normals." The last one is a fright sound made by Seiichirou Kitano, the main character of the manga series *Angel Densetsu* by Norihiro Yagi.

PAGE 73
Ms. Eight-Feet-Tall, or *Hasshaku-sama* (literally "Lady Two Meters Forty Centimeters Tall"), is a scary story introduced on the 2ch occult board. It concerns a mysterious woman wearing a white hat and dress, who is tall enough to see over a two-meter-high fence and whose appearance is heralded by the "popo, popoppo, po" seen on page 71.

PAGE 81
The **cycling anime** Tomoko has been watching is *Yowamushi Pedal*, in which an otaku boy joins his high school's competitive road-racing team.

PAGE 82
Tomoko is making a reference to Hiroto Kiritani, a shogi player turned investment guru who tried **living solely on stockholder perks** offered by the companies in which he held shares. Kiritani is also known for zipping around on an ordinary utility bicycle.

PAGE 82
Cumming by Climax Bike!! is a reference to the Japanese porn series *Akume Jitensha de Iku!*

TRANSLATION NOTES 2 ·······················

PAGE 91
Yukkuri Let's Play videos use the electronic Yukkuri Voice Changer app instead of the vid maker's unaltered voice to sound like a nonspecific synthesized voice.

PAGE 92
NEET is the acronym for "Not in Education, Employment, or Training." It was first used in Britain but has been widely adopted in Japan to describe the increased number of people who are either unemployed or disengaged from the working world.

PAGE 93
Hikikomori is another popular term in Japan to describe people who withdraw from society so much that they refuse to leave their homes, sometimes even their rooms.

PAGE 93
In both posture and appearance, **future Tomoko** in Tomoko's daydream resembles Shiro, the little sister of the sibling gaming duo in Yuu Kamiya's light novel series, No Game No Life, which has been adapted into both anime and manga.

PAGE 101
The logo on Komi's laptop, **DULL**, is a pun on the name of PC manufacturer, DELL. The original Japanese used "DEBU," which means "fatty."

PAGE 104
Rope eyes (rape eyes) is Internet slang for dull, expressionless, lifeless eyes.

PAGE 108
Tokyo Teleport Station is one station away from the Exhibition Center (Big Sight) Station on the Rinkai line. Both stations are on Odaiba, a man-made island in Tokyo Bay that's home to many large-scale entertainment and tourism facilities, including the Fuji TV building with its spherical observation room and the sixty-foot-tall Gundam giant robot statue shown on this page.

PAGE 108
Tomoko's imagination shows a scene from Volume 6 of the horror manga series Hakaijuu, where the spherical observation room on the Fuji TV building gets repurposed as a bomb to fight monsters.

PAGE 108
"Humans are like trash!" is a quote from the villain Muska in the Studio Ghibli animated film Laputa: Castle in the Sky.

PAGE 110
Lotti is a reference to the Chiba Lotte Marines baseball team, whose home stadium is QVC Marine Field.

PAGE 110
The **Gull Colle** logo used here is a parody of the title logo for the online card game Kantai Collection, or ~KanColle~, mentioned earlier. The team mascot for the Marines is a seagull.

PAGE 114
2:50 is a reference to Japanese male comedian Egashira 2:50, who usually performs wearing only black skintight pants like those here.

PAGE 116
"I have to get her knocked up!" is a reference to a September 2013 2channel thread "Name any characters about whom you distinctly remember feeling, 'I-I have to get her knocked up!'—No trolling!" One of the responses was Mokocchi!

PAGE 116
"I'd invite you to a tea party" is a reference to a scandal that broke in August 2014 over Osaka Diet member Kei Yamamoto having invited middle school girls via LINE, an Internet messaging service, to a "tea party" at his office. Komi's response, "Kimoin da yo," is a related reference to entertainer Terry Itou's comment on the incident on the morning show SUKKIRI: "Koitsu kimoi mon!" ("This guy's creepy!")

PAGE 116
KOMI STYLE is a take on AYA STYLE, a pinup calendar featuring famous voice actress Aya Hirano, in which she wore her bikini top upside down.

PAGE 119
Poceri is a reference to Pocari Sweat, seen written on the bottle later as "Pocali." This is a popular Japanese mild sports drink.

PAGE 119
"This is no time to be buried in sand!!" is a reference to an image meme of a panda leaping over a barrier with the caption "This is no time to be eating bamboo!!"

PAGE 120
The **odd-looking sun** is drawn to look like the Stand Sun, from "Stardust Crusaders," the third arc of the manga series JoJo's Bizarre Adventure.

PAGE 121
Nanpa is the Japanese word for a man hitting on a woman. A **reverse pickup**, or gyaku (literally "opposite") nan, is when a woman hits on a man.

PAGE 131
The **danger of talking to oneself in the mirror** meme came from "Gestalt Breakdown," a Japanese scary story that went viral. It was first published on the web around 2010. In it, the author mentions learning about this supposed experiment conducted by the Nazis, in which subjects were made to say, "Who are you?" and talk to their reflections daily, eventually going mad. The story details the frightening effects of this behavior on the author's friend who tries it himself and ends with the question, "Am I really me?"

PAGE 132
Akahata56 Jam is a parody of the real brand Aohata55.

PAGE 132
DoubleSo is a reference to the brand name DoubleSoft.

PAGE 136
Wall-bang, or kabe-don, is a term that has recently been used for supposedly romantic situations, where a guy hits his arm against the wall next to a girl as a way to corner her, either possessively or hostilely. This technique is better known as a way to indicate displeasure at a noisy neighbor, hence Tomoki's comment that he's already done it to Tomoko.

PAGE 138
Miyaneya is a news and information program broadcast weekday afternoons on Yomiuri TV.

PAGE 138
AoKA's arrest refers to a member of the Japanese pop duo Chage & Aska, who was arrested on May 17, 2014, for suspected possession of illegal stimulants. The incident mentioned in the sidenote was back in 2009, when Chage & Aska announced an "indefinite suspension" of group activities, after being together for thirty years.

PAGE 139
These two comic strips refer to an **incident** in summer 2014 involving Square Enix and the manga series High Score Girl by Rensuke Oshikiri.

VAMPIRE

A legendary immortal being that drinks the blood of humans.

Likes the blood of virgins.

Hates the blood of sluts.

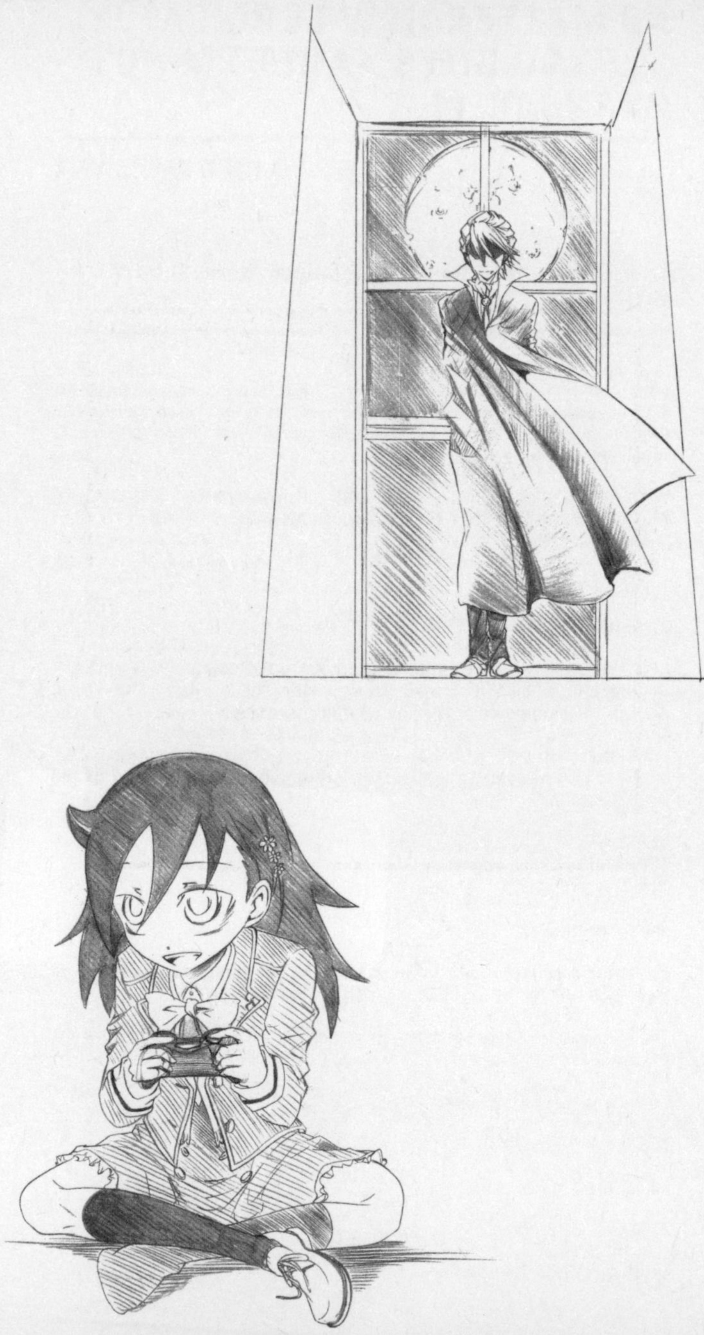

NO MATTER HOW I LOOK AT IT, IT'S YOU GUYS' FAULT I'M NOT POPULAR! ❼

NICO TANIGAWA

Translation/Adaptation: Krista Shipley, Karie Shipley
Lettering: Lys Blakeslee

WATASHI GA MOTENAI NOWA DOU KANGAETEMO OMAERA GA WARUI! Volume 7 © 2014 Nico Tanigawa / SQUARE ENIX CO., LTD. First published in Japan in 2014 by SQUARE ENIX CO., LTD. English translation rights arranged with SQUARE ENIX CO., LTD. and Yen Press, LLC through Tuttle-Mori Agency, Inc.

English translation © 2015 by SQUARE ENIX CO., LTD.

Yen Press
1290 Avenue of the Americas
New York, NY 10104

www.YenPress.com

Yen Press is an imprint of Yen Press, LLC. The Yen Press name and logo are trademarks of Yen Press, LLC.

The publisher is not responsible for websites (or their content) that are not owned by the publisher.

First Yen Press Edition: May 2015

ISBN: 978-0-316-34201-8

10 9 8 7 6 5 4 3 2

BVG

Printed in the United States of America